Before the Taliban

To Jackie

*the first person to make me believe I could
and to all the Afghan women*

Before the Taliban
Living with War, Hoping for Peace

Mary Smith

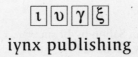

iynx publishing

First published in the United Kingdom in 2001 by

iynx publishing
Countess of Moray's House
Sands Place
Aberdour
Fife
KY3 0SZ

www.iynx.com

A CIP catalogue record for this book is available
from the British Library

ISBN 0-9540583-3-X

Typeset in Sabon by Brinnoven, Livingston
Printed and bound by Creative Print and Design, Ebbw Vale, Wales

Contents

Acknowledgements

Grateful thanks to Tommy Reeves, Liz Niven and Tom Pow for their encouragement while reading the book in preparation, and for their support to Jon, David, family and friends.

— 1 —
Introduction

As WAS USUAL when it came to goodbyes, Sharifa enfolded me in a damp farewell hug, her eyes red from weeping. Blinking hard, I croaked past the egg-sized lump in my throat, 'Please, don't. You'll start me off again and I've cried too much already over the last few days.'

Sharifa pulled back sharply, demanding, 'What are you crying for? You made the decision to leave us. If you are so upset about it, don't go.'

For a moment, changing my mind seemed such a stunningly simple solution to ending the misery, I almost agreed. Then I thought of the ordeal of the endless round of farewell dinners I had just endured. Each one had started with an air of forced gaiety as we laughed too loudly at not-very-funny jokes before lapsing into tense silences. Each one had ended in tears. I could not go through it all again.

Wordlessly, I shook my head and walked across the tarmac to where the tiny plane was waiting, its engines running.

Leaving was proving to be more painful than I had ever anticipated. It was heart-breaking knowing that it would be many years – if ever – before I again saw the friends now clustered together waving goodbye. There was, however, no time to drown in my sense of loss. With the plane taxiing down the runway, five-year-old David needed reassurance concerning his own doubts about our going away. Tugging at my sleeve, he demanded anxiously, 'Are you sure there are sheep in Scotland? If not, we'll have to come back because I really want to be a shepherd when I'm big – like Iqbal.'

'Yes,' I said, 'there are sheep in Scotland but first you have to go to school. After that we can consider shepherding as a future career.'

Satisfied, he soon fell asleep – maybe to dream about running wild on the mountain with his friend Iqbal. I let my own eyes close. Instantly, three years of memories jostled for attention as the plane flew over the jagged peaks of the Hindu Kush, taking us away from Afghanistan.

During those three years working, along with partner Jon, for a small NGO concerned with health care in Afghanistan, there had been many emotional highs and lows. Along with a demanding workload, there had been excitement, occasional moments of terror – such as when armed robbers, demanding dollars I didn't have, tied me up and poked a pistol in my ear. There had been anger and sadness, but, as well as tears, there had been lots of fun and laughter.

In particular there had been the overwhelming warmth and acceptance shown by the Afghan women who had become my friends, allowing me to share a part of their lives.

Apart from the over-emotional, soft-hearted Sharifa, there had been acerbic, sharp-tongued Latifa, Habiba with her snobbish aspirations, gentle Maryam with her practical good sense. I knew I would never need the *nishani* [remembrance gifts of handkerchiefs and embroidered cloths] to help remind me of them.

Nor would I ever forget the village women who bravely agreed to be pioneers, joining with me to establish the first Female Health Volunteer training project.

These women had learned how to prevent infants with diarrhoea dying of dehydration, to teach their neighbours all they learned, to deliver babies safely. They had been so excited when they received their hand-made certificates after passing the final exams. They had been even more excited when I showed them an article, accompanied by a group photograph, about their achievements, that I had written for a national newspaper back home.

'Are people in your country really interested in reading about us?' asked Fatima in wonder. 'We're poor. We can't even read and write. What is so special about us?'

I remembered when another group of women friends, this

time in the city of Mazar-i-Sharif, were discussing a child who had died of tuberculosis, two days after her mother had died of the same, supposedly curable, disease. Benazir had burst out fiercely, 'The men of Afghanistan have destroyed our country with their endless war. We can't sit forever waiting for peace because even if they stop fighting tomorrow they won't do anything about our children's health. We have to do things ourselves. Even if we can't do much, we have to try.' And they wondered what was so special about them?

When I once mentioned the many books on Afghanistan I had read before coming to live there, they wanted to know what was in them. I wished I had kept my mouth shut. Mostly they were books written by men, concentrating on Afghan men and *their* war. Scant attention was paid to women other than to reinforce western misconceptions that in a society dominated, particularly in the public domain, by men, all women are suppressed and passive victims.

By the time I arrived in Mazar-i-Sharif, I had read so much about the mujahideen I felt I was personally acquainted with the more famous commanders. They were so frequently interviewed in their mountain strongholds it was amazing they had found time to fight a *jihad* against a world super-power. I had also swallowed the stereotyped image of Afghan women – amorphous shapes shrouded in the burqa (that tent-like garment which covers the wearer from head to toe) imprisoned, usually in the name of Islam, behind high walls.

My friends were shocked, and hurt. 'Does everyone in your country believe that about Afghan women?' they had demanded. 'How could these people write that? They don't know us, they never talked to us. You know that it isn't true!'

I had tried to point out that not everyone from the West had the opportunity I had had to come to Afghanistan and learn for themselves. They had to rely on what they read in the newspapers or the books other people wrote. Those who came to report on the war did not live in the country for three years, nor did they meet many – if any – Afghan women.

'Oh, well,' said Jemila, 'you'd better write a different book.'

David stirred beside me as the engine's changing drone indicated we were coming in to land in Pakistan. 'Is Daddy coming to Scotland too?' he asked sleepily.

'Yes, but not until Christmas,' I replied cautiously. 'His work isn't finished yet.' I need not have worried. David was so used to our nomadic existence, not seeing Jon for weeks on end, that he seemed to think it quite normal that his father – who had an extra year's contract to fulfil – would not be joining us until later.

At least while Jon was still in Afghanistan, it would be relatively easy to keep in touch with friends but how, I wondered, would it be in the future?

I remembered Benazir's farewell speech at the last *mehmanni* [dinner party] organised by the Health Volunteers and a new group of students. She had said, 'We hope you will come back one day to see how hard your students have been working. You will be happy at how healthy the people of Mazar-i-Sharif have become.'

Wondering how many years it would be before I ever returned to Afghanistan, I had smiled through my tears, saying, 'I am sure you will be successful. Let's hope that Taliban never come here to stop your work.'

Benazir had snorted. Tossing her head indignantly, she replied, 'They have been at the gates of Kabul for months, but still they could not take the city. Dostum will never let them reach Mazar. Don't worry, we will go on working for the women and children of Afghanistan. No one can stop us now.'

Six months later, on 27 September 1996 the unthinkable happened. Taliban captured Kabul.

Thousands of miles away in Scotland, I scoured the papers for news, terrified that the media stories of Taliban bringing peace to Afghanistan meant the fall of Mazar-i-Sharif was imminent.

Hearing Jon's voice on the telephone from Islamabad in Pakistan brought some reassurance, 'Don't worry. Taliban are nowhere near Mazar. Everyone here is all right,' he said before describing the 'river of lights' made by the headlamps of thousands of vehicles full of refugees fleeing from Kabul. The citizens of Afghanistan's capital city were obviously less enthusiastic about Taliban's peace than the media.

The so-called 'peace' brought by the fanatical zealots, whose brand of Islam was virtually unknown anywhere else in the Islamic world, came with a dreadful price. Ex-president Najibullah and his brother were dragged from the UN compound – their refuge for four years – tortured and hanged, their mutilated bodies displayed in public.

People from ethnic groups – particularly Uzbek, Hazara and Tajik – known to oppose the extremist, predominantly Pushtoon Taliban were targeted – many were beaten, imprisoned or killed.

The new regime introduced harsh laws. Music was banned and televisions, videos, satellite dishes and cassette players were destroyed. The amputation of a limb was the punishment for thieves; stoning to death was that for adultery.

Girls' schools were closed, women were banned from working, from leaving their homes – even to seek medical treatment – without a male escort. Taliban soldiers entered the city's hospitals, dragged sick women from their beds and threw them into the streets.

Journalists vied with each other to produce the most graphic horror stories about Taliban's appalling treatment of women. Newspaper reports abounded, almost pornographic in detail, of women being publicly beaten or whipped with chains by young Taliban soldiers for violating the strict dress code.

It seemed inappropriate for me to be writing about my women friends safe in Mazar-i-Sharif and Hazara Jat. Perhaps the ups and downs of their daily lives, the shared laughter at silly jokes, would trivialise what was happening to women in Kabul? I put away the draft of the book Jemila had once instructed me to write.

Then Benazir sent me a video tape of her daughter's second birthday party. Benazir, as glamorously made up as an Indian film star, danced sexily with her husband, surrounded by other dancing couples and hordes of giggling children. With not a burqa in sight, it was as though Taliban did not exist.

There were also many messages from the women reminding me that Taliban did not control all of Afghanistan, that not all Afghan women had been silenced, that there was still hope.

I began to write again, for it seemed doubly important that the voices of my women friends should be heard. For one thing, as reports of Taliban's excesses continued, I seemed to hear in the west the frightening sound of a collective sigh and millions of shoulders shrugging as if to say, 'That's Islam for you.' I wanted to shout, as I had heard Latifa once do, 'This has nothing to do with Islam.' For she, too, understood that the obsession with controlling every aspect of women's lives had no Islamic justification.

Secondly, Benazir, Latifa, Sharifa and the others wanted the world to know that not all Afghan women had been silenced, as their sisters in Kabul had. I began to write again.

In August 1998, however, Taliban finally, at the third attempt, captured Mazar-i-Sharif. The previous year, Hazaras, helped by turncoat commanders who had earlier appeared to be pro-Taliban had routed the invaders. Benazir had written then, 'Mazar is free again and I am back at the clinic, Mash 'Allah, but to get to work I must pass the stinking bodies of Taliban soldiers lying dead in the streets. I hope they take them away soon.'

Taliban exacted a heavy revenge the following year. In the first two to three days, they systematically hunted out and massacred around 8000 Hazaras – mostly men but women and children too, especially boy children so that they could never grow up to fight against their Taliban oppressors. Few people in the West were even aware of the slaughter. The media kept everyone's attention riveted to the prospect of the ethnic cleansing of the Kosovars. The cold-blooded murder of 8000 Hazaras in far-off, non-European Afghanistan could not compete.

Desperate for news I searched the internet for Afghan websites, e-mailed and telephoned people working with aid agencies in Pakistan. I talked with refugees in London, who were equally desperate to find out about the fate of relatives in Mazar-i-Sharif.

Naeem called from Peshawar. He had got Maryam and the children safely out. His assurances about other friends, however, were not enough to give me peace of mind. I had lived too long in Afghanistan, absorbed too many of the customs. No one gives bad news, such as of the death of someone close, to people who are far away. Jawad tried to convince me, 'You know I hate this custom. Remember how I felt about my cousin? I promise I would tell you if anyone you know has died.'

Jawad had been horrified to learn of his cousin's death over a year after it happened. They had grown up together, inseparable friends until Jawad's work took him away from the village. Only when he had returned on a visit did his family give him the news of his cousin's death. He had told me then, 'I was angry that at the time when I should have been praying for him and remembering him, I was happy at finding a new house in Mazar and taking my family on picnics. I was so upset when I learned he had died, but everyone else had already had their time of sadness and couldn't share mine.'

Gradually, I began to hear news from other sources. Latifa sent a message. Whoever had written it for her said, 'I am not allowed to go to work and they have given my husband my job. My duty is at home now.' I was relieved to know she was alive and well although I could imagine her fury at being forced to stay at home. Jemila fled to Pakistan with her mother, from where she wrote: 'I often remember the happy times we had in the clinic. I still cry when I think about the pregnant women I used to see. Who will help them now at the time of delivery?

We were beginning to move forward slowly but now they want to force us backwards again. The lives of Afghan women will be worse than in the books you told us about.'

I looked again at the manuscript I had been writing. It was no longer about the reality of Afghan women's daily lives. It had, tragically, become a history book. It was about a time, albeit a recent time, when women had been tentatively moving forward, reaching out to grasp opportunities and freedoms that had suddenly, violently, been snatched away.

That history is important to Latifa, Sharifa and Maryam and many other Afghan women. They wanted people to understand the reality of their lives, not to be dismissed as passive victims accepting whatever fate dealt them. They welcomed me into their lives with warmth, generosity of spirit and humour. Allowing them to tell their own stories is a way of ensuring that Afghan women's voices will never be completely silenced.

— 2 —

Flea Bites, Power Cuts and Women with no Trousers

THERE WAS NO fan above the table, which had 2000 flies crawling over it and the bones of at least three sheep under it.

Everyone else in the restaurant sat cross-legged on carpeted platforms, heaped plates of meat and rice in front of them, or lolled back comfortably on grubby cushions sipping from steaming glasses of green tea. The waiter had hastily led us to a conventional table and chairs, tucked away at the back. He tugged a huge, greasy curtain around the table to hide me from the fascinated gaze of the other – all male – diners. It was unbearably hot and airless.

'The hot weather', Naeem said informatively, pulling back the curtain on the assumption that I would prefer being stared at to suffocation, 'starts every year on 15 May.' Just our luck to arrive the week after it started, I thought, exhaustedly trying to soothe my tired, hungry and fretful child.

When Naeem had suggested eating out to celebrate our arrival it had seemed a sensible idea, not least because I had discovered by then the power supply was so weak it took an hour to boil a pint of water, never mind cook a meal.

We had walked through dimly lit streets to the restaurant he had chosen. It was shut. Anyway, we discovered later, it was not a restaurant but something called a 'Wedding Cloup' in which wedding receptions were held.

Apologising profusely, Naeem led us on. The first kebab house had no nan left. Neither had the second. The third had no kebabs but plenty of nan. Naeem bought up the left over bread and we returned wearily to the first kebab house. Near the door, two cooks, sweating profusely and obviously unconcerned about the bread shortage in their own establishment, were busily turning skewers of meat sizzling over long braziers of glowing coals. A blast of heat and smoke met us as we sidled past into the dining area.

This day, our first in Afghanistan's northern city of Mazar-i-Sharif had not turned out as I had expected. For a start, our arrival, less than two hours after taking off from Islamabad's International Airport, had been disorientating.

Previous journeys into Afghanistan had involved cramped travelling in an overloaded jeep on tortuous roads. In those days, with civil war still raging in Kabul, we had worked, for security reasons, from a base in Quetta, in Pakistan. Driving over high mountain passes and across bleak deserts it had sometimes taken several days and nights to reach our destination in the heart of Hazara Jat, Afghanistan's remote, mountainous central region. Such lengthy travel did, however, provide the opportunity for a gradual mental preparation for whatever lay ahead.

The sight of jets lined up on the cracked tarmac of Mazar-i-Sharif's runway, bombs piled haphazardly beside them, made me wonder how 'stable' our new base really was. The dry, dusty landscape was not encouraging. Devoid of trees, or hint of greenery, it stretched endlessly towards the distant horizon. Only there, did the hazy outline of mountains offer the eye some relief from the flatness.

It was David's first trip to Afghanistan but, at two and a half years old, he was unconcerned about his surroundings. Crowing with delighted recognition as he spotted his old friends, Naeem and Reza, he rushed towards them.

After throwing our luggage into the boot of an ancient, beat-up yellow Volga taxi they had borrowed, and with Reza at the wheel, we headed towards the city. The two men vied with each other, like excited schoolboys, to draw our attention to such wonders as tarred roads, electricity pylons, television aerials and telegraph poles.

As he pointed to a satellite dish on a mud roof, Naeem asked, 'Do you believe you are in Afghanistan?' Without bothering to wait for a reply, he answered his own question, 'I've been here nearly a month and still can hardly believe that this is *my* country.'

Naeem and Reza were both from Hazara Jat. Their Afghanistan had no electricity, no telephones, no running water, tarred roads or plumbing. Although well acquainted with such twentieth-century accoutrements through living in Pakistan, they had assumed that their entire country, with the possible exception of Kabul, which Naeem remembered seeing as an awe-struck child, would be like Hazara Jat. Guilty of the same assumptions – since my own previous travels in Afghanistan had been confined to Hazara Jat – I shared their wonder and disbelief.

The sight of uniformed traffic policemen on the city's broad, tree-lined boulevards, seemed to confirm for us that we had arrived by mistake in some other world. We pointed and exclaimed – like country bumpkins – over each new sight.

As Reza threaded the vehicle confidently between jeeps, trucks, spluttering Russian motorcycles and carts pulled by camels, donkeys or men, we glimpsed hospitals, X-ray laboratories, schools. There were even cinemas, and, through the vehicle's open windows, we caught snatches of Indian film music blasting from the many video and music cassette shops lining the thoroughfare.

Naeem had enthusiastically described the office accommo-dation he had rented. 'It is very big with lots of rooms,' he said, 'and it is a completely new building.' Only his obvious pride in it made me hide my dismay when I first saw what was to be our 'home' for the foreseeable future.

Of hideously ugly concrete, it was so new it was not even finished. 'Our landlord', Naeem remarked, 'is building another two floors on top.' The basement, ground and first floor, where the main office accommodation, kitchen and staff rooms were situated, were ours.

The stairs had no railing and every door and window led onto barrier-free balconies. To reach the dining room involved traversing a narrow, open verandah twenty feet above the

ground. A half completed flight of concrete steps led to the
second storey whose open window frames jutted out over
an even higher, vertigo inducing, drop. This was where I
discovered David, minutes after our arrival. The entire place
was a death trap for an active, inquisitive, two-year-old.

The inside walls had not even been plastered and Naeem's
attempts at interior decoration – leprosy posters secured
with the aid of carpet tacks – had done little to improve
the appearance of the place. He had purchased grotesquely
cumbersome chairs with plush covered seats (sure to be itchy
in the heat) and three desks. His computer sat on one of them,
balefully denying him access to his files. Its cables and wires
appeared to have multiplied in transit and yards of flex criss-
crossed the floor to where a dangerously overloaded adaptor
was plugged into a socket.

Sensing that I was less than happy about the arrangements,
Naeem decided to give me all the bad news at once. The
electricity supply was, he admitted, often weak, frequently
erratic and, sometimes, non-existent – but, he hastily assured
me, something called a three-phase connection would solve
that. Despite the two large bathrooms, complete with western-
style loos and showers, we would have to use the latrine in the
compound. 'Only for a few days', promised Naeem, 'until we
sort out the water supply.'

'There is no water?' I was appalled.

'As soon as the underground tank is ready, we'll have a
mains water supply. For now, what water we need is delivered
by donkey cart.'

It was then that he had suggested we go out to eat, probably
to prevent me discovering further unpalatable facts about our
living conditions. He was apologising for the tenth time about
the filthy state of the restaurant when I interrupted to ask how
difficult it had been to obtain permission for us to set up our
office in the city.

'It was easy', he replied, 'The Foreign Ministry wants aid
agencies to come here so they were happy to give permission.'
Looking suddenly doubtful, he added, 'They want us to open

lots of clinics in the city. When I told them we worked in Hazara Jat, they said it was important to work here as well – and they want us to make regular reports about what we are doing.' He shrugged, 'I'll take you to meet the Foreign Minister in a few days and you can explain things to him.'

Not relishing the prospect of explaining to a Government official that we had no money to open clinics in the city, I wondered if our stay in Mazar was going to be shorter than we had hoped.

The kebabs arrived. The long skewers held tiny chunks of meat, interspersed with the occasional piece of tomato and, tastiest of all, little blobs of white fat from the *dumba* [the Afghan sheep's fat tail]. Delicious though they were, we were too exhausted to do full justice to our long-awaited meal and were soon ready to go back to the office.

Scooping up a weary David, Reza chivvied us along, 'We must be back before ten o'clock because of the curfew. No-one is allowed on the streets after that.'

David fell asleep as soon as he lay down, and I collapsed, thankfully, beside him on the mattress in the ground floor room – generously allocated to us because it was the coolest. Five minutes later, there was a power cut, the fan stopped whirring and any illusion of coolness disappeared. The initial excitement of our arrival was replaced by gloomy doubts and pessimistic thoughts.

Next morning David and I both woke scratching furiously at numerous flea bites. Hot, sweaty and horribly itchy, with no immediate prospect of a bath in sight, I trailed David disconsolately across the compound to the latrine. Groping for the light switch, I stifled a yell when my hand brushed against the sticky softness of cobwebs. When illuminated by the weak bulb, the webs which festooned the walls were of a size and thickness that indicated spiders of fearsome proportions.

The foot-rests on either side of the hole were large blocks of sun dried mud and I kept a tight grip on David while he straddled what appeared to be a bottomless pit. Shuddering at the thought of him demonstrating his independence by deciding to use the toilet alone, I resolved to buy a plastic potty until our indoor toilets were usable.

'Mazar is famous for fleas', said Reza, authoritatively, when I complained about our bites. 'They go away in the melon season,' he added enigmatically. Needless to say, that was weeks away. Watching David and me as we scratched our way through breakfast, Naeem suggested a trip to the bazaar to find insect repellent and antihistamine cream.

The city centre, dominated by the impressive blue-domed shrine – or *mazar*, from which the city takes its name – was laid out with tree-lined, two-lane avenues around a central square. An imposing eight-storey building on one corner was, Naeem informed me proudly, a proper hotel.

'Does it have a restaurant?' I asked hopefully.

Naeem shook his head, 'The owner became fed up with the Party Commanders who came to Mazar for meetings with General Dostum. They stayed there and ate in the restaurant but never paid their bills, so he closed it down to save money.'

The shops around the hotel had obviously been established in the days when tourists still came to Afghanistan. They boasted a wonderful array of Afghan rugs, carpets, antiques. Several large carpets were laid in the middle of the road. Jeeps and trucks drove over them. Seeing my surprised look, Naeem grinned, 'I think foreigners like old rugs best, no?'

Further round the square were smart, glass-fronted shops selling up-market consumer goods. Air conditioners, fridges and cookers were mostly Russian, women's fashions, including high-heeled shoes and shiny, slinky blouses were imported from Iran. There were countless well-stocked pharmacies and several bakeries, whose mounds of biscuits and pastries displayed in the windows seemed to attract more flies than customers.

On the wide pavements in front of these shops, however, modern city planning gave way to the colourful confusion of the more traditional eastern bazaar where traders set up stall using anything from enormous woven baskets to wooden hand carts to iron-framed bedsteads. Here everything from padlocks to rubber-soled shoes to imported plastic tat; from cheap cosmetics to baby clothes to glass bangles was on offer.

There was an amazing diversity of ethnic groups – Uzbeks, Tajiks, Turkomen, Hazaras and Pathans. Some Uzbeks shared the high cheekbones, small noses and slanted eyes of the Hazaras, whom they call their 'cousins'. The two tribes boasted of sharing Genghis Khan as a mutual ancestor. Giving the lie to this, other Uzbeks had facial features more strongly Turkic in appearance.

Despite the seemingly normal, cheerful bustle and hubbub of the bazaar, Mazar was clearly a city prepared for war. The streets were full of uniformed soldiers and militiamen, each armed with the ubiquitous Kalashnikov. Many also strutted about with rocket launchers strapped to their backs. Not all belonged to General Dostum, who – invariably described in the press as a warlord – controlled the city. Other parties had a presence in Mazar-i-Sharif and there were Tajik militia, loyal to Ahmad Shah Masood and President Rabbani's Jamiat-i-Islami group, as well as Hazaras belonging to Hisb-i-Wadhat.

Yet, however unsettling Mazar's signs of military activity were, it was nothing to the astonishment produced by the number of women seen everywhere.

There were women hidden beneath the folds of burqas, resembling mobile shuttlecocks, the material falling in pleats which swirled to the ankle from a tightly-fitting headdress. A fine mesh panel allowed the woman only a restricted view of where she was going. Many wore the less concealing chaddar – like a large sheet – while a surprising number opted for daringly wispy little headscarves which concealed nothing of their hair.

Naeem nudged me. 'Look to your right,' he whispered. Three girls, in their late teens, had stopped to examine an array of cosmetics. Each wore a wisp of gauzy stuff on her head, western-style blouses and long skirts, which reached almost to their ankles. The real eye-opener was that they wore no *tunban* [the traditional, baggy, drawstring trousers

with which Muslim women cover their legs]. True, not much
above the ankle was on display, but I had never seen an
Afghan woman without her trousers, and, in shock, I stared
openly. Naeem asked, yet again, 'Can you believe you are
in Afghanistan?'

Not only were women highly visible on the streets, Naeem
said there were female nurses, midwives and doctors, women
teaching in schools and colleges, and working in offices. Neither
I, nor my two colleagues, had ever dreamt that Afghan women
played such a large role in life outside their homes. We had been
vaguely aware that education for girls was possible in the major
cities, but our imaginations had not stretched beyond that.

As I began to meet some of the women of Mazar-i-Sharif
I had to accept that all I believed I 'knew' and 'understood'
about women in Afghanistan had been based on much too
narrow a field of contact.

Aquila, a refugee from Kabul working for a UN agency,
described herself as a feminist – a word that would have no
meaning to the women I had met in Hazara Jat. She talked
of freedom for women, surprising me with her outspoken
support of ex-President Najibullah, who, she declared, had
been an advocate of *huqooq-i-zen* [women's rights]. She was
condemnatory of the mujahideen, who, when they had assumed
power, had immediately set about attempting to push women
back into their traditional house-bound roles. 'They are not
Muslims,' she declared. 'They know nothing of Islam.'

One day, Aquila, disdainfully indicating the chaddar I
always wore when outside our office, demanded, 'Why are you
wearing that thing?' Known as a *chaddar-i-namaz* [a prayer
chaddar or shawl] the huge, all enveloping semi-circular length
of fabric covered everything but the face.

'I think it is important that foreigners working here adopt the
local customs, including dress.' I replied, with a priggishness
that now makes me blush.

Aquila's response was to hoot with laughter. 'I am more
local than you will ever be, but I would never dream of wearing
such a thing. It might be all right in rural areas where the

women aren't free, but not in the city. If you really want to cover your hair, buy a *rooasarie*.'

I bought a couple of these Iranian triangular headscarves to wear in the office, but, though rather abashed by Aquila's comments, I could not bring myself to go outside without wearing more than a large handkerchief on my head. I was troubled about the morality of adopting a dress code seen by Aquila as repressive, but welcomed the small degree of anonymity the chaddar offered. As the summer heat increased, however, I exchanged my *chaddar-i-namaz* for a smaller, lighter version, wondering, as I sweated even then, how those women hidden under stifling, veiled burqas did not die of heatstroke.

For, despite Aquila's talk of city women being 'free', many did still cover themselves completely when they went outside. Did these women then have no freedom at all, I wondered. Was their outer covering a sign of imprisonment and oppression – and did they regard it as such?

Aquila believed so. Had she lived in London in the 'sixties, she would undoubtedly have burned her bra, and for her, throwing away her chaddar held the same symbolic meaning. But she still covered her hair, if only with a small scarf, when she went outside. When I queried this, she replied, 'It makes life easier. If I go without any headscarf – as I did in Kabul – the soldiers shout abusive remarks. Most of them are illiterate, uneducated peasants.'

Aquila, whose family had been part of Kabul's elite professional class, shared a concept of 'freedom' for women similar, in many ways, to Western feminist ideals. Her conversations were peppered with words such as equality, empowerment and women's rights.

On the other hand, Zohra, who worked as a domestic servant in another UN office did not consider herself 'free'. Quite the reverse. She felt a terrible sense of shame that because her husband, who had been a teacher in Kabul, could not find work, she had been forced into becoming the family breadwinner.

'My mother and grandmother taught me that if I was a good wife, my husband would take care of me and our children,' she complained. 'Well, I was a good wife. I kept his house clean, cooked his meals and looked after the children, keeping them quiet when he was resting. I was a good wife.'

Walking to work was an ordeal Zohra could barely endure. Never before having had to leave the house alone for anything, she scurried through the streets of the city, glad to hide her face in the flowing folds of her faded burqa.

I puzzled over this word 'freedom', which, in relation to women, obviously had many shades of meaning in Afghanistan. I wondered how many Afghan women shared Habiba's views, how many agreed with Sharifa? One thing was clear – exhilaratingly so. At least here in Mazar-i-Sharif, with so many women in public life, I could discard the mantle of honorary male which, in Hazara Jat, had been so often bestowed on me.

There it had usually been men who had answered my questions about Islam, customs, cultural belief and social conventions. Not only did they explain their own views, they presumed to speak on behalf of women as well.

I had seen how difficult women's lives were in terms of the work they did, the health problems they suffered, but knew little about how they felt about these things. What did they think of their situation? Did they even think about it? Or did they just accept the hardships of their lives as inevitable? Was I seeing oppression, discrimination, lack of power in their lives only because I was a foreigner from a vastly different culture? Now, with three years in Mazar-i-Sharif ahead of me, I hoped to learn from women themselves what life was really like for Afghan women.

Soon after my arrival, Naeem suggested we interview a woman for the position of office cook. 'Suggested' is perhaps not the appropriate word. He gave me to understand that if this poor woman, who had come begging for work, was not given immediate employment, the death of her two children from starvation would be for ever on my conscience.

It was for less altruistic reasons that I was delighted at the thought that a woman would join our team. As was the case in every office in Quetta, all the support staff – cook, cleaners, chowkidars – were men. Since arriving in Mazar and seeing so many women in jobs with other NGOs and UN agencies, I had felt it was time our organisation stared practising some gender equality.

There were other, more selfish, reasons. I wanted to make friends with Afghan women. Much as I liked Naeem and Reza and enjoyed their company, there were constraints imposed by Afghan culture on mixed-sex friendships. Certain topics of conversation were off limits. Naeem may have taken it in his stride, but I could not see myself casually explaining that my headache and bad mood were because my period was due to start. I needed to have some women around me during the next three years.

Latifa, hidden in the folds of a patched and faded burqa, appeared the next day for her interview. She greeted us nervously, not knowing that with Naeem firmly on her side, unless she let slip that she was a wanted criminal, her appointment was a foregone conclusion.

Sitting cross-legged on a mattress (we had bought soft cotton-filled mattresses as a more comfortable alternative to the itchy, plush chairs which were only used when we *had* to sit at a desk), she threw back her veil to reveal a strikingly attractive face with high cheek-bones and finely-shaped eyebrows. A dark mole below her full bottom lip gave her a coquettish appearance, and her big, dark brown eyes were bright and lively.

Latifa's eyes, I soon learned, left one in no doubt as to her mood. They could twinkle humorously or glint flirtatiously. When she was angry their dangerous flash warned everyone to stay clear.

On this occasion, describing her circumstances, her huge eyes were clouded with pathos and her story tumbled out breathlessly. Both the speed of delivery and the unfamiliar Kabul accent allowed me to grasp only one word in ten. Naeem did better – but he had heard it before – and translated for my benefit.

Her husband had gone to Iran to look for work, leaving Latifa and their two children in Kabul. She had not heard from him since his departure, and when heavy fighting had erupted close to their home she had been forced to flee to Mazar-i-Sharif. From the little money her husband had left her, she had paid an advance for a small room. Now there was no more money, the rent was due, her children were hungry and she was desperate to find work.

'My husband always looked after us,' she murmured, brushing away tears. 'I have never had to look for a job before. I'm not educated, so all I can do is cook and clean.'

She shot me a look before continuing, 'But I don't know what foreigners eat so I might not be able to cook what you like.' She looked downcast for a second before adding hopefully, 'I can do chips?' Naeem assured her, a bit tactlessly, I thought, that I could eat anything.

There was no need for further discussion. Offering Latifa the job, we were rewarded with a ravishing smile which made her dark eyes dance with delight.

Chicken Soup to Clear the Tubes

I WAS AWAKENED at seven o'clock next morning by Latifa knocking insistently on my door. 'Drink!' she commanded, handing me a glass. 'It's good for people who smoke. Clears the tubes.' It was scalding hot chicken stock.

Sipping sleepily, I followed her upstairs, where I found Naeem, grinning happily, drinking his 'medicine'. Reza, a non-smoker, looked slightly sulky, but was mollified by an extra large helping of *halwa*. Since our usual breakfasts had been dry nan and tea, we greeted with delight the delicious combination of wheat flour and sugar cooked in oil into which Latifa had thrown a handful of plump, juicy sultanas.

Satisfied that her first morning's culinary endeavour met with approval, Latifa cheerfully bustled off to continue the preparations for our chicken lunch. We could hear her laughing with her daughter, Tamana, a rotund and robust toddler who in no way resembled a child facing the threat of starvation, or even mild hunger pangs. 'I think she is happy with her job,' commented Naeem with a smile.

Although my personal thoughts had been more along the lines that Latifa seemed extraordinarily cheerful for a penniless woman whose husband had apparently abandoned her to bring up two small children alone in a war zone, I kept quiet.

It was not long before we discovered that Latifa had bent the truth a bit when describing her unfortunate situation. On her third day at work, full of excitement, she announced that her husband had written from Iran saying he would soon be home.

'How did he know where to send a letter?' I asked, genuinely astonished and intrigued by the workings of such a sophisticated grapevine. After all, she had told us that she had heard nothing from her husband since his departure, and she had left Kabul without being able to get word to him.

Looking sheepish, Latifa launched into a rapid and voluble story, very little of which I could follow – as she well knew. I asked no more awkward questions, not even when her husband, Moh'd Ali, turned up in Mazar, within days of Latifa receiving his mysterious letter.

We never learned the whole truth, although it seemed that Latifa's husband had been in Mazar-i-Sharif all along. Neither Naeem nor I pursued the matter, justifying our reluctance to challenge Latifa's version of the facts by agreeing that she really needed the job. Perhaps she thought we would not have given her the job had we known she was not having to cope alone? Maybe she thought we would have offered her husband, who was unemployed, the job instead of her?

We both liked her enormously. Her bubbly personality and ready laugh brightened our days – and she was a brilliant cook.

After her interview, I never again saw Latifa wear the burqa. Instead, pushing Tamana in a large, old-fashioned pram – the kind nannies used to use in London parks – she walked the half mile to work wrapped in a *chaddar-i-namaz*. This she exchanged, once indoors, for a small *rooasarie*, filling me with envy at how, with a quick twist of the ends, she contrived to keep it in place. I never learned this knack, having to resort to tying mine, gypsy fashion, at the back of my neck to keep it from slipping off – though I was proud of the fact that I could wear a chaddar as though to the manor born.

Latifa had a slender figure which showed to advantage the western style skirts and tops – bought at the second-hand clothing bazaar – she wore over slim legged *tunban*. I asked why she had worn the burqa that first day.

She shrugged. 'I never wore it in Kabul but men here, especially Uzbeks, are old-fashioned. I borrowed it from a neighbour for my interview in case the *rais* – the boss – did not like women going about without a veil and refused me the job.' She added, with a smile, 'I didn't know then that Naeem doesn't worry about such things. If Reza was the *rais*, though, he would never have given me the job. He isn't happy about me being the cook because he thinks a man should have got the job.'

Naeem confirmed that Reza had been opposed to appointing Latifa – or any Afghan woman for that matter – to work in the office. The two men, although they had grown up almost next door to each other in the Jaghoray district of Hazara Jat, held totally different attitudes to the phenomenon of Afghan women being free.

Naeem welcomed it wholeheartedly. He began immediately to look for a house to rent – sure that his wife, Maryam, would be happy in Mazar. He was delighted that his daughter, Fatima – as well as his sons – would be able to attend school and have a chance to fulfil her ambition to become a doctor.

Where Naeem rather liked the idea of Maryam being free to have her hair done at the beauty parlour, go out to visit friends or shop in the bazaar while he was at work, Reza clearly did not.

He expressed doubts on the wisdom of sending for his family. 'He is old-fashioned,' complained Naeem. 'Also, he is so careful with money he is afraid that if his wife was free to go to the bazaar without him she would spend all his money.'

Reza certainly hated to part with money. Occasionally, when with him in the bazaar, I had tried to buy fruit for David, only to return empty handed because Reza had become incensed by the prices. Since no locally grown fruit was available at that time of year, choice was limited to small overpriced mangoes or wizened, blackened objects, scarcely recognisable as bananas.

In vain did I try to convince him that the cost of transporting produce from Pakistan inevitably meant prices were higher than in Quetta. Wimpishly, I would give up, sneaking off with Naeem later to buy a mango for David. On the other hand, when I realised that shopkeepers, assuming all foreigners worked for the UN, put their prices up whenever they saw me approach, there was none better than Reza to help with hard bargaining.

However, it was not only Reza's miserliness that made him more cautious about his family coming to Mazar. In Jaghoray, the only women with whom he had had any dealings were family members. He was used to other women effacing themselves in his presence, turning away and covering their faces. Suddenly he was confronted every day with women who strode past him on the street as though he did not exist.

When visiting UN offices and Government departments, he met many working women, some of whom chatted freely to him, as though unaware that he was a man. Even more galling, some spoke down to him, showing they thought themselves of a higher status than a mere driver. Coming to terms with women assuming such a high profile in public life presented Reza with huge difficulties.

His biggest problem was that his upbringing had conditioned him to believe that women who did not remain safely cloistered at home must be totally immoral. Suddenly, he was being expected to change lifelong beliefs almost overnight.

For all that he disapproved of working women, Reza soon found a hundred different reasons to spend time in the kitchen with Latifa. The building often rang to the sound of her laughter, which always – even on the most innocent occasion – sounded as though she had just enjoyed hearing a particularly smutty story. Lunch-times became hilarious occasions as she entertained everyone with a stream of jokes – most of which went right over my head, even with Naeem's efforts to interpret. The joke, however funny in Dari, totally lost its humour in translation.

Latifa often teased Reza for his narrow-minded attitude towards working women. He would hotly deny that he thought they should be locked up at home. Invariably, though, he qualified his denial by saying, 'If a woman has no husband to support her, of course she must work to feed her children.'

Latifa, who never hid the fact that she would not give up her job, even if her husband found work the next day, would laugh cynically. 'Oh, Reza, if only I had a husband like you! I could stay at home all day, cooking and cleaning, not seeing anyone, not talking to anyone, waiting for you to return to tell me how hard you work in the wicked world outside.'

I worried that her joking had gone too far the day I heard her ask Reza, who was wiping tears of laughter from his eyes, 'Don't you wish you had married me? Should I leave my husband and run away with you?' Not catching Reza's laughing reply and thinking I had perhaps misunderstood (not an uncommon occurrence), I glanced at Naeem. From the intent way he was concentrating on his food, ignoring the laughing banter, I knew I had not been mistaken.

He obviously shared my discomfiture, explaining later, when we were alone: 'Reza is not used to women talking like that. He may not understand that Latifa is joking and read more meaning into it than she intends. You'll see, it will all end in tears.'

Amused at Naeem's use of what I had considered a very British expression, but troubled by his prophecy, I went to talk to Latifa in the kitchen.

I often spent time there with her, enjoying watching the casual way she chucked a handful of this or a large pinch of that into the cooking pot. An instinctive cook, she judged everything on look, smell and feel, producing mouthwatering local dishes some of which, she confessed, she had never cooked before. Mantu, an Uzbek dish of dumplings stuffed with mincemeat, became a favourite dish in the office, as did her fried leek fritters.

On this occasion, I asked tentatively if she was sure that Reza understood she was joking when she talked about running away with him. Her eyes flashing fire, Latifa expressed her opinion of Reza. 'He makes me crazy. He thinks men are up here, women down there.' Her hands waved about in demonstration of where Reza placed women on his evolutionary gender scale. 'He keeps his wife locked up in the house and would beat any man who dared to talk or joke with her, but it is all right for him to tease me and make dirty remarks. He has two faces – like many Afghan men.'

Although not condoning Reza's attitude, I suggested that

he found it difficult to know how to behave towards women who worked outside their homes, mixing with men, talking freely to them. Latifa snorted, 'He'd better learn quickly. He's not in Hazara Jat now. He must see that things are changing in Afghanistan.'

'What about Gulbedin?' I asked. 'He doesn't accept these changes. He wants women back at home.' In those pre-Taliban days, the then prime minister of the Kabul Government, Gulbedin Hekmatyar, was the fundamentalist bogeyman. One of his first acts on taking office had been to ban women from appearing as newsreaders on Kabul television, publicly announcing that a woman's place was in the home.

Latifa shook her head, 'He can't push us back into purdah now, there are too many of us. So many women have lost their husbands and sons in the war that they have to go out to work, or they would starve. Gulbedin isn't going to feed them.

'But anyway, why shouldn't women be able to work? I don't want to sit at home all day. I enjoy working. I like to have my own money and decide how I want to spend it. Reza will have to get used to seeing us around. He'll have to accept that if we talk to men, even enjoy a joke with them, it does not mean we are too free.'

I was becoming used to the various shades of meaning in this word *azad* [free]. Latifa used the word to describe women, like herself, who found employment outside their homes without having to ask their husband's permission, and who had control over their own earnings. Women who were free were able to move about the city without having to conceal themselves in the burqa or be chaperoned.

Latifa believed women should be free to talk with male colleagues without being considered by them to be of loose morals, tagged with the label of being 'too free'. But then, although Latifa declared that her own daughter would never be forced into an arranged marriage, she thought her neighbour's teenage daughter was too 'free' because she was secretly meeting a boy of whom her parents disapproved.

In the meantime, work on our office premises moved

frustratingly slowly – sometimes even going backwards. Our landlord, who was, naturally, a big commander (*all* commanders were described as big; there were, seemingly, no small ones) had disappeared on military business somewhere out of the city. We suspected this was an excuse to release him from the obligation of solving the building problems.

We were still buying water, which was delivered in forty-gallon oil drums, by an old man with a donkey cart. In our waterless bathrooms, we had been managing nicely with bucket baths, until the plumber – who had forgotten to instal any water pipes – came back to dig up the floors. Having thus rendered both bathrooms totally unusable, he disappeared – for five days. When he finally returned to complete the work and connected everything up to the water tank, no water appeared. Someone, somewhere along the system was waiting for a bribe – which eventually, in desperation, we paid.

The fleas were as vicious as ever – and the melon season still hadn't started. On one occasion, sitting for dinner between Naeem and Reza, both of whom remained totally unmolested, I collected eight new bites. Principles, and all regard for the ozone layer, went out the window as I went on a spraying frenzy. The walls, the carpet, even the mattress were squirted with some foul-smelling pesticide.

This helped for a time, and being able to spend more hours asleep instead of scratching at bites, I could face with greater equanimity the other problems we confronted on a regular basis.

Naeem and Reza, having installed the almost useless electric cooker, bought a one-ring kerosene stove. With the addition of an enormous kettle, a frying pan and a large spoon, they believed the kitchen was fully equipped. Latifa, insisting that a few other items of kitchenware were needed, suggested a shopping expedition during which we could buy in bulk our rice, beans and lentils.

In the wholesale market we wandered in lanes lined with huge sacks of rice, several kinds of lentil, red and white kidney beans and wheat. Hundreds of fat pigeons strutted about, occasionally taking flight as an overloaded handcart threatened to run over them. Moments later, they would re-alight on the road, smoothing ruffled feathers, before continuing their banquet of spilt grain.

I pointed inquiringly at piles of reddish coloured rocks. 'For washing your hair,' said Latifa. 'You break them up and when you put some pieces in water they become foamy. It makes your hair shiny and beautiful.' I noticed, however, when visiting Latifa's house that her shampoo of choice was Silvikrin.

Reza pointed out sacks of poppy heads, openly on sale. 'People boil them to make medicines,' he explained, 'to help them sleep or as painkillers.'

'Some mothers use them to make a syrup to stop their babies crying,' Latifa added, her tone registering disapproval.

After almost an hour of poking and prodding and sniffing at endless sacks, Latifa and Reza had bought nothing. The shopkeepers, hearing their goods dismissed as both inferior and expensive, began to look less friendly. The children were restless. Naeem sighed, glumly muttering, 'Latifa is every bit as penny-pinching as Reza. This is going to take all day because they are both determined to prove they can find the best bargains.' Leaving them wrangling over the price of rice, Naeem and I took the thoroughly fed-up children off for ice creams.

The shopping finally finished, an unusually quiet Reza drove us back to the office. After helping to carry the heavy bags up the stairs, he strode, stony faced, out of the kitchen, huffily refusing an offer of tea.

Shrugging eloquently at his retreating back, Latifa commented, 'He is sulking because I got a better price for *lubia* [red kidney beans] than he did. He thinks shopping is a man's job – that women will be easily cheated because we don't know how to deal with shopkeepers. I showed him a woman can manage just as well – even better – than a man.' Reza, I reflected, had as much to learn about these Afghan city women as I.

His pride was further dented a few days later, when we

were all invited for lunch. We hardly knew our hostess, Farida, whom I had met only briefly when renewing my visa at the passport office where she worked. A few days later she called at our office to issue the invitation to lunch.

Although her family was from Mazar-i-Sharif, Farida and her sisters and brother had grown up in Kabul, where their father had worked for Najibullah's Government. After the mujahideen came to power, the family had prudently returned to Mazar, where they still owned property. She and her brother had studied in Moscow and spoke fluent Russian, as well as their Uzbek mother tongue, and Dari.

When lunch was served, Farida and her sisters ate with us – something that would never have happened in Reza's home in Hazara Jat. Dinner parties there were men-only affairs, cooked by invisible women who remained in the kitchen.

The conversation turned to the war and politics. Reza, who gathered most of his news from gossiping shopkeepers, taxi drivers and Hazara friends, who understandably only ever saw things from the Hazara point of view, held forth at considerable length.

Farida, who gained her intelligence from close contacts with Government officials, both civil and military, listened quietly for a while, then politely but quite firmly told him he was wrong. I don't think Reza took in a word of her argument, so stunned was he by the fact that a woman had contradicted him – in front of other people, at that. He lapsed into a surly silence for the rest of the meal.

When the television was turned on – tuned to a Russian programme featuring half-naked girls disco dancing – and Farida asked Naeem for a cigarette, Reza's expression of outraged disbelief made me glad I was wearing my chaddar. I could use it, as Afghan women do, to hide my mirth.

Driving back to the office Naeem asked, 'How did you enjoy the *mehmanni*?'

Reza sniffed. 'It's very different from Jaghoray,' he replied. 'Did you see those women on television?' As the screen was similar in size to that of a small cinema, Naeem could hardly have missed it. He nodded, remarking innocently, 'I think it was some kind of sporting event.' They both turned to me, in some alarm, as I snorted helplessly into my chaddar.

Reza was much happier at another lunch. Our host, referred to as Engineer, was clerk-of-works for our landlord and was therefore supposed to supervise the work still be done on our part of the building. The invitation was, we suspected, to keep us from complaining too much when things were not done.

Engineer was a Pushtoon and kept his women securely hidden away so Reza could relax, safe from any further culture shocks, and enjoy his lunch. After eating, I went behind the curtain to meet Engineer's wife, who he told me proudly, had been educated in Kabul.

'She knows French,' he added, 'so you can talk to each other.' As I hadn't spoken French since leaving school, this was not reassuring. Fortunately, she didn't and although we struggled at times we managed to communicate in Dari.

I fear I was an enormous disappointment to the women of Engineer's family. His wife, his mother and his sister, waiting to greet me in the *zenana* [women's section] were dressed in the most gorgeous and obviously expensive clothes. Every movement and gesture they made was accompanied by the swish of silk and satin. They also wore gold – vast quantities of it – on their fingers, around their wrists, their necks, in their ears and in their noses.

I felt like a dowdy moth sitting next to a group of colourful butterflies. My only jewellery was a cheap silver and turquoise ring, which, to my horror, Engineer's sister spotted. 'Show me,' she commanded. Embarrassed, I sat watching them pass the ring from one to another, exclaiming over it as though it was the most wonderful, expensive piece of jewellery ever designed.

Whenever a man entered the compound a warning shout went up, giving the women time to pull the curtain across the window in case they were glimpsed with their heads uncovered.

Although he would have balked at having to provide so much

gold, Reza would heartily approve of such gender apartheid, I thought as I finally rose to go.

The heat steadily increased and, even with two air conditioners running, the temperature in the office was over eighty degress Fahrenheit. Occasionally Latifa escaped the fiery furnace of her kitchen to catch the slight breeze on the balcony. From there she could carry on a conversation with our neighbour, Shireen, whose compound we overlooked.

Shireen's family lived in a traditional, mud-built, beehive-domed house which they abandoned during the summer, which they spent entirely out of doors. At night, much to my envy, they slept beneath the stars under a large, mosquito-netted pavilion.

Joining Latifa on the balcony one day, I queried the blue–green iridescence covering the roof of Shireen's cow's shed. Fascination turned to horror when she explained that Shireen was drying her tomatoes in the sun. 'They are very tasty in *shurwa* [soup] in winter, when no fresh ones are available,' she assured me, puzzled by how green I must have turned. The entire crop was covered in enormous bluebottles. Even now, listening to anyone extol the superior flavour of sun-dried tomatoes, I remember that shimmering carpet of flies gorging themselves on Shireen's tomato crop.

— 4 —
Condoms and Abortions

LATIFA WORKED AND TALKED, usually simultaneously, at top speed.

'*Ahista bollo*' [speak slowly] I would beg, as she rattled off a story. Patiently, she would start again, slowing her speech until, caught up once more in her tale, she would unconsciously speed up again. I was constantly asking her to repeat things, puzzling over unfamiliar words, sounding them in my head before attempting to try them out – sometimes not sure if I had the correct meaning.

When we talked about health, pregnancies and childbirth, I was more confident, having already absorbed a more extensive vocabulary. So when two of Latifa's friends arrived one day to ask the *kharijee* [foreigner] for contraceptive advice I was on reasonably safe ground.

Nafissa, a mother of six, wanted to stop taking oral contraceptives, blaming them for her headaches. A brief description of the intra-uterine device and how it worked filled them with disgust. Latifa grimaced, 'Ugh! I wouldn't like something left inside me. It's not natural.'

When I suggested condoms as an alternative to the pill or IUD, Nafissa exploded into ribald laughter while the younger woman, Shafika, giggled and hid her face in her chaddar. Led by Nafissa, the discussion degenerated into lavatory humour.

All over Afghanistan children use condoms as playthings – even the word *pakana* means balloon. I began to understand why both Afghan men and women were reluctant to consider condoms seriously as a means of contraception.

Surprisingly – for she was usually the leader in such ribaldry – Latifa was quieter than the others. Wondering if she was more amenable to the idea of using condoms, but embarrassed to say so in front of her friends, I mentioned the subject when next we were alone. Latifa heard me out looking, I thought, a bit miserable, before replying, 'I think I could persuade Moh'd Ali to use condoms but, for now, there is no need. I am pregnant.'

'Mubarak! Congratulations!'

She looked sourly at me. 'I told you before, I don't want another baby. It was an accident.'

Before I made some inane 'cheer up, it's not the end of the world' remark, Latifa's next words rendered me speechless.

'I am not going to have it. Tomorrow, I am seeing a doctor who will end the pregnancy. I may need a day or two off work, if that is all right?'

I nodded, dumbly. Although a dozen questions were forming in my head, I found myself unable to ask a single one. What kept me silent was shame. I suddenly realised how patronising my attitude had been to the news of Latifa's pregnancy.

We had once talked about family sizes, and when I had said that for me, one was enough, she had replied, 'It would be nice if David had a sister, but you might have three more boys before you got a girl. I'm lucky to have one of each because Moh'd Ali and I don't want any more.

'Now that I have a job, we can afford to send both Farid and Ruckshana to school when they are older. If we had more children, their future would not be so good.'

Acutely embarrassed, I wondered now if Latifa had been insulted that day by my obvious surprise at her words. Why should she not use the same arguments as Western couples for limiting the size of her family? Because she was Afghan, Muslim, uneducated, a woman from the Third World? Had I even taken her words seriously, I wondered, wincing at the tactless way I had just offered congratulations, despite her obvious misery that she was pregnant.

Realizing that she was still talking, I tried to concentrate on her words. 'I asked', she repeated with more than a hint of impatience, 'if you would come with me to the hospital tomorrow? I would like to have someone with me.'

I nodded my agreement and Latifa murmured goodbye, leaving me to my uncomfortable thoughts.

Her announcement that she wanted an abortion had shaken me because, despite the fact that Latifa herself had told me that she and her husband only wanted two children, I was still holding fast to the Western notion that all Afghans want large families. Didn't received wisdom state that people in developing countries always have lots of babies because so few survive to adulthood; that children are an economic necessity to work on the land and support their aged parents?

It was embarrassing to have to accept that I had been so guilty of blindly swallowing the stereotype image of Muslim women – those shadowy, burqa-clad figures, hidden away behind high walls, producing babies year after year.

I had been excited by the idea that I would be able to learn the truth about Afghan women's lives, from women themselves, and been delighted when it seemed that Latifa and I could become friends. Now I recognised how little effort I had made to rid myself of preconceived ideas – was indeed horrified to realise that I had not even been aware of harbouring such prejudices. If I was to understand anything about Afghan women's lives, I was going to have learn to keep my mind, as well as my ears, open.

Thank goodness Latifa had forestalled my inane 'cheer up, it's not the end of the world' remark. Our friendship, scarcely begun, might not have survived that.

Next morning, as we walked the short distance to the 'Do Sat Bistar' – the 200-bed hospital – Latifa tried to answer my many questions. 'It's allowed,' she explained, 'if the pregnancy is dangerous for the mother. Two doctors must agree and,' she added, with a slight smile, 'the husband must sign a form giving his permission.

'Of course,' she continued, 'some doctors won't agree to an abortion, saying it is against Islam. Others don't even accept that pregnancy can be dangerous for a woman, or they think that it is Allah's will that women suffer in childbirth. A friend of mine, who had six children, had to act like she was crazy –

screaming and tearing her hair, crying that she would kill herself – before the doctor agreed to an abortion. He asked for her husband's signature, telling him his wife was mentally disturbed. When she came out of hospital, her husband had taken her children away and divorced her for being insane.'

My pace slowed as I listened in horror to Latifa's tale. She touched my arm, urging me on. 'Don't worry, my doctor is all right,' she said. 'I know him from Kabul. He will understand that this pregnancy would be dangerous. Last time I was very ill with *khon-i-fishur* [high blood pressure].'

In the consulting room, rather than displaying signs of incipient insanity, Latifa greeted the good-looking young doctor warmly, jokingly asking him how many wives he had collected since she last saw him. Turning to me, she explained, 'He has two wives already, but he still chases after the nurses.' She gave a throaty chuckle, adding, 'Some of them don't run away very fast either.'

When the doctor said that he would first have to confirm the pregnancy, Latifa laughed, 'There's no need – I know.' The doctor was adamant.

'First we check. I'll give you a prescription for an injection. Come back after two days.'

I asked how an injection was used as a pregnancy test. In faltering English (he was already fluent in Polish and Russian, as well as Uzbeki and Dari, he was apologetic about his weak English, while I apologised, shamefacedly, for my weak everything) he explained, 'If there is no bleeding within twenty-four hours, the woman is pregnant. If she starts bleeding she is not pregnant.'

Was it a drug to induce an abortion? The doctor shook his head, 'No, no, that would be illegal.' Latifa took the proffered prescription and rose to leave. 'We'll go to the medicine shop on the way back to the office.'

I pleaded with her not to use the injection when I saw, in tiny English print, a warning that it was to be avoided 'if pregnancy is suspected'. Latifa shook her head, 'The doctor said I must do it. If I bleed then I won't need the operation.'

There was no bleeding. Forty-eight hours later, however, Latifa was not, as she had expected, making her way to the hospital for a termination. She was indignantly marching up and down my room, fuming about her husband. He was refusing to give permission for the abortion. Without her husband's signature, the doctor would do nothing.

'He says he is afraid Allah will be angry with him.' She snorted. 'He, who never prays, is suddenly thinking about Allah!

'I know it is only because he hopes it might be a boy. He is worried that if anything happens to Farid, he will not have a son. He has promised that this one – whether it is a girl or a boy – is the last. It is easy for him, he won't have to suffer the problems I'm going to have.'

In the short time I had known her, Latifa gave the impression of being adept at ensuring Moh'd Ali accepted whatever she wanted. This time she admitted defeat. He would not change his mind.

Over the next few weeks, it became clear that Latifa had not exaggerated her health problems. She became increasingly depressed and ill. Apart from severe morning sickness which prevented her from eating properly – even tea made her retch violently – her blood pressure was high. As she went, almost silently, about her work, I couldn't help comparing this tired, anxious Latifa with the vivacious, fun-loving young woman she had been when she first began working with us.

Her husband, Moh'd Ali, now desperately concerned about her ill health, regretted not signing the consent form. In a fit of remorse, he had taken over the cooking and cleaning at home. With the ghost of a grin, Latifa said, 'He won't wash the clothes though, in case the neighbours see him.'

Gradually, as the morning sickness lessened, Latifa began to brighten, but, although reconciled to the arrival of another baby, she was still resentful of how her feelings had been ignored.

'What gives my husband the right to decide these things?' she demanded, rhetorically. 'I have a mind. I am capable of making decisions about my body.'

When I ventured to ask if Islam gave husbands the right to make such decisions, Latifa snapped back, 'This has nothing to do with Islam. All his talk about Allah has been forgotten now. It is because men have to be in charge of everything – even things they don't understand, like women's bodies and having babies.'

With a sudden chuckle, she added, 'I think after this baby comes out, it will not be difficult to persuade Moh'd Ali to use condoms.' It was good to hear her laugh again and, although she was never really well throughout her pregnancy, the old sparky, gregarious Latifa began to reappear.

When she had started working with us, Latifa had asked permission to bring with her her eighteen-month-old daughter, Ruckshana, because she was still breast feeding her. I had been delighted, selfishly hoping the little girl would be a companion for David, whose demands for attention took me, too often, away from my desk.

The two children of course hated each other on sight. Ruckshana became enraged with jealousy when Latifa, amused by David's fascination for watching her nurse her daughter, would casually offer him a breast. Ruckshana's protests at this could be heard all over the building.

Feeling sorry that he had no companions of his own age, Latifa invited David to her home so that he could play with her son, Farid.

Four refugee families lived in the house, each family paying rent for one room while their landlord lived rent-free in a relative's house. Latifa's room was tiny and she had to cook outside in the compound, where Moh'd Ali had built a mud fireplace on which to balance her cooking-pot. The families shared the only outside latrine – though it was evident that many of the children rarely reached it in time. When David and Farid vanished outside to play, I tried not to dwell too much on typhoid, worms and other unpleasant things – comforting myself with the fact that Farid was a healthy enough child.

He and David became good friends but their occasional play times together did not solve the problem of keeping David

safely occupied while I was working. I had to find someone –
soon – to help look after David.

Through the Hazara community grapevine, Naeem heard
about a woman looking for work. Plump and pretty, Sharifa
had a ready smile which made her whole face light up. She, her
husband and five children rented a room in a house shared by
three families.

Her room was bare, apart from a couple of thin, cotton
mattresses, a few cushions, some bedding and, incongruously,
a large fridge, which took up a huge amount of space. She
caught me eyeing it curiously and gave a rueful laugh. 'That
fridge was my pride and joy in Kabul. It was the only thing we
had left when we came here – but the electricity is so weak in
this house that I can't use it.'

With Naeem's help in translating, I explained what Sharifa
would be expected to do – basically prevent David from leaping
to a certain death from a balcony or drowning himself in the
water tank. Sharifa had such a reassuring aura of motherliness
and unflappability about her that I hired her on the spot.

Hoping that David, who had disappeared to play outside
with the children, would also take to her, I went in search
of him. He was gazing, enraptured, at a large and very dirty
sheep. Sharifa gave him some vegetable peelings which, to his
delight, the sheep graciously accepted from his hand. David
was soon chattering happily to Sharifa, one arm still lovingly
draped round the sheep's neck.

Next morning, over breakfast, he asked excitedly if Sharifa
would be coming to play with him. Delighted that he had taken
such a shine to her, I foolishly began to make plans for the
hundred and one things to be done that day. When Sharifa
arrived, David promptly burst into noisy sobs. She had, of
course, arrived without the sheep.

Poor Sharifa, not understanding the cause of his tears
and already nervous about looking after a foreign child, was,
understandably, distraught by this reaction to her. Instead of
working, I had to spend the morning consoling them both.

The presence of the sheep may have made that first day

easier, but in the long term would have made little difference. As a child minder, Sharifa was a disaster. Most of her energies were directed towards making David go to sleep, rather than entertaining him. After gossiping over tea and boiled sweets (she could crunch up a dishful at one sitting), sleeping was her favourite occupation.

Understandably, David, an active child, was not happy about this turn of events. Nor was I. On the few occasions she did succeed in making him sleep in the afternoon, I was awake half the night playing with him. More often, Sharifa would doze off and David, seizing his chance, would scoot off to climb the scaffolding, or something equally life threatening until someone spotted him and alerted me.

By the time I realized just how hopeless the situation was, it was too late. I knew too much about Sharifa's troubled life to be able to inflict further misery by dismissing her. Until my departure for Hazara Jat in a few weeks' time we would manage somehow. What would happen after my return, I postponed thinking about.

I couldn't condemn Sharifa for wanting to sleep. In her shoes I would certainly have wanted to do the same. I was sure too that if I had five children of my own, the last thing I would have wanted to do was look after someone else's child – unless, of course, I was as desperate as Sharifa to earn some money.

Her husband, Jawad, brought home a pittance from his work as a handcart puller, casual labour which carried no certainty that he would be hired from one day to the next. Every morning, along with dozens of other hopefuls, he waited at the transport depot for the arrival of trucks loaded with a variety of goods – cigarettes, tea, sugar, wheat, cooking oil. Once everything was unloaded it was transported on hand carts to the bazaar merchants.

It was back-breaking, soul-destroying work. In the fierce summer heat men, usually working in pairs, laboured and sweated as they pulled and pushed the overloaded carts through the crowded streets. Animal rights protestors in the West would activate against such work – if donkeys were doing it.

Although Sharifa was easily moved to tears when hearing of someone's misfortune – or when she remembered her own losses – she was quick to dry her eyes and find something to smile about. I marvelled at her ability to keep cheerful when, on a visit to her home so that David could renew his acquaintance with the sheep, she told me something of her recent past.

She had loved Kabul – the Kabul before the mujahideen came to power. 'We were not rich, but we had a good life. My parents lived with us because my mother had no daughter-in-law to help her in the house. My brothers left Afghanistan when the war began, before they had married. We had a nice house and *auly* [compound or yard] with some *toot* [mulberry] and almond trees.'

She sighed wistfully, 'Oh, I used to love the almond blossom in the spring. We went for picnics in the park or by the river.' Sharifa's eyes crinkled with pleasure at the memory. 'Jawad', she continued, 'had regular work then and we always had enough food. We could buy new clothes for the children every *eid*.

'And it was a good time for women. There were lots of women doctors, teachers, women in offices. Many of them attended Kabul colleges, some even went to Moscow to study. They were free to go about in the bazaars without fear of being bothered. Many of the young ones even wore miniskirts, though my family would never have allowed me to wear one.

'When the mujahideen took Kabul, they told us that they had freed Afghanistan and it would be a true Islamic country. As Muslims, we did not want communism so, of course, we were happy to hear this, but we did not understand why suddenly an Islamic Government had to put up the prices of everything – wheat, oil, fuel. Feeding the children became difficult.'

That was not the only unwelcome change the mujahideen brought to Kabul. Sharifa told of the soldiers shouting abuse at women who did not cover their hair. There were stories of women being raped. Shops sold out of burqas and chaddars as women rushed to cover themselves in protective layers. Young girls, determined to demonstrate some defiant spirit, took their mothers' traditional white burqas to be dyed in more appealing colours.

Then the various parties which formed this new coalition Government began to squabble over the division of power. Soon, renewed fighting broke out. People became afraid, not knowing what to expect.

Sharifa fell silent for a few moments, lost in her sad memories. She gave a shrug before continuing, 'Jawad talked then about leaving Kabul. I did not want to leave. It was my home. Besides, my parents were too old to move. I couldn't leave them. Then one day, there was no more reason to stay.'

Sharifa's eyes filled with tears. 'My husband and my father were not at home the day a rocket hit the house. It was completely destroyed. My mother was killed instantly. My sister, Marzia, was badly injured. I only got a few cuts, nothing serious.

'When Jawad returned, he told me rockets had also landed in the bazaar, killing many people. We waited for my father to come home, but he never did. We searched everywhere, went to all the hospitals. It was horrible. There were bodies there – some had no heads, no-one could recognise them. One woman came to look for her husband. She only knew it was him from his shoes – brown and white ones. I can still hear her screaming. Maybe one of the others was my father.' Tears streamed, unchecked, down Sharifa's plump face.

Her voice husky with emotion, she continued, 'That was when we left Kabul. All we had was the clothes we were wearing, and my fridge. I don't know how it had survived. Jawad wanted to sell it, but I refused. It was a wedding gift and means such a lot to me. He was really bad tempered about it, especially when there was so little space for everyone on the truck. It was full of *mohajireen* [refugees] finally forced to run away. The women and children were crying, the men were angry. We had lived through so much, but we could not take any more.'

Sharifa dried her eyes. Her sadness was replaced by anger – anger that in the end it was her own people, not a foreign army of occupation, that had forced her to become a refugee in her own country. 'My mother and father – and my sister's husband – were Muslims and it was Muslims who killed them. It was Afghans fighting other Afghans that drove us out of Kabul.

'The mujahideen said Najibullah was a communist, but my children had shoes to wear when he was president. They had food to eat. Do you know how it feels when your children are hungry and you have nothing to give them? I wish Najibullah was still in power. I don't understand this kind of Islam.'

No, I could not tell Sharifa that I would have to find someone else to look after David.

Sometimes though, especially on busy days, I dreaded having to make the customary daily enquiry about her health. Whenever Afghans met, custom demanded a ritual litany of greetings, beginning with, 'How are you?' The correct reply to which was an echoed, 'How are you?' followed by, 'Are you well?' answered by, 'Are *you* well?' The process was repeated regarding every member of the other's household, the other's happiness, tiredness and well-being.

Amongst Hazaras, especially, the salutation always included the phrase, 'May you never be tired!' to which the response, 'May you live long!' was inevitably given. Once, even twice, would have been manageable, but the entire thing could be repeated several times, like a stuck record.

I used to stutter and stammer, in a desperate attempt to keep up my end of the catechism, until I realised that no-one actually listened to the replies. In the beginning, not knowing how to end the ritual, I had frightening moments imagining the entire day spent asking 'How are you?' Then quite by accident I discovered that if at some point in the proceedings I raised palms and eyes heavenwards, murmuring that my good health was thanks to God, it neatly stopped further questions. We could go forward towards a real conversation.

Whoever had spent an interminable amount of time assuring me of her excellent health and happiness, might then – and only then – admit that she was ill, or her house had burned down the night before.

Not Sharifa! She was the only Afghan I ever met who, when asked how she was, began immediately to list her complaints. Anything from dizzy spells to kidney pains, headaches, back ache, sore toe joints or aching legs – even, on particularly bad days, a combination of several at once. She had spent a fortune (which she could not afford) consulting doctors who simply prescribed expensive, and useless, tonics, vitamins and antibiotics. When one lot of pills had no effect, off she would go to a different doctor.

What Sharifa, along with countless other women in Afghanistan, really needed, was expert counselling to help her come to terms with the traumatising effects of the war. Not only had she suffered the tragic death of her parents, loss of her home, the misery of becoming a refugee, her future was a gaping black hole which offered no security for herself or her family. For the women – and men – of war-torn Afghanistan, however, there was no such help available.

All I could offer were large doses of tea and a sympathetic ear. Talking, remembering, having a good cry now and then seemed to provide some temporary relief of Sharifa's symptoms, but sometimes I was too busy to listen, and there were days when, patience exhausted, I gave instead of sympathy a sharp retort. Then, a look of hurt on her normally cheerful face, Sharifa would back away, leaving me to deal with a nasty combination of emotions: guilt at not providing the support she needed and helplessness because I could do so little anyway, all mixed up with anger about everything connected with Afghanistan and its endless war.

— 5 —
I Won't Sell My Sister

SHARIFA HARDLY HAD the chance to enjoy the benefits of an extra income before Jawad lost his job. Heavy fighting between rival political factions closed the main supply route into Mazar-i-Sharif; with no trucks arriving at the depot, there was no work available.

'I know the road closure is not his fault,' complained Sharifa, 'but he's not even looking for another job. Now that I'm earning money he thinks he can sit about and do nothing.' Latifa nodded, without commenting.

'At least Moh'd Ali helps you in the house,' added Sharifa. 'Jawad does nothing.'

Latifa and Sharifa regularly gathered round my desk for our morning tea and gossip break. Latifa was glad to have Sharifa around, with whom she could talk at her natural speed. She must often have been frustrated by my repeated requests that she slow down or repeat things I had not grasped.

It must have been irritating too to hear me stumbling through a tale, sometimes searching painfully slowly for the words I needed. We managed because we wanted to understand each other. Often, when I was talking I would realise, half way through a sentence, that I did not have the necessary vocabulary to finish whatever I was saying. The women would indicate they had grasped my meaning anyway, urging me to continue the story. The result was that I formed a bad habit of never quite finishing sentences. Amongst friends this was not a problem as they generally understood what I intended to say. Strangers, wearing puzzled expressions, would wait expectantly for me to supply the final verb which in Dari always comes at the end of a sentence.

The friendship between Sharifa and Latifa was mainly one of circumstance rather than choice. Their personalities were too different. Sharifa was a kinder person than Latifa, without the latter's acerbic tongue and quick wit. Sometimes I could see Sharifa – though she was no shrinking violet – looking faintly embarrassed at Latifa's banter with male colleagues. Sharifa reacted to any confrontation with tears – Latifa, eyes flashing dangerously, met it head on with relish.

Occasionally friendly relations between them were punctured by stiff silences – usually when Sharifa took offence at something Latifa had jokingly said – until one or other found something ridiculous in the situation and the breach would be healed with laughter and hugs.

Latifa had little patience with Sharifa's endless aches and pains, and even less for her complaints about her husband's behaviour. Her own husband, apart from when he refused his consent for the abortion – something that still rankled – was given no chance to think that he was lord and master in their home. She frequently scolded Sharifa, 'You are too weak. You shouldn't let him behave the way he does. If he doesn't have a job then he should do something in the house. If you are buying the food, he could at least cook it, or watch the children. Stand up for yourself.'

Sharifa's round, plump face would start to crumple, and as tears threatened to flow, Latifa would hastily change the subject.

Whenever I saw them together, I felt that Moh'd Ali and Latifa did regard each other with genuine affection. They talked to each other, shared private jokes whereby a word or look from Moh'd Ali provoked a gurgle of laughter from Latifa, and they spent time together with their children. The appearance of domestic harmony on display in their home may have been for my benefit, but it felt natural and comfortable.

In Sharifa's house, whether or not guests were present, Jawad did nothing to help. Often he went out without bothering to tell Sharifa where he was going or when he would return. 'I'm still supposed to have his meal ready to put in front of him the moment he returns,' she complained, 'How am I supposed to know when he's coming home? If it's not ready he says I am lazy.'

The arrival of her youngest sister, Marzia, and her six-week-old baby daughter, Shahnaz, brought additional problems into Sharifa's already difficult life.

When the family fled from Kabul, Marzia had gone to stay with another sister, Chaman, who lived with her husband and small son in Pul-i-Khumri, a town about three hours south of Mazar. At the time of Shahnaz's birth, Sharifa had worried about Marzia's lack of motherhood skills. 'She did not know which end of the baby to feed and which to clean,' she grumbled.

Despite the overcrowded conditions in their one room, Sharifa wanted Marzia and her baby to live with them. Jawad did not, and made it clear that he did not expect his young sister-in-law to be a long-term guest in his home. Complaining about having another mouth to feed (though, as Sharifa pointedly remarked, he didn't have to feed her), he became increasingly surly and quick tempered.

Marzia was beautiful, with rosy, dimpled cheeks and clouds of dark hair cascading down her back. Her eyes sparkled with humour, reflecting her bubbly personality and irrepressible sense of mischievous fun. An inveterate giggler, her refusal to take life too seriously sometimes infuriated Sharifa. She was also the most forgetful mother I ever met.

Accompanying Sharifa to the office on occasions, she would leave Shahnaz asleep somewhere and wander off to drink tea in the kitchen, or play with David – who adored her – outside. The baby would wake, hungrily demanding food and attention, but her mother would be out of earshot. When the lusty yells became too much to bear one of us would scoop up the well-swaddled bundle (Shahnaz, wrapped in layers of cloth bound with embroidered bands, usually resembled a badly tied parcel) and set off in search of her mother. Marzia, gigglingly accepting her daughter, would produce a well-filled breast and a blessed silence would descend.

Knowing of the tragedies that had already touched Marzia's life, I sympathised with her longing sometimes to shirk the responsibilities of motherhood. After only a few years in school, she had been kept at home to help her mother. At only fifteen, her parents had arranged her marriage to a man who already had two wives, and who took a fourth shortly after.

Before she had turned sixteen, Marzia, already pregnant, was widowed when her husband was killed by sniper fire in Kabul. She had moved back to her father's house, the house that was soon afterwards destroyed in the rocket attack that killed her parents. Marzia's arms and legs bore an unsightly network of shrapnel scars, a permanent reminder of the horrors of that time.

Being so young and pretty – and unattached – she was soon attracting a lot of attention from the men in their neighbourhood. 'Some of them come to ask Jawad if they can marry her,' said Sharifa, 'but I think she should wait until Shahnaz is older. No husband is going to be happy while his wife is breast feeding another man's child.'

Knowing that Marzia's coming and goings were being closely monitored by their neighbours, Sharifa, at Jawad's insistence, made Marzia wear a burqa outside. 'People will talk about her, saying she is too free,' she explained, an apologetic note in her voice.

The slightest lapse in what the community considered acceptable behaviour for a young widow, would lead to the wagging of malicious tongues. And any gossip about Marzia would bring shame on Jawad. As head of the household, it was his honour and good name that were at stake. Until she was safely married again – when the burden of honour would be transferred to her husband – Marzia would have to wear her burqa and show exemplary behaviour.

When discussing what they referred to as 'good' and 'bad' behaviour, Sharifa and Latifa were resentful of the attitude of those men who believed that unless shrouded in a burqa, women were immoral. 'Marzia', said Sharifa, 'would not do anything "bad" whether or not she wore a burqa.'

This reminded Latifa of a joke often told in Kabul: 'There was a very religious man who was always telling people what a good, clean life he led. Of course he insisted his wife was always veiled. One day he went to a prostitute on the street. He was very surprised at the high price she quoted for her services. Wanting to check if her beauty really warranted such a fee, he raised her veil. With a big shock, he saw it was his wife.'

She and Sharifa roared with laughter. Latifa, when she had her mirth under control, added, 'Why can't men understand that if a woman's heart is clean, she will not do anything wrong whether she sits at home or goes out to work, whether she hides herself under a chaddar or not? And if she wants to go with other men, she will find a way. What I wear makes no difference to whether I am a good Muslim and in the end it is Allah who judges us, not men.

'What makes me angry', she continued, 'is those people in the Government, like Hekmatyar, saying that women should stay at home for their own protection. If he means we need to be protected from men, why does the Government not teach men how to behave? It is not our fault that men run behind us, so why are we blamed and told we should stay at home or hide under a burqa?'

Her words brought an echo of the warnings given at home, advising women not to be out alone after dark – in case they are raped. Men commit the crime, but it is women who – for their own protection, of course – are punished by having to surrender a part of their freedom. Even when a rapist is found guilty and punished by the legal system, is there not still, even in our 'enlightened' society, an element of blame attached to the woman? Should she not have known better than to be out alone after dark? Didn't wearing a short skirt and make-up indicate that she was 'asking for it?'

Latifa's point that women were held responsible and blamed for the bad behaviour of Afghan men was sadly still true in our society, where women had supposedly achieved freedom and equal rights.

Although in the eyes of Latifa and Sharifa, women in

my country enjoyed a level of freedom beyond their wildest dreams (something my very presence amongst them without my husband proved) I found myself wondering gloomily if that freedom was not still a very fragile thing.

Could women ever be completely free, or would men's possession of the ultimate weapon of control – rape, or the threat of it – always be a constraint? Women in Britain might be crashing through glass ceilings to become top business managers, but on a basic, very fundamental level, they had hardly advanced much further forward than Sharifa and Latifa.

I was still deep in such depressing thoughts when Latifa poked me in the ribs. 'I was asking', she said, aware that I had not been concentrating, 'how could I find time to get into trouble, anyway? I am busy all the day here, and when I go home I am busy with housework all evening until I go to bed.' Sharifa obligingly repeated the punch line that I, following my own uncomfortable train of thought, had missed, 'Then Moh'd Ali keeps her busy there!' Latifa patted her stomach, the bump still barely showing and Sharifa beamed in delight as we laughed at her joke.

Next morning, though, she arrived at work looking as though she had never enjoyed a joke in her life. Her relationship with Jawad, who was still adamant that Marzia should not stay with them for much longer, was rapidly deteriorating. 'He is angry all the time. Marzia is doing almost all the work in the house, so he has nothing to complain about, but he picks a fight over everything I say or do. It is my duty to take the place of our mother at this time in her life. Who else she could she be with? Chaman is too young to teach her anything.'

Burying her face in her hands, Sharifa sobbed, 'I wish our mother was still alive. I need her, too.' Looking up, her face streaked with tears, she wailed, 'Last night, Jawad was so angry with me, he beat me.'

Sharifa's husband was a scrawny little man, half her size. One good wallop and she could have laid him out flat. Without thinking how unsympathetic it sounded, I said so. Through her tears, she stared at me in open-mouthed astonishment. 'Oh no, I couldn't do that,' she spluttered. 'He would divorce me.'

She hid her face again, her shoulders shaking. Putting a comforting arm around her, I suddenly realised she was convulsed, not by sobs, but by giggles. When she could manage to speak, she said, 'I never would dare to hit him, but just picturing it makes me feel better.'

Wiping her eyes, she continued, 'He didn't really hurt me. Just slapped me. But I don't understand why he's started to hit me. In Kabul he wasn't a bad husband. We argued, you know, like everyone does, but he never lifted his hand against me.

'He has changed since we came here. He hates having no job. And hates that I am working, because he thinks the man should earn the money to support his family. I understand that he feels bad about not being a proper husband. If he had a good job I could stay at home, but I'm frightened that if I stop working we'll starve. I don't see why he doesn't look for other work. Other men find work, why can't he?'

Sharifa shrugged her shoulders wearily, adding, 'All this complaining he does about Marzia is not the point. If she left tomorrow, he would still be bad-tempered with me.'

'What happened last night to make him hit you?' I asked.

'When the landlord came for the rent a few days ago, he saw Marzia. Yesterday he came and told Jawad that he wants to marry her. He is very rich and has offered a good price, a lot of gold. Jawad said we should accept his offer, but I refused.

'He is a horrible man, and too old for Marzia. He is a *rish-i-safeed* [a white beard]. He doesn't even have any teeth.' Sharifa shuddered.

In the ensuing argument, Jawad had lost his temper and slapped Sharifa before storming out of the house.

A week later, things became worse. When Jawad reluctantly informed the landlord that he could not marry Marzia, he retaliated by threatening to evict the family if they did not accept his offer. Sharifa told her husband that he could beat her as much as he wanted, she would never agree. The landlord evicted them.

Sharifa began planning to move somewhere nearer to the centre of Mazar, telling me, 'Jawad might find a job more easily if we lived in the city.' He had other ideas.

David and I, calling to see 'his' sheep, discovered Sharifa, once again in floods of tears. Jawad had not only refused to look for a room in the city, he had decided that they would move to the refugee camp, where they could live rent-free.

'He isn't thinking about what my life will be like. There is no electricity, so it will be too hot in summer without a fan, and freezing in winter. I'll have further to travel to work, and have even more work to do at home. Water for cooking and washing has to be brought from a pump – and you can be sure Jawad believes that is women's work. Worst of all . . .'

Here, Sharifa's voice broke as her sobs redoubled. 'Worst of all, he is selling my fridge. If we moved to a room in the city we might have been able to use it but, in the camp, it would be useless. That fridge meant more to me than my wedding gold. In Kabul, I used to make ice-cream for the children and, since we came to Mazar, I have been promising them that one day I'll make it for them again. It was like saying, "one day things will be better", but I can't say that any more. It is an old fridge now, so he won't even get a good price for it.'

I tried to comfort her, but there was little I could say. Even the distant prospect that one day things might indeed be better did nothing to compensate for the loss of Sharifa's precious fridge.

Hoping to take her mind of it, I changed the subject, asking how they could move to the refugee camp, which was supposedly for people newly arriving from Kabul or other parts of Afghanistan. Having already found rented accommodation, the family was technically not entitled to the plot of land and tent allocated by the UN.

'Oh, that's no problem,' she said. 'Anyone can get a tent. The camp is full of rich people from Mazar-i-Sharif who own houses in the city. They rent out their own houses, or give them on *grau*, then move to the camp, claiming the monthly rations the UN gives.' *Grau* was a mortgage system whereby ownership of a house, or piece of land, was transferred – temporarily – on payment of a lump sum. At the end of a mutually agreed time, the original owner had to repay the money to take back his house. In this way, people raised capital, often to invest in building another house – which could then be let or mortgaged.

A few days later Jawad collected their tent and the family, with their few belongings (minus the fridge), and moved to the camp situated on a tract of barren desert at the edge of the city. The UN referred to the families living there as DPs – Displaced Persons – as though, one day, they might all be tidily put back in their proper places. As far as Sharifa and the thousands of others in the camp were concerned, the mere 200 miles they had travelled from their former homes in Kabul constituted a psychological barrier as great as if they had crossed an international border. They called themselves *mohajireen* [refugees].

As Sharifa had predicted she had to fetch all the water for the household from one of the rows of standpipes which ran at intervals through the camp. There were also rows of latrines, whose overpowering stench remained in the nostrils long after leaving them.

Attempts at providing other services, including a kindergarten, were made by various agencies. Sharifa, who was familiar with kindergartens in Kabul, was disappointed and angry to discover there was neither a toy nor a colouring book in sight. The children sat in silent rows while the young women in charge chatted amongst themselves until it was time to go home. 'It is a waste of time – the children are bored, they learn nothing. I only send mine because at least they get some milk every day.'

There were a few clinics run by various NGOs, outside which patients queued for hours in the heat to see a medical worker who had no time to do more than issue hastily scribbled prescriptions for antibiotics and tonics.

Once assigned their plot of land, all the refugees erected their tent as a temporary home until they had constructed something more permanent, by digging underground rooms. Building their houses in this way provided people some protection against the extremes of heat and cold. Sharifa's was reached by descending a few steps cut in the bare earth. The walls rose above the level of the ground and the canvas tent provided an extra protective layer over the mud roof.

'I feel like a *taberghow* [a marmot],' grinned Sharifa as she emerged to greet me the first time I visited her new home. At first, Sharifa's room felt delightfully cool after the scorching heat outside, but it was an illusory coolness. Within minutes, the slightest movement caused profuse sweating from every pore. A heavy curtain covering the doorway increased the room's stuffiness, but the moment it was lifted, hundreds of flies swarmed in. On the bare mud walls, in a vain attempt at brightening the place, Sharifa had tacked some pictures – a photograph of her and David I had taken and, from a magazine, a bright red sports car zooming through some lush green countryside. Outside the entrance door, Jawad was building a small lean-to which would serve as the kitchen.

The whole camp was a dreary, depressing place. Only a barbed wire perimeter fence was missing to complete the impression of a prison camp rather than a place of refuge. How anyone could *want* to live in that place if they had a choice completely baffled me.

Sharifa, being Sharifa, soon cheered up and found things to laugh at – such as my attempts to help fetch water. Sweat dripping from the end of my nose, on which my glasses, having slid down, perched precariously, I struggled to carry two buckets to her home. Water slopped out at every step to mingle with the dust, coating my feet in thick, sticky mud. By the time I deposited my buckets in her doorway, they were half empty. Thoroughly exhausted, I collapsed onto a mattress, wondering how on earth Sharifa found the energy to laugh.

6

Go Safely, Come Back Quickly

THE MELON SEASON finally started and, as Reza had predicted, the fleas disappeared. Within days of the first truck-loads of melons arriving in the bazaar, there were, mysteriously, no more fleas. I suspected they had died of heat stroke. By then, the city was like a furnace. Occasionally, a wind blew – hot and dry and full of dust which it deposited on everyone and everything. I was eagerly anticipating the cooler climate of Hazara Jat's mountains, where I was to begin a new health training project for village women. It would also be a relief to put some distance between David and the cholera epidemic which in recent weeks had held the city in its grip, killing hundreds of people, mostly children. Much to David's disgust, I banned his consumption of the locally made ice-cream. Explanations that it might contain germs which would make him terribly sick led to him worrying about the Afghan children he saw eating ice-creams. 'Look, mummy, that boy will be sick, won't he?' To my reply that this was a possibility, he continued, 'Will he die? Is that boy going to die, Mummy?' Then, without waiting for an answer, in Dari, to the terrified child, 'My mummy says you're going to die if you eat that!'

Naeem and Reza, convinced that everything edible in the bazaar was potentially lethal, would have starved had I not reassured them that provided rules of hygiene were followed scrupulously by everyone, we would be in no danger. Jawad issued instructions to Latifa that all salad stuff and fruit must be washed thoroughly in water that had been boiled for at least twenty minutes. None of us – nor any of our children – became sick.

There were occasional lighter moments. Marzia, filling in for Latifa who had taken a day off, served up a cucumber salad in a rather soggy state. Puzzled, Naeem asked how she prepared it. Marzia, with a shrug replied, 'Well, I never heard of boiling cucumber before, but I'm sure that's what Latifa said you wanted.'

Cholera or no cholera, I refused to give up our daily feasts of juicy melons. The streets of the bazaar were lined with melon sellers every few yards, their fruit piled in pyramids beside them. There were enormous water-melons with thirst-quenching scarlet flesh, although my favourite was the giant rugby-ball-shaped variety, some of which could weigh up to seven kilos.

I did scrutinise each fruit carefully after someone warned me that unscrupulous growers sometimes inject water into the melons to plump them up. Though how I was going to detect needle marks, I wasn't sure.

As well as preparing teaching notes for the work I would be doing in Hazara Jat, I had reports to write, both for our donors and for the Mazar-i-Sharif civil servants.

When I submitted our first report, giving an account of the number of clinics established in Hazara Jat, and details of forthcoming field tours, it was accepted with considerable coolness. Summoned to the Ministry, Naeem and I were questioned, in the discreet diplomatic way of Afghanistan – an hour and several glasses of tea before coming to the point – about our future plans.

'You will, I think be opening some new clinics soon?' asked Mr Khaliq, nodding encouragingly at us.

'Yes, indeed,' I replied enthusiastically, 'We expect to have funding for one in Mazar by next year.'

Mr Khaliq looked expectantly at us. 'Oh, and there is our new project for women health volunteers in Hazara Jat,' I added, 'If women can be trained as health workers they can do a lot to improve the health of women and children. There is a great need for mother and childcare work.'

Mr Khaliq was not remotely interested in our work in Hazara Jat. 'There is a great need for health work, here, in this city,' he reminded us gently. 'We need many clinics and many

doctors need work. This is why you were given permission to
come to Mazar-i-Sharif. We believed you wanted to help us.'

We assured him we did want to help but that our budget was
too small to allow us to open lots of clinics all at once.

We were invited several times to take tea with Mr Khaliq
and discuss our future plans. On each occasion Naeem and
I reiterated that we would definitely open a clinic in the city
within the next few months, and Mr Khaliq pointed out that
there was a need for 'many clinics'. Finally, I could take no
more diplomacy and, to Naeem's horror, announced that if
our organisation was not wanted in Mazar we would leave.
We would, I hinted, consider Kabul as a possible base for
our office. It worked and, for a while at least, the pressure
to expand our project well beyond the bounds of budget and
reason eased. In the meantime, Jon was touring in Hazara
Jat calling us whenever he reached a place with a radio
link to Mazar. This was not to find out how we were, but
to give us lists, endless lists of things the clinics needed –
medicines, spare parts for jeeps, stationery, bits for generators.
Naeem, Reza and I would race round the bazaar trying to
find everything, hoping we were not missing our few precious
hours of electricity when it was (just) cool enough to work in
the office.

At least I had hopes that the childcare problem would
be resolved when we returned from Hazara Jat. Things had
not improved. Sharifa, tired and depressed by the necessity
of coping with her husband's bad moods and increasingly
violent outbursts, had become even less able to keep David
amused. One day I produced David's paddling pool, guiltily
using vast quantities of our precious water to fill it. Although
we now had 'city water' piped into our tank, during the melon
season, farmers on the city's outskirts used most of it before
it reached us. David had eagerly jumped in, splashing with
glee. Minutes after reaching my desk, however, I heard his
loudly voiced protests as Sharifa, having decided it was too
dangerous to remain outdoors any longer, forcibly dried and
dressed him.

Naeem offered to help by taking David, with Sharifa, to the bazaar. Gratefully I waved them off, expecting at least a couple of hours on my own. Shopping with David in tow always took a long time because of the mutual fascination between him and the shopkeepers. At first, they had baffled him – and alarmed me – by addressing him in Russian. I was afraid that if we were mistaken for Russians we would encounter a great deal of hostility, but Naeem assured me there was no anti-Russian feeling in Mazar-i-Sharif.

For years there had been strong trade links between the various countries of the USSR and Afghanistan. The bazaars were full of Russian products – from air conditioners through all manner of electrical and household goods to children's bicycles. Many of the Uzbeks who were officially Afghan nationals still had family connections in neighbouring Uzbekistan, from where they had originally come. Some still took their wives across the border to give birth so that their children had dual nationality and the right to two passports.

Even so, I was happier once the traders realised that David understood Dari – a discovery that so delighted them that he was plied with dried fruits, almonds and sweets. Each outing to the bazaar entailed calling on his various friends, at whose shops he used to like to 'help'. Even the soldiers – who were more inclined to steal money than give it away – used to slip some Afghanis in his pocket.

Unfortunately, Sharifa did not like wandering around the bazaar. 'She said it was too hot,' Naeem explained, 'and insisted on staying in the jeep with David. When I got back, she was sound asleep and David was escaping through the window.'

Watching Marzia play with David one day, making him shriek with laughter, I realised how much more suited she was as a child-minder than her exhausted older sister. David adored her and she seemed genuinely happy to play with David, teaching him games she remembered from her, not so distant, childhood.

When the rest of our Pakistan-based colleagues arrived in

Mazar-i-Sharif in early autumn, there would be a vacancy for extra support workers. I wondered if Sharifa would prefer to be a 'general worker', helping Latifa in the kitchen, making tea for guests, and doing some cleaning. Anxiously, for I was afraid she might see it as losing status, I broached the subject.

'I know I am not so good at doing things with David, but I really love him. I would miss him.' She blinked back the ever-ready tears, 'I'm going to miss you both when you go to Hazara Jat.'

'We'll miss you when we are away,' I told her truthfully, 'and when we come back you will still see David. And if you are employed by the organisation instead of by me personally, your future will be secure. When I leave Afghanistan you will still have a job.'

Sharifa nodded agreement, asking, 'Is there any chance for Marzia to have my job with David?'

'I was hoping you might suggest that,' I grinned at her.

Marzia had needed no persuasion. 'I've wanted to find work for a long time,' she said delightedly. 'But no-one would allow me to bring Shahnaz with me. I can't stand being in the house on my own when Jawad is there, and if I can earn some money to pay for me and Shahnaz, he might not be so angry all the time.'

She would have been happy to accompany me to Hazara Jat to look after David there, but Sharifa swiftly vetoed this idea. 'What would the neighbours think?' she demanded. 'How would I know she was behaving herself?'

At last departure day arrived. Sharifa hugged me tightly, the customary 'go safely, come back quickly' ending in choking sobs. Assuring her, with the obligatory 'Insh 'Allah' thrown in, just to be certain that we would be back before she had time to miss us, I clambered into my corner of the jeep.

David, unmoved by Sharifa's emotional farewell, was already ensconced in his car seat – the only one of us, with the exception of Reza in the driving seat, to have enough leg room. An unimaginable number of boxes and bundles – the results of Jon's shopping lists – had been stowed in, behind us, beside us, under our legs and feet, to be delivered to the clinics. Naeem shared the front passenger seat with Iqbal, the paramedic in charge of the Waras clinic, who had come to Mazar to accompany us to our destination.

At Pul-i-Khumri Reza took a right turn and we discovered we had reached the end of civilization – at least in terms of road conditions. Swearing and apologising alternately, Reza swung the jeep around the boulders that littered the narrow, winding track.

Sometime in the late afternoon, I asked where we would spend the night. Reza shrugged, 'No idea. None of us have ever been on this route before. Don't worry, we'll find somewhere.'

No-one in their right mind travels after dark in Afghanistan, because of bandits. Fortunately, soon after the sun disappeared, we reached a cluster of mud houses which boasted a *samovad* (tea-house), where we could have dinner and stay the night.

Iqbal, David and I spread our bedding on the floor of the room in which we had eaten. David was instantly asleep, but despite being exhausted after travelling for over twelve hours, I lay awake for a long time. It was no cooler here than Mazar, and since electricity had ended at Pul-i-Khumri, there were no fans to stir the hot air. Tossing and turning, I envied Naeem and Reza enjoying the coolness of the rooftop. Until, that is, they appeared equally bleary-eyed in the morning, having spent the night providing dinner for mosquitoes. 'Now you know how I felt about Mazar's fleas,' I remarked.

We made better progress on our second day; only two punctures and an over-heated engine. I, for one, was grateful for those extra stops as Reza, obviously possessing a cast iron bladder, would otherwise have driven for eight hours without stopping.

It was three wearying days before we arrived in Waras. Keeping David amused for hour after hour in the jeep was exhausting, although fortunately he slept a lot. How he achieved this with the constant bouncing and juddering over rock strewn 'roads' I have no idea. Any attempts I made at nodding off were instantly thwarted when my head, with a neck-wrenching twist, slammed against the window. It was, however, worth staying awake for the scenery. The dramatic, rugged mountains of the Hindu Kush formed a constantly changing backdrop – their kaleidoscopic colours varying from slate grey through earthy brown to rosy pink – as we travelled towards Bamiyan, the capital of Hazara Jat.

This small, nondescript town and its surrounding areas is steeped in history. It was once part of the ancient Silk Road, covering the route that led between Balkh and Tashkurghan, to Taxila, far-away in Pakistan's province of Punjab. Caravans laden with luxuries stopped to rest in Bamiyan's fertile valley before continuing their arduous journeys. I enjoyed showing David the huge Buddhas carved in the rosy sandstone cliffs. They were, he declared 'good giants' – presumably in contrast to the giants, inevitably bad, which often featured in his story-books.

Four years before, Jon and I had spent a happy day playing at being tourists in Bamiyan. A young mujahid acting as impromptu tour guide, had escorted us up, inside the smaller – at thirty-five metres – of the two Buddhas. Despite our guide's insistence that it was 'thousands and thousands of years' old, it was probably built in the latter part of the third century AD. The larger of the two, some few hundred metres along the cliff face, is an awesome fifty-three metres and was undoubtedly carved later, probably in the fifth century.

Naeem and I tried to take David for a closer look at the smaller Buddha, but the maze of adjacent caves – once used as monastic cells, sanctuaries and accommodation for visiting pilgrims – were occupied by mujahideen of the Jamiat-i-Islami Party. The commander was not around and no-one else would grant permission for us to visit. Watching the cook empty tea-pots and other slops out of a cave entrance to run down the cliff side, I wondered how much of the Buddha would be left intact by the time Afghanistan's war ended.

We arrived at the clinic shortly before dusk on the fourth day of travelling. Although Waras was in Bamiyan province, it had little in common neither with the fertile Bamiyan valley, nor even of its neighbouring district of Panjau. Here, the lack of sufficient water and the poor land combined to make farming a precarious existence. There was no fruit grown in the area surrounding the clinic and only a few parts of the precious land were given over to vegetable crops. Apart from the *alaf* [animal fodder] all other land, including the rock-strewn mountain slopes, was used primarily for wheat.

It was utter bliss to stretch out after dinner, glass of tea in hand, relishing the fact that I would not, at four o'clock next morning, have to clamber, bleary-eyed, into my corner of the jeep for another bone shaking twelve-hour journey. The prospect of being able to sleep for as long as I wanted next morning was wonderful. I had forgotten that two-year-olds have much more efficient recuperative powers, and next morning David, thoroughly refreshed and ready for action, woke at dawn. Excited about seeing cows and calves, sheep, goats and donkeys – all within reach – he couldn't wait to be out exploring his new world. Iqbal's field assistant, Hassan, volunteered to take him around the village and the two became instant friends. So much so that when David needed to go to the toilet, he was insistent that his Uncle Hassan should take him. I laughed at Hassan's consternation. 'What should I do?' he asked helplessly, having obviously never had anything to do with that end of childcare – despite having six children of his own.

By lunchtime, David had ridden his first donkey and overcome his initial fear of hens. While pleased at his new-found bravery, I was less delighted when I caught him kissing one on its beak.

Iqbal's clinic was a small, dilapidated building on the edge of the village. The mud walls were a foot and a half thick, while the flat roof was constructed of straight poplar tree-trunks, interwoven with branches topped by several layers of mud. The tiny windows were designed more for keeping out the bitter cold in winter than for allowing in light. A large room, where we gathered to eat, drink tea and entertain guests, doubled as sleeping quarters for the staff – driver Abdul Ali,

cook Ibrahim, field assistant Hassan and Iqbal. What had
been the former resident's kitchen had become a small, dark
consulting room.

A separate entrance led to Ibrahim's hell-hole of a kitchen,
which was never cleaner than filthy. Because it was dark in
there, he thought no-one noticed the dirt. Next to a small
storage area – occupied by mice – was the guest room, which
David and I shared. It had an adjoining bathroom – a bare,
narrow room with a small hole in the bottom of one wall
through which the bath (a metal bucket) water could run.
When any of the other staff wanted to take a bath David and I
were evicted from our room. The men, modest to the point of
paranoia, were seemingly terrified in case we peeked.

After a few days, I stopped reaching for a light switch when
it grew dark, waiting instead for someone to light the pressure
lamp, known as the *gaz*. To my shame, I never learned the
knack of lighting these temperamental things and I was useless
at keeping them alight when the pressure began to fall. If
the light dimmed, furious pumping was required to raise the
pressure, followed by some mysterious twiddling of a red knob.
Whenever pushed, by necessity, to attempt any of this myself,
I invariably plunged the room into darkness or set the entire
contraption alight.

In time, too, I remembered the pit latrine, a hundred yards
from the clinic, had no flush. It had no door either. A curtain
made of old sackcloth – full of holes – suspended over the
entrance gave only the illusion of privacy. The occupier was
expected to cough loudly at the approach of another party.

When I was in occupation, no amount of coughing prevented
women – who, amongst themselves, had none of the men's sense
of modesty – from joining me. Many a medical consultation
was conducted while I squatted, flushed with embarrassment,
over the hole.

'Go and see Dr Iqbal,' I'd plead, but in vain. The women
who followed me to the loo did so because they were too shy
to mention gynaecological problems to a man. They would
be clutching little packets of paracetamol, prescribed because,

overcome by horror at discussing such personal matters, they had instead complained to Iqbal of headaches.

Each morning a queue of patients, the majority of whom were men, formed outside the clinic long before we had breakfasted, and the cook distributed numbered tickets on a first come, first seen basis. Iqbal, assisted by Hassan, spent the mornings in the consulting room. Lunch was only served when he had seen the last of his patients.

Iqbal's fifteen-year-old sister, Basma, readily agreed to look after David for part of each day. Wondering why he was often not interested in lunch, I discovered that the pair of them spent the mornings on a round of social visits to Basma's friends in the village. David was plied with fried eggs, yoghurt and hot, fresh nan straight from the tandoor. Life was a lot more exciting than it had been for him in Mazar-i-Sharif.

After a few days settling in, Iqbal and I began the process of recruiting volunteers for our training project. In the surrounding villages, we had to talk first to the *'mooie-safeed'* [the white-haired ones] without whose blessing nothing could happen.

'We want', explained Iqbal, 'women to come to class to learn how to make your children strong and healthy. We will teach them what we have learned and then they can teach the other women in the village. Then your children won't need to take medicines all the time.'

The village elders would call together the rest of the men to discuss the matter together, including the fact that Iqbal would be acting as my translator.

Once I urged Iqbal to remind the men that we wanted the women to *volunteer* for training – not simply be told by a village elder that they had to attend. He pointed out that most of the women were sitting on an adjacent rooftop, listening to the discussion, and were quite capable of deciding among themselves who would attend.

While I was less sure about this than he, I let it drop for the time being. I was by then too distracted by David's efforts to catch chickens to worry about anything other than what to do when a two-year-old leaps twenty feet off a roof after a squawking bird.

In the days before the classes were due to start I became increasingly doubtful that any women would turn up. Not one had approached us about the training course. 'Don't worry,' Iqbal tried to reassure me. 'The men were happy about the project. The women will come to class, you'll see.'

Despite asking for the names of likely students so that we knew how many might be attending, none had been put forward by the morning of the first class.

When You Can Eat Sugar . . .

BY THE TIME five bemused-looking women hesitantly entered the staff room I was so nervous I forgot the welcome speech that I had been rehearsing in Dari all morning.

'You'll have to translate for me,' I murmured to Iqbal, while trying to smile confidently at the women now seated around the room. I wanted to go home whenever my gaze rested on the two women who had arrived spinning wool, and who, with grim expressions, continued to do so throughout the introductory speech. I interpreted their expressions to mean they considered they had far more important things to do than come to silly lessons. They reminded me of those women who used to sit knitting around the guillotine.

When, through Iqbal, I began asking about the health issues which most concerned them, I was pleased to see them lay aside their balls of wool and begin to look interested. Before long a lively discussion, led by one of the wool spinners, developed. I had to keep reminding Iqbal to translate for me, as he became involved in the conversation.

Iqbal smiled reassuringly, 'They want to learn about pregnancy and deliveries, diarrhoea and "weakness" [their description of malnutrition]'. As those were the main subjects on which I had prepared lessons I gave a sigh of relief.

We must have said something right because the next day three more women appeared for class, and within a week we had thirteen on the training course – a larger number than we had dared hope for. Every day more women asked if they could join. Feeling that any more students would make the class too big we noted their names, promising a place on the next course.

The staff room was not an ideal location for our classes.

Ibrahim and Abdul Ali couldn't resist popping their heads around the door to see how we were getting on. Kulsom offered the use of her guest-room and we decided on daily two-hour teaching sessions.

Before long the class, which at first I had regarded as a single entity, dissolved into individuals as I learned everyone's names and came to know each distinctive personality.

Habiba was easy to remember – she hardly spoke. If asked a question, she whispered her response so softly it was difficult to hear her. Nickbacht and Chaman, the one talkative and intelligent, the other equally talkative though usually on a subject quite unrelated to the one under discussion, were the wool spinners.

In her late forties, Aquila – Iqbal's mother – was the oldest in the group (Iqbal had tried to dissuade her from attending, telling her she was too old to learn anything). The youngest was her sister-in-law, Hassan's sister, Kulsom, who was a pretty, rosy-cheeked young woman in her mid-twenties. 'When she was young, everyone said she was the most beautiful girl in Hazara Jat,' Iqbal said, clearly proud of his aunt's reputation.

I never forgot Jemila's name. She was a robust, strikingly attractive young woman, but what made her so memorable was her aggressively argumentative manner. She relentlessly queried everything Iqbal and I said, unwilling to believe anything without proof, though once convinced she was a wonderful ally.

I came to like her very much and was deeply impressed by her when I learned that she, carrying her four-month-old baby, along with Suraya, who was also pregnant, and Aquila, walked for more than an hour each way to attend the classes. This took up a huge part of their working day. Although they had less field-work to do when the men harvested the wheat, the women's work was, literally, never done.

Their day began with the early morning preparation of tea and making nan. All work around the house – sweeping floors and cleaning, cooking, fetching water, washing and mending clothes, looking after the children – fell on the women's shoulders. They were responsible for attending to the chickens, milking the goats and sheep (and the cow, if they were lucky enough to own one), making yoghurt and butter. It was the women who spun the wool from the sheep and wove the gilims, a task they did in their 'spare time'.

Accepting that there was likely to be resistance from the women if I plunged in and started teaching things which, I suspected, would be contrary to existing health practices, I was prepared to move slowly. For the first few sessions I encouraged them to talk while I listened, learning as much as I could about their local beliefs.

Although some were found throughout many parts of Afghanistan, others were more localised, and, even within the small geographical areas from which the women came, there were differences of opinion. For instance, all the women were in agreement that a baby should not be born directly onto the floor, but had different ideas on what made the best landing mat!

'Someone should catch the baby in their hands,' explained Kulsom.

'No, no,' disagreed Jemila, 'the best thing is a cushion made from dried animal stool crushed into a powder. It's nice and warm for the baby.'

When I asked what they did to help women during deliveries, I expected to hear of various local traditions – perhaps herbal preparations or massage. It was a surprise when they answered with one voice, 'Pray!'

Although I hoped that by the end of the course more practical ways of helping might have been accepted, I encouraged them in the meantime to keep on praying.

The women did have a number of 'cures' for a retained placenta, although they could hardly be called 'traditional'. 'If the woman smokes a cigarette it makes her cough and that often works,' said Aquila, 'or firing a gun outside the room.'

Nodding in agreement, Nickbacht added, 'They're good ways and sometimes the men in house take the door off its hinges.'

'How does that work?' I asked.

Nickbacht shrugged, 'We don't know. No one can explain it, but it works – at least it does sometimes. For some women, though, nothing works and they bleed to death.'

On the subject of the causes of ill health, the women were unanimous. The main culprits were *djinn* [nasty, malevolent little spirits], closely followed by the mistake of eating the wrong balance of 'hot' and 'cold' foods.

Every item of food and drink in Afghanistan is defined as either 'hot' or 'cold'. Oil, meat and rice are 'hot' while yoghurt, *dogh* [whey] and cucumber are 'cold'. It is not that certain foods are considered unhealthy, but that a person could become ill by consuming them in the wrong combination.

I spent ages making lists of foodstuffs, trying to work out which hot and cold combinations caused which illnesses until, thoroughly confused, I gave up. I suspected it was not something a foreigner ever could learn. It was probably a genetic inheritance passed by way of the umbilical cord from generation to generation.

The women, pleased by my interest in their beliefs – if somewhat puzzled by my ignorance – encouraged me to write down further confusing dietary details. Thus I learned that although milk is considered healthy it is also believed to rot teeth. It is also a 'windy' food, as are goat's meat, cow's meat and barley bread.

My professed liking for barley bread amused everyone. Not only is it known to cause wind – farting is a dreadful breach of etiquette – it is only eaten when wheat for 'proper' bread was in short supply. No one admitted to enjoying it.

If the sickness – be it diarrhoea, the common cold or pneumonia – is caused by the wrong combination of foods then the cure is to omit certain items from the diet. This treatment is called *perhez* [fasting]. At best, it is a harmless though ineffective treatment but, too often, the patient takes *perhez* to dangerous extremes. Out goes the yoghurt, the milk, eggs, meat, vegetables and oil. Deprived of almost everything nutritious, small children and the elderly, already weakened by the original illness, become prey to other infections.

Expecting the concept of bacteria and lack of hygiene as major causes of ill health to be strongly opposed, I arrived in class with my teaching aids and a great deal of trepidation. Surrounded by jugs of water, salt, glasses, soap and buckets, Iqbal and I explained about microbes, how they are spread and how they can cause many preventable diseases, such as diarrhoea.

Some of the women were nodding thoughtfully, though I could see that Jemila, for one, remained unconvinced. 'How do we know these microbes exist when we can't see them?' she demanded.

'Just watch,' instructed, Iqbal, busily filling a glass with water into which he dissolved a spoonful of salt. Holding the glass aloft he said, 'You can't see it, but you know there is salt in this water. It is the same with microbes. You can't see them, but they are there.'

Suraya spoke up, 'We know *djinn* exist although we can't see them. You said microbes most often attack babies, old people and children who are weak?' I nodded. 'Well,' she continued, 'those are the people usually affected by *djinn*.'

This provoked an animated discussion, which resulted in a general consensus that it might be worth hearing more about these microbes, especially how to protect against them. They were not particularly impressed when I produced a bar of soap.

Hand-washing before eating plays an important part in Afghan culture, particularly when there is a *mehmani* [dinner party]. Usually the sons of the host bring round water in an *aftawa* [jug]. Starting with the most important people in the room, a bowl is placed in front of the guest, who holds his hands out under the stream of water from the jug. On such formal occasions soap is sometimes provided. After the meal, the ritual is repeated and small hand towels are passed around. When there are no guests, people simply douse their hands in cold water, without bothering about soap.

I promised the students that the humble bar of soap could go a long way in helping them kill dangerous microbes. They watched with obvious scepticism as Iqbal and I arranged our buckets and jugs of water. We invited everyone to take turns washing their hands, first in plain water, then again with soap. As they exclaimed in horror and disbelief at the different results and saw the dirty, soapy water in the buckets, I knew that for the first time since classes began, I really had them on my side.

So enthusiastic were the women to hear more about how to wage war on microbes that the class overran by almost an hour that day. They listened open-mouthed in horror as we explained how flies liked settling on dirty things – like the animal and human turds around their houses – and picked up tiny particles, laced with millions of microbes, on their sticky feet.

'What happens when flies come in our houses? Where do they land?' I asked.

'On our food,' they replied in unison. By the time Iqbal had translated my little lecture on the digestive system of a fly (unable to eat anything hard, they first vomit on their food – our food – then stomp on it with their filthy feet), the women were hooked. They wanted to know more and more – how could they prevent flies coming in their houses, how could they stop their children shitting too close to home.

'We need latrines in every village,' said one.

'Yes,' another agreed, 'and we need to use the soap ourselves, not keep it for guests.'

Listening to them chatter, reminding each other of when it was important to wash their hands, I began to feel more confident than since the course began.

Iqbal was euphoric. 'From now on it will be easy,' he remarked.

Of course it wasn't. The women had to persuade their husbands that soap was not a luxury item for special occasions, but a household essential. Some husbands were far from happy about this development. It was the students' first lesson on how difficult it was going to be to teach others the new health messages they were learning.

However, after our microbes lesson, the women remained highly motivated and their enthusiasm made them willing to be more open-minded about whatever other strange ideas I might have up my sleeve.

Jemila was still the most argumentative. One day her baby, normally a quiet, contented infant, was crying persistently. 'Jemila, why don't you feed him?' I asked in exasperation.

'I have just finished drinking my tea. It was hot.'

My incomprehension showed. Jemila sighed heavily at the stupidity of this foreigner who had set herself up to teach them things, when she clearly knew very little herself.

'The tea was hot. So now my milk is too hot for him to drink. He'll have to wait until it cools down.'

I explained that breast milk remained at a constant temperature – perfect for babies at all times. Jemila explained that everyone knew breast-milk became hot when a mother drank hot tea, just as it became cold when she was outside in cold weather.

By then we were well into autumn and it was already bitterly cold, so, realising that words would never convince Jemila, I suggested she stand outside for a while. Handing the still squawking bundle of baby to Nickbacht, Jemila headed for the door. The rest of us had another cup of tea while we waited. (Ibrahim always provided a collection of filled thermoses, glasses and sweets at the start of class.)

When Jemila returned, shivering, she expressed some milk onto the palm of her hand and delicately dipped the tip of her tongue into the milky puddle. 'Oh, it's normal!' she exclaimed in wonder. After gulping down a much-needed glass of hot tea, she repeated the experiment. The whole class was riveted, watching with bated breath. I half expected her to burn her tongue and shout, 'Told you so.'

Silently, taking her baby back from Nickbacht, Jemila speedily offered him a milk-swollen breast. The wailing ceased, and peace at last descended on the class.

Jemila's skill at playing Devil's Advocate was useful in role-plays. Working in pairs, the health volunteers had to pass on their newly learned health messages. When Jemila was playing the part of a non-co-operative mother, the students really had their work cut out. They often became angry with her.

Jemila defended herself, saying, 'You know how long it took before I accepted new ideas. It won't be easy making other people change their ways. If I acted like you had convinced me easily, you would think it was going to be just as easy in the villages. It isn't. And becoming angry with a mother who doesn't agree with you won't help.'

I knew she was right, though I hoped that not all the village women would be quite as stubborn as Jemila.

Along with learning about the causes of diarrhoea, its treatment was a topic of equal, if not greater, concern to the students. More than any other illness, it was blamed for most of the deaths of small children.

Lovers of pills and potions and knowing the names of almost every antibiotic known to man, they were hoping I was going to bring them some new wonder-cure. They were, therefore, extremely disappointed when I produced from my bag of tricks nothing more exciting than sachets of oral rehydration drinks. And horrified when we told them that not only was it vital to replace fluids, but that it was important to keep feeding their children.

'That's not proper medicine,' Jemila pointed out dismissively. 'We need strong *goli* [pills] to cure diarrhoea.'

Explanations on the need to replace fluid lost through diarrhoea fell on deaf ears. Our experiments with half-dead flowers brought to life after a drink of water, and leaking plastic bags collapsing in on themselves to demonstrate dehydration, did nothing to convince them.

'We know diarrhoea is dangerous. Our children die from it. That's why we need strong medicine,' cried Jemila. 'If we give them food it makes them shit even more. We want to stop the diarrhoea, not make it worse.'

I don't believe we would ever have convinced them had it not been for the arrival at the clinic one morning of a ten-month-old girl.

Lying limp in her distraught mother's arms, her eyes – too dry to even shed a tear – were unfocused and unblinking. Other patients, and those students who were present, had shaken their heads despairingly, convinced it was too late to save the child.

She had been given the usual treatment – nothing to drink, no food (not even breast milk) and a cocktail of antibiotics bought over the counter in the bazaar.

Dripping ORS drop by drop into the girl's mouth was a long, painstaking process. Despite their scepticism, Jemila and Aquila, Suraya and Nickbacht took turns in administering the drops. Occasionally I overheard and ignored muttered comments about the uselessness of such actions. By mid-afternoon the little girl had revived sufficiently to breast feed again.

The students watched the child suckle, their expressions a mixture of astonishment and delight. A few days later the mother returned for more ORS, bringing her happy, smiling daughter, unrecognisable as the child who had been so near death's door.

As the word spread, mothers stopped the students to ask about ORS and their seemingly miraculous curative powers. 'If it goes on like this,' remarked Iqbal, 'the clinic's stock will run out before the next delivery arrives.'

In class one day Jemila said, 'You'd better show us how to mix that stuff properly. A lot of children in my village have diarrhoea just now.'

Before we started on lessons about healthy pregnancies and deliveries, the students requested a class on family planning. It was the contraceptive pill they most wanted to hear about.

'Is it true', asked Kulsom, 'that if a woman takes the family planning *goli* for a while, then has another baby she won't have any milk?' Someone else wanted to know if forgetting the pill meant the woman would have twins. Others were concerned that they might be left infertile if they took the pill for too long.

This worried Kulsom, who said, 'It's not that I don't want any more babies it's just that I'm tired – I'd just like to have a rest before the next one.' As she had had four babies in six years this was not surprising.

Nickbacht, a mother of seven, commented, 'It used to be that babies came every two years. Now it is often every year. It is harder for the younger ones now.'

Her explanation for the increased birth-rate caused laughter but general consensus from the others. 'It's since the war started and so many men went to join the mujahideen,' she said. 'They don't have sex while they are on duty, so when they come home they want it all the time until they go away again. If they come home once a year, then once a year their wives become pregnant.

'If there is ever peace again and the men are at home all the time, it will go back to every two years. When you can eat sugar whenever you want, you stop wanting it so much.'

There was much giggling and hiding of faces in chaddars when I asked the women to tell me what they knew about how babies are conceived. A few ribald remarks were made amidst increased giggles, making me explain hastily that I did not want a description of the physical act. While it was clear that the 'how-to' aspect of procreation was undoubtedly understood, there was little knowledge of the process of conception.

There was some confused murmuring about male and female eggs and someone declared that a woman could not become pregnant unless she was sexually satisfied.

Nickbacht, the wool-spinner, snorted. 'If that was true, how come there are so many children running around.' This smart rejoinder, provoking much laughter from the women, made Iqbal blush furiously.

Poor Iqbal often had cause to blush as the women teased him unmercifully, telling him that as an unmarried man he wouldn't know about these things yet. When condoms were handed round during a birth-spacing class, the women promptly blew them up like balloons, laughing and making jokes that he refused to translate for me.

On one occasion he was so embarrassed he left the room, leaving me to demonstrate – with an inadequate vocabulary and the help of a broom handle – that a condom cannot be fitted correctly if it has been stretched to its full extent and snapped like a rubber band.

He said later that he could not bring himself to translate the 'coitus interruptus' method that was next on the list, a method advocated by the Prophet Mohammed. It had the added proviso that it was an acceptable method only if the woman gave permission to have her pleasure interrupted. I suspected that what really did for him was the sight of his mother, Aquila, dangling an unrolled condom from her forefinger, asking laconically if her classmates knew *anyone* with anything large enough to fill it!

The wool-spinning Nickbacht was one of the brightest students as well as the one most determined to make the project work. During classes on pregnancy we had stressed the importance of regular antenatal checks and it was Nickbacht who suggested that the students brought all the pregnant women from their villages for a check-up. Iqbal agreed enthusiastically.

On the appointed morning, however, it all went disastrously wrong. The women, busy with household chores, could not reach the clinic by eight o'clock, by which time, of course, Ibrahim had distributed the appointment numbers to the men already waiting. Iqbal was unperturbed, 'Don't worry, as soon as I finish seeing the men, we'll do the antenatal checks.'

By the time he had seen the male patients, none of whom were prepared to give up their places in the queue, most of the women had left to prepare midday meals for their husbands. Nickbacht, in a filthy temper, went home.

In class that afternoon, she rounded furiously on Iqbal. 'We had to work so hard to persuade women to come to the clinic this morning and you just wasted everyone's time. Now they are all angry with us.'

Iqbal's attempts to apologise did not appease her and she continued, crossly, to berate him.

'How can we hope they will listen to us in the future. They think we are are useless.'

Finally, Iqbal cried, 'I have said I am sorry. What more can I say?'

Nickbacht smiled slowly before replying, 'You can say that every week, one morning will be for pregnant women and children. You can tell the men not to come that day. They have all the other days – but not our day.'

Iqbal's jaw dropped. He muttered in English to me, 'Did you put her up to this?' I shook my head. No, Nickbacht had come up with the proposal herself, although, judging from the other women's expressions of determination, they were right behind her. Iqbal had to agree. The men of the district had to agree. The women were beginning to flex their muscles.

They didn't stop there. All the women knew, often first-hand, of babies who had died of neo-natal tetanus. The horrible symptoms displayed by the tiny victim – the jerky arm and leg movements, the back-arching spasms – made them think the baby had died of fright, and the disease was known locally as *tars* [fear].

When they heard that an anti-tetanus vaccine was available through a local representative of AVICEN – an organisation that provided a vaccination service – Nickbacht, once again, went into action.

'Why', she demanded, 'can't he come to the clinic on our antenatal day? We could bring all the pregnant women.'

When approached with the request, the vaccinator agreed. That morning, Ibrahim came banging on my door, 'Quick, quick, come and see your women!'

From every direction, a great sea of women was approaching the clinic. The students, looking like little tugboats guiding huge liners into dock, bustled about, organising their patients. It was an incredible sight and I was overwhelmed with pride and admiration for Nickbacht and her co-students.

Watching her stride towards the clinic, I thought about how her life might have been had her circumstances been different – definitely a career woman, a high flier, an achiever. Then I realised that in her own way, in her own place, Nickbacht was already becoming all of those.

— 8 —
Social Etiquette
and Toilet Training

AQUILA WAS THE FIRST to make overtures of friendship outside class. Possibly it was out of a sense of duty to her son's *mudder under* [other mother], a role bestowed on me by Iqbal when he was studying in Pakistan.

It is the name given to a father's second wife by the children of his first wife, even when she is very much alive and probably living in the same house. In my case, when Iqbal was a young student he 'adopted' me as a temporary mother. Over the years I had added Hassan's son to my family when he came to live with us in Pakistan when he was studying in school.

Aquila had been pleased to learn that her son had found an 'other mother' to care for him while he was so far from home. The title had stuck partly, I suspected, because Afghan men never use a woman's first name. A married woman is always 'wife of . . .' until she has a child, when she becomes 'mother of . . .', even to her husband. Iqbal knew me well enough to understand that I would not accept being referred to as 'wife of Jon', although most of the men in the area usually called me 'mother of David'.

Aquila often invited me and David to spend time at her home, where, to my relief, I gradually lost the uncomfortable status of honoured guest. Dinner invitations came from other students with increasing frequency – much to the delight of Ibrahim, who was also glad to have a night off cooking.

At first I welcomed and accepted all invitations, hoping they would allow me to form closer links with the women. As a teacher I was treated with respect, and kept at a distance and I often missed the easy companionship I had enjoyed in Mazar with Sharifa and Latifa.

Unfortunately, the dinner parties tended to be rather formal occasions to which the local *bozorg* [big people] were also invited, providing little chance to chat freely to the women. This was not because, as was the case in Jaghoray, the women were not allowed to attend, but simply that the men tended to dominate the conversation. If the women and I struck up a conversation of our own, a sudden silence from the other end of room indicated that the men had stopped to listen. They would smile and nod at me in what I assumed they intended as encouragement. Such rapt attention to my faltering attempts at social chitchat produced in me instant tongue-tied embarrassment.

One evening, when Iqbal announced that we were going to dine at the home of one of the students, I sighed wearily. 'Are you too tired?' he asked. 'It's all right. We don't have to go if you want to stay at home.'

'Are you sure Chaman won't mind?' I asked. 'I don't won't to cause offence.'

Assuring me that it was 'no problem', Iqbal sent a message to Chaman with our apologies. 'You are free here to do what you want,' he told me. 'There is no rule to say you must accept an invitation to dinner.'

Of course there was, and by the afternoon of the following day so many people had asked me why I had not gone to Chaman's for dinner that I felt an absolute heel. I vowed never to refuse another invitation – which meant that when I accepted Kulsom's invitation the following week I caused even more offence to Chaman. In class I felt her gazing at me reproachfully, and I'm sure my attempts to apologise and explain only made matters worse until, in time, she forgave me my faux pas.

Being treated as a *bozorg* made me uncomfortable. Big people are fussed over, and they are never allowed a moment's privacy. They seemingly don't want it either. Their status is threatened, feelings are hurt and face is lost if left alone for a couple of minutes. Their hands get kissed a lot and everyone rushes to help them put on their shoes. Every move a big person makes is closely monitored, as people try to second-guess what his next whim might be.

Worst of all, *bozorgs* are followed to the toilet. Fortunately, the clinic staff and Iqbal's family accepted – even if they did not understand – my wish for privacy when answering a call of nature. Unfortunately, they were not always quick enough to stop others when we were in someone else's house. The clinic latrine's holey sackcloth was unsettling enough: in most villages there was not even that much.

When other people 'went outside', they melted into the landscape in a way I found impossible to emulate. Whichever bush or rock I crouched behind left me feeling embarrassingly visible – even when I had succeeded in shaking off my pursuers. If I had been a proper *bozorg*, I would have accepted – demanded even – that someone carry the water jug (or, in my case, the toilet paper) for me. Not being a truly grand person, I refused to allow others to attend the wiping of my bottom.

When Iqbal left on a tour of the more distant villages we gave the students a holiday as I did not feel able to continue with classes alone without his help in translating. With Basma and David I made impromptu visits to some of the students and, at last, the honoured guest barriers began to come down.

The men were usually out at work in the fields and, not being accompanied by Iqbal (as clinic in-charge, a *bozorg* in his own right) news of our visit did not reach them in time to rush back to the house to greet us. With no men fussing around, ordering tea, plumping up my cushions, asking about my health and happiness every two minutes, the women were much more relaxed, especially when Basma assured them that I was happier in the kitchen than the guestroom.

David was quite a useful icebreaker. He enjoyed chattering to the women – providing there were no kisses – and was delighted when the younger girls swept him off to join them in their dances.

From when they were toddlers, girls learned the local dances, some of which were accompanied by traditional songs about engagements and weddings. In place of an instrumental accompaniment, the performers made a sort of raspberry-blowing sound between pursed lips. I often met groups of girls by the well, practising together while waiting their turn to draw water. Up to the age of eleven or twelve the girls' dancing was considered a harmless, childish pastime. After that age, it would have been shameless for a girl to dance where men could see her.

In the privacy of my room, I asked Basma to teach me some dance steps. She giggled, 'I was too shy to learn to dance when I was small. If anyone laughed at me, I cried.'

The main step, executed with fists on hips, consisted of a sideways jumping movement with both feet together. With David as our only audience, Basma and I practised together. We were hopeless, making David shout with laughter when we fell over in a tangled heap. Through his giggles, he declared, 'Mummy, only girls dance, not old women.'

By the time Iqbal returned my room at the clinic had turned into a social club for the women. Aquila, Jemila and Suraya were regular visitors and when classes resumed they often called in for a glass of tea before their long walk home. Kulsom, along with her year-old-daughter who loved playing with David's toys, came most days. Nickbacht, the wool-spinner, dropped in when she could find the time and, gradually, other women from the village took to calling in for a chat.

Another student who became a regular caller was Zohra, who lived almost an hour's walk in the opposite direction from Aquila and Jemila. Her village, with almost forty households, was the largest in the catchment area yet she was its only volunteer. Mostly, two women from a village attended class so working alone was going to be difficult enough, but Zohra had the added handicap of coming from a village whose leader was the most cantankerous, obstructive and ignorant man I met in the whole district.

On our first meeting he had laughed outright at our proposed project, declaring that there was no need to teach the women anything. When he realised that women from the other villages were attending, not wanting to be left out, he sent Zohra. She had not been a volunteer but was chosen by Moh'd Ali because 'the other women are too busy with their work to waste their time, but Zohra is so lazy and useless, she won't be missed at home'.

She was a gentle, pretty young woman in her early twenties and, in the beginning, almost as shy as Habiba. She was soon, however, one of the most enthusiastic students and wasted no time in putting into practise all that she learned in class – at least in her own home.

Hassan, the clinic's field assistant, told me one day that when talking to some people from Zohra's village they had been full of praise for how the training had transformed her. Her house was spotless, her children were regularly scrubbed clean and she had persuaded the pregnant women in the village to attend the antenatal clinic.

Next time I met Moh'd Ali, though, he was still laughing. Zohra had been trying to persuade everyone to use soap. He thought this a ridiculous idea. 'Look at me! I have reached the age of sixty and I have never touched a bar of soap in all my life.'

Looking hard at him I saw an almost bald, white-haired old man with a deeply-seamed face and maybe three or four teeth. He looked about ninety-five. I did not envy Zohra her task, and was full of admiration for her bravery and determination to make changes in that village

As my social circle widened my Dari was improving too – or at least, my confidence in using it grew. While Iqbal was away, David was the only person with whom I could speak in English – and by then he usually spoke Dari.

Basma and Ibrahim encouraged me, making me re-tell David's bedtime story in Dari. 'Ali Baba and the Forty Thieves' was the favourite – a story they knew well.

One night I recorded in my diary the topics of conversation the three of us had covered that evening. We had started – I don't know why – with burial procedures in our respective countries, followed by the Hindu custom of suttee. This had led on to dowry problems and general wedding expenses,

ending with an instructive half hour on the various animal
and insect life of the area. As far as I could tell, we had all
understood each other's point of view.

My growing confidence in understanding and being
understood made it easier to visit people on my own without
a translator. Sometimes, when out for a walk, I would call
on Nickbacht in the next village. I liked to stroll through
a small wooded area between the villages, enjoying the
glorious autumn red and gold of the leaves. They provided
the only real colour in the landscape now that the wheat had
been harvested.

Nickbacht's house was tiny – its only room having to
accommodate cooking, sitting and sleeping arrangements for
nine people. When I first crossed the threshold, I was aware
that she was watching me closely. Stepping from the bright
sunlight, it was difficult to see much in the dark room. As
my eyes adjusted to the gloom I was shocked by the miserable
conditions in which she and her family lived.

My gaze swept past the two or three tin trunks which stored
the family's possessions and took in the tattered, threadbare
gilims, whose once glowing colours were now a muted, sludgy
grey on the bare earth floor. Nickbacht indicated the crumbling
walls, blackened by years of smoke and soot from the kitchen
fires. 'In class, you tell us to keep our homes clean. Now you
have seen this, can you tell me how?'

I shook my head wordlessly. She was still watching me and
I realised that any expression of sympathy would instantly put
an end our nascent friendship. This proud, intelligent woman
was not looking for pity. As I sat down, narrowly missing a
lump of chicken shit, I remarked, 'No, but it might help if you
trained your chickens to shit outside.'

Nickbacht laughed. 'Not how a health volunteer should live,
is it?' she commented drily, as she started to make the tea.

Her life had been far from easy and yet she looked younger
than most of her contemporaries, with skin still unlined and
smooth, although she had several grandchildren. With her
slim, girlish figure she reminded me of Latifa in Mazar.

Nickbacht's parents had owned no land. Her father had worked as a casual, seasonal labourer, hired by wealthy farmers. Throughout her childhood, Nickbacht had led a nomadic existence, moving each year to a different village, a different labourer's cottage. She married young. How young, I wondered?

'I don't know,' she laughed. 'It was just after my first *kola shushtan*.' Menstruation was referred to as *kola shushtan* [the clothes washing time] because the women, regarded as unclean during their menstruation, bathed and washed their clothes when it ended. In other districts, it was called the hair washing time.

Nickbacht's husband was also a landless labourer so her peripatetic lifestyle continued after marriage. 'Each of my first six children was born in a different house. Then, my husband found this job and we've been able to stay put for some years. He doesn't earn much, but at least we have a roof over our heads, if nothing else.'

As Nickbacht walked part of the way back to the clinic with me she suddenly said, 'I'm glad you came here to run the classes. I was afraid that I couldn't learn anything because I've never been to school but now I know I'm not stupid. Now I feel that I am doing something really useful.' I returned to the clinic feeling about ten feet tall.

We had sailed through pregnancy and childbirth in class. The women were particularly eager to learn about how to make deliveries safer and how to recognise danger signs. When we moved onto the topic of infant nutrition, I was therefore taken aback at how contentious a topic it was.

The women thought a newborn baby was incapable of sucking at the breast for the first few days and nobody allowed their babies to have the *pila* [colostrum] believing it to be dangerous for them. Yet, when a cow calved, the *pila* was a highly-prized delicacy. When I pointed this out, Jemila was quick to reply, 'Oh, yes, it's very good for humans, but we don't give it to babies.'

Very few babies were given any solid food before nine

months, or even older. The first food was often a piece of dry bread – almost the last foodstuffs to be given a child were vegetables. And as for eggs, they were forbidden until after the child could talk, for given before then, the child would develop a speech defect.

To every suggestion I made, the women had a counter argument. Mashed potatoes? 'Oh no!' they cried in horror. 'Potatoes are *khonuk* [cold].' I was very relieved that this subject had not been earlier in the course, before the women had accepted many new ideas already.

Surprisingly, it was Jemila who proved to be my strongest ally in introducing a healthy diet for infants. After four daughters, she had given birth to a longed-for son and was desperate enough to make him strong and healthy to try, cautiously, some of our suggested weaning foods. The fact that David had obviously thrived on mashed potatoes, eggs and vegetables as an infant helped her believe that perhaps they would do more good than harm. I knew once Jemila was on my side, she would persuade the others.

Then Suraya, the only one of the women who could read, became convinced. I had given her a UN booklet in Dari, which included amongst its health messages a section on nutrition. She struggled through this, reading it to her children, her husband, her mother-in-law and anyone else she could make listen to her.

Towards the end of the course the students began to panic about the exam. Throughout the training we had been constantly evaluating and assessing what the women had learned. Sometimes, though, it was not easy because if one student did not answer a question immediately, all the others shouted out the answer. Iqbal and I were not sure if the woman had simply been taking time to formulate her reply, or hadn't known the answer. It was he who suggested testing each student individually.

I was taken aback by the importance the women attached to the *imtihan* [exam]. They wanted desperately to do well in it, even though they had already proved their competence in the practical work they had been carrying out as health volunteers over the past weeks. Suraya, whose reading skills far outweighed her writing ability, demanded that Iqbal write up notes on all the lessons for her. He refused.

The usually rather vague Chaman surprised him by handing over several sheets of closely written notes. 'Could you please check if this is correct?' she asked. It turned out to be a summary – a detailed one – of everything covered on the course.

'Who wrote this?' asked Iqbal. Chaman smiled, shyly, replying, 'Well, I tried to remember everything we've learned and my son wrote it down as I told him. Is it all right?' Iqbal promised her she would have no problems in the exam. Soon most of the students were dictating what they had learned to literate members of their families, bringing in reams of notes for Iqbal to check.

We spent two days over the examination. Each student was questioned on theory and asked to do practical tests such as preparing oral rehydration drinks, demonstrating on our 'baby' (made from old tights stuffed with cotton wool) how to tie and cut the cord. Everyone, as we expected, passed with flying colours.

Many of the women's husbands approached me in the days following the exams. They would start the conversation by stating that they didn't suppose Kulsom or Chaman or whoever his wife happened to be, had done very well. 'Oh, yes, she did,' I would assure him, 'She did very well indeed.' Husband would look pleased – as if he had answered the questions himself. 'But what', he would ask 'was her number?'

They only wanted to know because they felt their own status was at stake. If a woman had done badly, her husband would feel shame; if she had come first, it would be his glory, not hers, and he would feel able to gloat amongst his friends.

Eventually the men gave up asking me as I repeated the same story – all the woman had passed the exam and were now qualified Female Health Volunteers.

Iqbal wrote by hand beautiful certificates for the women,

and we organised a special 'graduation' lunch to be held in the clinic. Ibrahim and I worked like slaves for two days. He prepared the traditional *mehmani* fare – meat stew, Kabuli rice with its carrot, raisin and almond topping and *subzi* [a spinach-type vegetable which is gathered from the mountain in summer and dried for use in the winter].

I cooked western-style alternatives with what was locally available. There was a thick vegetable and rice soup, and for dessert, *kishta* [dried apricots] cooked, sieved and mixed with yoghurt.

Cooking in the tiny, dark, windowless kitchen was a nightmare. A hole in the roof was supposed to draw the smoke up and out, but it never did and the kitchen (not only ours but in all the houses) was always full of dense smoke. No wonder so many women had endless problems with their eyes.

The occasion was a tremendous success. When we had first thought of the lunch I had been uncertain about whether the women would be allowed to attend without their husbands. I needn't have worried. All thirteen students arrived, even shy little Habiba. Hassan, Abdul Ali and Ibrahim brought the water for hand washing and waited on the women before joining the company to eat. Not a giggle nor a smirk nor a remark indicated that this was not the usual way of doing things.

Later, bursting with pride, each woman stepped forward to accept her certificate. And, I thought, as Iqbal clicked away with his camera, they had every reason to be proud of themselves.

A few days before the end of the first training session my room began to look as though I was about to embark on a new career selling fresh produce. There were carrots from Kulsom, eggs from Zohra, some tiny turnips, more eggs, yoghurt, and even a live chicken.

They were gifts, brought by the women when they heard that David was ill. He had suffered the occasional episode of diarrhoea, but nothing worrying until now. This time it was serious and days of severe diarrhoea and vomiting – often both at once – followed.

When he developed a high temperature I started him on a course of antibiotics, which made him anorexic. Refusing to eat anything, he rapidly lost weight. Trying to keep up his fluid intake was a constant battle. It was one of the worst times I ever spent in Afghanistan.

David was fractious and clingy, hating me to be away from him, so most of my time was spent cooped up in our room with him. I carried on with classes, as much as anything because I needed those couple of hours away from him. Leaving him sobbing in Basma's arms was horrible and I felt terribly guilty.

After all, David hadn't chosen to be trailed around Afghanistan, exposed to all kinds of bugs and infections. I knew – logic and my own medical knowledge told me – that he would recover, but that was no comfort. Mothers can never be comforted when their children are ill. We always fear the worst. Perhaps we are afraid of tempting fate by daring to say aloud that we know our child will soon be better – just in case?

I was deeply touched by the women's support and concern. Their kind words of comfort often caused my eyes to fill with tears. Iqbal, who believed that women's tears were a sign of some inherent weakness in us, became impatient with my emotional displays.

The women, however, understood. They felt especially sorry for me because, far from home, I did not have the close family network they so much depended on in times of crisis. Offering themselves as a substitute, extended family, they gathered round me.

Eventually the diarrhoea stopped and I began to believe that David would live after all. It's amazing how a child's perfectly formed sausage-shaped solid stool can bring so much joy to an anxious mother! He had become so thin that the first time he went out to play, his trousers fell down. He thought it was hilarious. I wanted to cry.

Once free of the infection, he began eating like a horse, and after we passed the frightful, cantankerous stage children go through during convalescence, he made a rapid recovery. My

guilt and anxiety were – at least temporarily – laid to rest.
I stopped bursting into tears whenever anyone said anything
nice to me.

9

Blessings on the Goat

BEFORE THE SECOND training course began I went to stay in Iqbal's village to enjoy a few days' holiday, gossiping with Aquila and the other women.

By then, I had succeeded in shrugging off my honoured guest status and, to my relief, the family had stopped killing things for me to eat. At first I was afraid they would bankrupt themselves as they slaughtered goats and chickens left, right and centre whenever I put in an appearance.

Afghanistan's rules of hospitality are horribly expensive for the host. Dinner for a guest has to be banquet and must include meat (chicken, goat or sheep), rice, vegetables and sweet dishes.

A host's reputation is based on the number of dishes that appear. Seven dishes constitutes a good spread, anything less makes him look mean.

In Aquila's village, there were four households, all related to each other and at first each family insisted on providing a dinner for me. As they had to invite everyone else in the village, we were rarely less than twenty people, which meant another goat had to be despatched. They also had a habit of bringing the hapless goat into the house and leading it around the guests to be blessed. Hassan, interpreting the expression on my face as one of alarm at being confronted with my dinner still alive and bleating, stopped his son from bringing the goat to me.

While not enthusiastic about looking the goat in the eye, what concerned me more was, if that was dinner still parading around very much alive, when would we finally eat?

Eventually the family realised that I was not going to blacken their name by telling everyone I had not been given the full seven courses while in their home. It also become acceptable for me to sit in the smoke-filled kitchen chatting with the women instead of in the guestroom, with someone appointed to entertain me.

In the kitchen I watched Fatima, Hassan's wife, making *ash* [pasta] by hand, wondering if it had reached Italy, from much further east, by way of the Silk Road. The simple flour and water pasta was served with whey and oil which had been boiled together. Another frequently eaten dish was *qruti*, which was made by reconstituting *qrut* [a type of cheese made from curd, dehydrated until its texture resembles a rock] in hot oil. Into bowls of this greasy liquid we threw torn-up nan until most of the liquid had been absorbed. A filling dish, it actually tasted better than it sounded – provided one did not have to eat it too often.

Sometimes I would wander alone up in the hills behind the village, marvelling at the desolate, awesome beauty of mile after mile of hills and mountain peaks. The landscape held me so completely enthralled that I would return without having glanced at a page of the book I had brought. The hillsides, bare even of their coats of wheat now the harvest was in, were brown – but I had never known before how many shades of brown existed.

On a walk with Gul Chaman, who lived in the next village, she paused, pointing towards a narrow gully between two mountains. 'That is where Al Khatoon lives,' she remarked, conversationally.

'Who's she?' I thought it might be another recruit for the next health-training programme, although I could see no sign of a house.

Astonished by my ignorance, Gul Chaman launched into a colourful description of a dangerous apparition who walked the hills at night. Men, powerless to resist her enchanting allure, suffered dreadful consequences when they approached her. 'Some', she said, 'become dumb, or blind. Some die.'

As she spoke, I was struck by her quiet conviction that Al Khatoon was real, fact not fantasy. This was no bogey-man story to frighten children into being good, but one more example of the hazards – like plagues of grasshoppers or a high infant mortality rate – of life in Hazara Jat.

Nearly everyone believed in and feared Al Khatoon. There were regional variations in description – in some places she was reputedly endowed with enormous breasts with which she suffocated her victims. And her feet pointed backwards. Despite these bizarre characteristics, everyone agreed that her beauty was well-nigh impossible to resist. Back in Mazar, I learned that she was not a rural phenomenon but existed as *madar 'ol* in the cities.

The women laughed at my demands for more details about Al Khatoon. It was the shame-faced laughter of people who knew there was no such being, but who could not prevent the mouth drying fear they experienced when out alone after dark. One day I met a man who claimed to have really seen Al Khatoon with his own eyes.

Hussain had been a *mujahid* [a freedom fighter]. Now back working on his land, he was a taciturn man, whose surly demeanour seemed unlikely to entertain flights of fancy. 'Two of us were on a night patrol,' he said, 'and the commander warned us we were near where Al Khatoon walks. I didn't believe in her so I wasn't afraid. It was just after one o'clock when I saw her.'

He paused, his eyes distant as though he could still see the apparition. He looked at me, 'I could see her as clearly as I see you now. She was sitting on a wall, combing her hair, which was loose and fell right to the ground. She was the most beautiful woman I have ever seen. Somehow, I forced myself to turn and run away. When I looked back she had gone.'

Someone in the audience laughed. Hussain shot him a truculent look. 'Mock if you like. I know what I saw. And so did the soldier with me. I had forgotten about him until I stopped running, and found he had been running right alongside me. If we had taken another step towards her, she would have trapped us.' Watching him shudder at the memory of his lucky escape I realised Hussain would never be shaken of his belief that he had seen and escaped Al Khatoon.

Gul Chaman, sitting next to me, asked me if I was not afraid
to go out to the latrine alone after dark. Laughingly, I said I did
not think I need fear Al Khatoon. Hussain looked at me rather
oddly for a moment or two before replying, 'Take care. She
especially likes to get people who are not afraid of her.' That
wiped the smile from my face.

Iqbal told me a story equally strange. 'Do you remember
the woman at the antenatal clinic who was crying because
her husband had died?' he asked. I nodded. The woman, who
was about six months pregnant, had been tearful and anxious
about how she was going to manage when the next baby
arrived as her other children were too young to give any help
in the house or fields.

'Her husband, Ali Gul, was attending a funeral at the
capristan [graveyard]. You know the custom of the men
reading prayers for the dead all night, by the graveside?

'Just before midnight Ali went to the spring for water. When
he returned he was nervous, asking who else had gone to the
spring. The others said no one else had left the graveside. He
became very agitated, saying that when he reached the spring
he heard someone else moving about and called a greeting.
There was no reply but, although he couldn't see anyone, he
knew there was someone or something walking beside him
back to the grave.

'Everyone tried to convince him he was imagining it but he
became more and more afraid, saying it was a sign that he
would surely be the next to be buried.'

Iqbal paused while he poured a glass of tea. 'Go on!' I urged,
'What happened?'

'He went home,' continued Iqbal, 'too afraid to continue the
vigil. In the morning he complained of pains all over his body.
Someone sent for me. I examined him thoroughly but could
find nothing wrong. He was a healthy man, not yet forty, and
his heart was sound. He died that night.'

'Al Khatoon?' I whispered. Iqbal laughed. 'There is no Al
Khatoon. Anyway, she is visible and Ali Gul never saw anything
that night. I can't explain it. Maybe he just died of fright.'

Although it was reasonably safe to assume that Al Khatoon was the stuff of myths and legends, the same could not be said of djinn. They were written about in the Quran, in much the same way as the Bible mentions spirits that possessed people. Nasty, evil creatures, they were blamed for all kinds of sickness.

Women, as might be expected, were often suspected of harbouring djinn that had invaded their bodies. The custom of not allowing any woman from outside the family to see a baby until forty days after the birth was a protection against djinn being inadvertently brought into contact with the vulnerable newborn.

Tawiz [amulets] sold by mullahs, provided protection against djinn. Verses from the Quran were folded into a triangle and sewn into a piece of cloth, leather or metal. Everyone – adults, children, newborn babies, horses, cows, sheep and goats – wore them. The fact that children, despite the protective *tawiz*, still became sick was partly why the students were prepared to listen when I explained the power of soap in the fight against microbes. I certainly did nothing to discourage them from visiting the mullah to ask for prayers, blessings and *tawiz*. As long as they used soap too, I was happy.

At least a *tawiz* was harmless. Some of the other practices and advice given by the mullahs were not. Aquila told of a mullah suggesting that a mother whose son had a respiratory infection made him swallow a chicken's saliva, and mullahs often blew into the mouths of supplicants, passing on another few million microbes.

As if Al Khatoon and djinn were not enough to contend with, everyone worried about the threat of someone casting the 'evil eye' on them, their children or their animals. No one openly praised a child for its looks or intelligence, but if one did, inadvertently, say something nice, the phrase, 'Mash 'Allah' [Thanks to Allah] had to be added.

Marzia, Aquila's sister-in-law, told me of an accident that happened to her brother, Zahir, as a result of someone putting the evil eye on him.

'He was coming back from the mountain where he had spent the day cutting *butta* (a low scrubby bush used as firewood). The load on his back was taller than he was. A friend of my mother was talking to her and, when she saw Zahir approaching, she said, "Your son is a strong lad. You are lucky to have a boy who works so hard." The next day Zahir fell and broke his leg. You see,' concluded Marzia, 'she had put the evil eye on him.'

The incident had occurred twenty years before, but Zahir's mother had never again spoken to the woman she held responsible for her son's accident.

The women loved the opportunity to re-tell stories of the evil eye and other superstitions, and I was an enthusiastic listener. They were, at first, a little hesitant, afraid that I would laugh at them. It did not take long to set their minds at rest. Anyone whose compatriots thought it unlucky to walk under a ladder, who touched wood instead of saying 'Mash 'Allah' and who thought black cats were lucky (in Hazara Jat, the opposite is true) – was hardly in a position to mock their beliefs.

Soon after returning to the clinic, I saw something of the havoc and horror of what the evil eye could reputedly do.

A couple arrived one morning, bringing their *doganagi* [twins]. They were in a pitiful, severely malnourished state. Both were extremely dirty and their heads were covered in scaly cradle cap. At three months old, each baby boy weighed two kilos.

The mother, looking utterly exhausted, complained of having too little breast milk. She wanted us to give powdered milk. They had already bought some, but it was too expensive; they could not afford more. She produced a filthy feeding bottle, its teat encrusted with dried milk, which she offered to one of the babies. Even if they could have all the powdered milk in the world, I feared the twins had little chance of survival.

The thought of teaching this exhausted woman how to prepare feeds, impressing on her the need for scrupulous hygiene, filled me with despair. Would she accept that the water must be boiled? It would mean a lot of extra work as well as the expense of using extra fuel. Would she sterilise the bottle and teat? If she really had not enough breast milk, feeding the babies diluted cow's milk using a cup and spoon would be a safer alternative to milk formula in a bottle. But it would be time consuming and she would need huge reserves of patience and a great deal of support.

As Iqbal and I talked to the couple, I wondered how much support the woman would receive from the man sitting so silently by her side. He hardly seemed to be listening, and at Iqbal's suggestion that Suraya and I visit their home to help the mother learn how to feed the babies, he shrugged hopelessly.

'It won't do any good,' he muttered. 'They will not live. They are sick because someone put the evil eye on them. I only came today because she', he nodded in his wife's direction, 'forced me when I told her I couldn't buy more milk powder. I know they will die, whatever you do.'

Wordlessly, I stared at the man, unable to believe that any father could so callously dismiss his sons' chances – albeit slim ones – of survival. His wife, cradling the babies in her lap, imperceptibly tightened her hold on them and lifted her eyes to meet mine. They glistened with unshed tears and the desperate appeal they held needed no words. I suggested a day and time for our proposed visit, and she nodded.

After their departure Iqbal filled in the details of the story. The couple had suffered the death of three children already – only one daughter survived. 'You can imagine', said Iqbal, 'how happy they were when twin boys were born. People from all around congratulated them on their good fortune.'

A few weeks later, a fire had broken out destroying most of the family's wheat. 'The men had been working very late at night, threshing the wheat,' said Iqbal. I had seen men in the clinic village work half the night at this task. Several shared one threshing ground so there was always a sense of urgency to complete the job.

Iqbal continued, 'Someone left the hurricane lamp behind and it must have blown over. It was an accident, but that man, Nabi, says it was the evil eye. He thinks someone was jealous of his good fortune in having two sons arrive at once. He says his wife's milk drying up proves he is right.'

Suraya met Iqbal and me at the twins' home. While the mother, Nickbacht, went off to make tea I looked round the clean, neat guestroom. In a corner of the room, bedridden, reclining on piles of cushions, was her mother-in-law – almost blind from cataracts – the epitome of the ancient, cackling crone.

Nickbacht returned with hot, sweet milk – a luxury. 'Don't say anything,' warned Iqbal, seeing my angry expression and knowing I was thinking that milk should have been for the twins.

'At least we know there is a cow,' I whispered back.

When Nickbacht, with seeming reluctance brought the babies to us, they looked weaker and dirtier than only a couple of days before.

The mother-in-law cackled something – incomprehensible to me – which made her daughter-in-law bow her head as though in shame. Suraya's face darkened in anger. She repeated, slowly enough for me to follow, what had been said, 'The mother-in-law is blaming Nickbacht for the boys' ill health. She says that she herself raised nine children, none of whom died, yet her daughter-in-law can not keep more than one child alive. She says she is a useless woman and is accusing her of bringing bad luck on the family.'

Suraya worked tirelessly to keep the twins alive. It was a difficult and frustrating task, made no easier by the father's lack of concern and support. There was no one in the household to share Nickbacht's heavy workload, and she was always exhausted. The old crone kept up her constant barrage of verbal abuse. The cow went dry and Nickbacht's sister-in-law, who lived next door, was reluctant to give milk from their cow.

Suraya battled on, spending so much time and energy – both emotional and physical – that I feared she, too, would become as exhausted as the twins' mother. For Suraya, pregnant herself, knew what keeping alive those pathetic little boys meant to

Nickbacht. Both her own sons had died shortly after birth and only two daughters survived.

Though still very much at risk, especially with winter fast approaching, the twins had begun to gain weight by the time I left for Mazar-i-Sharif a few weeks later. Along with the privileges that came with being adopted into Iqbal's extended family (being allowed to satisfy my inherent nosiness and urge to know the minutiae of their daily lives, many aspects of which would normally be hidden from outsiders) came the responsibilities of being a family member.

When one of Ali's lambs was lost one night, I was not exempted from going out on the dark mountainside to look for it, reassuring myself that wolves only took lambs in the winter. Stumbling about on a dark mountainside was a small price to pay for knowing that my days of being an honoured guest were over.

It also meant I shared the family's ostracism by Miriam's family, who never spoke to Iqbal's family. If any of them passed me on the path between, they simply pretended I was invisible.

Miriam was married to Hassan's brother, Ali. As children, he and Miriam had played together and fell in love when they grew up. Miriam's family had opposed the marriage so the young couple had eloped. Fatima said, 'They spent two nights in a cave on the mountain. When Ali and Miriam returned here a mullah performed the *nikah* (the religious part of an Islamic wedding ceremony) so that they were properly married.

'Miriam's family came to see us, saying they did not want *dushmani* (enmity) between the families, and since the *nikah* had happened, they would accept the marriage. Then they asked us to pay a bride price to show that we were not angry. They asked for a lot of things besides money – cows, sheep, a donkey.'

Aquila interrupted, 'It wasn't a donkey – it was a horse. They knew we didn't want any trouble so they became greedy. Miriam's father and brothers came to collect everything and have never spoken to us since.'

'What about Miriam?' I asked, 'Doesn't she see her family?'
Fatima shook her head, 'Even her mother hasn't spoken to her
in twelve years.

There was little sympathy for Miriam's plight amongst the
women. Miriam and Ali's elopement, which I was inclined to
view as romantic, courageous and the stuff of weepy films, the
village women viewed as foolhardy and stupid. In a culture
where family ties and loyalty are vitally important, it must
have been heart-breaking for the young Miriam to realise her
family had disowned her – especially when the women of her
new family barely accepted her.

The women were the keepers of the family's oral history,
and from Marzia (Iqbal's aunt, married to his father's brother)
I heard of the feuds that had started through disputes over
land. Marzia's mother and sister's engagement to two brothers
had started one such feud, and it is still unresolved.

'My grandfather had no sons so my mother and aunt would
inherit all his land. The *Arbab* [the chief of the area] was angry
because he wanted his own son to marry my mother. He was a
powerful man and Hussain Karbali, the brothers' father, was
afraid of him.

'You know the custom of *lungi* – when a boy marries, his
father gives gifts to friends? Well Hussain Karbali offered the
Arbab a very fine *lungi* – he signed a paper giving a large
piece of the land that should have come to my mother and her
sister.'

Marzia's family had been angry, but once a *lungi* has been
given, no one can ask for its return. Only Marzia's mother,
in her eighties and very frail, was still alive, still hoping that
before she died her family would win back her land. A ruling
that the paper giving the land had been signed by force had
been recently overturned amidst rumours and accusations
of bribery. Hopes of an amicable settlement were rapidly
disappearing amidst such rumours.

With almost every family struggling to eke out a living by
farming, it was understandable that land ownership was a
contentious issue. Marriages were arranged, often less with a

view to the suitability of the young couple than with an eye to increasing land-holdings.

Gul Sevre, Aquila's daughter, deeply unhappy about her future marriage, was a pawn in this game of land acquisitions. Her uncle Hassan had arranged her engagement to Moh'd Amir, seemingly to acquire more land. Moh'd Amir was in Iran earning money for the wedding. 'I hope he stays there!' exclaimed the normally placid Gul Sevre. 'I hate him.'

I asked Aquila if there was no way of stopping the marriage. 'It's too late,' she replied. 'Her father won't do anything to upset Moh'd Amir's family. Talk to Hassan. He is the one who wants to become a rich farmer by giving away my daughter in exchange for land. He is already using the land and he won't give it up because Gul Sevre is miserable.'

I did talk to Hassan about Gul Sevre's unhappiness. He considered for a few moments before replying, 'At the moment, Gul Sevre is upset, and I am happy she can talk to you about it, but I don't think you completely understand the situation.'

With a slight smile, he continued, 'You are assuming that Gul Sevre knows best what she wants, and you think I only want her to marry Moh'd Amir to get more land. Well, the land is important – you have been here long enough to understand that. It would, though, be possible to obtain the use of that land in other ways, through renting it or taking it as a *grau*.'

Watching me closely, he continued, 'You know Gul Sevre well. What do you think of her?' Not sure where the conversation was heading, I replied cautiously, 'She is a nice girl, and a hard worker in the house.'

Hassan shook his head, 'That is not what I meant. What about her intelligence?' I admitted that she seemed a little slow. In fact, Gul Sevre had a learning disability, caused, I suspected by oxygen deprivation during a long labour. I added quickly, 'That doesn't mean she isn't able to express her feelings.'

'I know that,' agreed Hassan, 'but what you don't understand is that because of how she is, it would be almost impossible to find a husband for Gul Sevre, except through family connections. If she didn't marry,' he continued, anticipating

my next argument that Gul Sevre had expressed a wish to
remain single, 'her life would be difficult. Her brothers will
marry and bring their wives to the house. You know how the
system works.

'Gul Sevre, as an older, unmarried girl, would have no status
in the house and, when her mother died, she would have no
protection from the ridicule of her sisters-in-law. Her situation
would be even worse than if she marries someone who, at first,
she thinks she does not like.'

His words conjured up a sad mental image of an unmarried
Gul Sevre, in ten years time. She would be the scapegoat for
any mistakes made by her sisters-in-law, the butt of their cruel
jokes – a drudge going about her thankless tasks, unhappy
and bewildered by her treatment. Hassan succeeded in making
me realise that, regarding Gul Sevre's future, there were many
factors involved which I had not considered before opening my
mouth.

So upset was I by this portrayal of poor Gul Sevre's future,
I quite forgot to ask if some other, more appealing, man
within the family network could not be found to marry her,
or to question the assumption that her brothers' wives would
necessarily be heartless and cruel.

None of the other women, with the exception of Gul Sevre's
mother, Aquila, were concerned. They agreed with Hassan
that Gul Sevre would be unhappier if she remained single,
saying she would soon become used to life with Moh'd Amir,
and that all girls felt the same before their marriage. Their
attitude made me feel as though I had run slap into a cultural
barrier, too high for me to cross.

Contemplating this, I realised, with something of a shock,
that for increasing periods of time I was hardly aware of this
barrier. Surrounded by people who really tried to make me feel
that I belonged, I had absorbed much of the culture and ways
of life – even to the extent of adopting local superstitions. I
knew if a cat was seen washing its face, a visitor would arrive.
If the teapot ran dry before filling someone's glass, I would say,
laughingly, 'Sorry, your mother-in-law doesn't like you.'

I was so accustomed to the women coming and going freely from their villages to class and to my room at the clinic that I had stopped thinking about Afghan women's lack of freedom. Their way of life, though physically harder and economically more constrained than that of most Western women, had begun to seem perfectly normal.

But then something like Gul Sevre being forced to marry a man she loathed pulled me up short. I was shocked, too, by the attitude of the women, who were unconcerned about Gul Sevre's unhappiness. Confused, I did not know where to direct my anger – towards men like Hassan who seemed to regard the acquisition of land as more important than a woman's future happiness, or the women who shrugged it off?

Suddenly I was a foreigner again.

10

Stereotypes and Misconceptions

THERE WAS LITTLE time to brood – the second training session, with ten new students, was beginning.

Some of the women were pregnant and were instantly adopted as training aids, frequently lying, like so many beached whales, around Kulsom's guestroom having their abdomens palpated.

The first to give birth was Shahnaz, who, although there was no family tie between them, asked Nickbacht, the wool-spinner, to be her midwife. Three days later, in defiance of the custom which prohibited outsiders seeing a new baby for forty days, Shahnaz, with baby, was back in class.

'Shahnaz is the best volunteer we have,' said Iqbal, one day shortly afterwards. I disagreed, pointing out that there were several women more able in class than she. Iqbal's admiration of Shahnaz was, however, for her beauty rather than her health-worker skills.

Personally, I thought the large-boned, rather coarse featured young woman with big teeth resembled a horse. 'Oh, but look at her eyebrows,' Iqbal urged, 'she has the most beautiful eyebrows in the world.'

Next day in class I looked at Shahnaz a little more intently, paying special attention to those eyebrows. I still couldn't see the attraction, although it made me realise that with so little on show, Afghan men had to assess women's beauty on individual features such as eyebrows, eyes and lips.

No wonder so many women, knowing how closely their facial features were being appraised by the opposite sex, kept their eyes cast down and covered their mouths when they laughed in public. Zohra, for instance, habitually put her hand over her mouth when speaking to men, even her husband.

There could be nothing alluring about Hazara women's

hands. Hard manual labour left them dry, calloused and wrinkled with broken, often dirty, nails. Nor was there much in the way of style or fashion about the women's clothing that might make some stand out from the crowd. Everyone wore the same shapeless dresses in either flowery printed polyester or a synthetic crushed velvet over a pair of *tunban* which were never colour coordinated.

Every woman wore a highly decorative waistcoat. Some were hand-embroidered, others had metallic braiding machine-stitched in various designs. These waistcoats served as the women's handbags. In the one very small pocket a box of matches was kept. Safety pins and threaded needles were stuck into the fabric, while medicine prescriptions were pinned securely inside the waistcoat.

Bunches of keys were also pinned, for safe-keeping, to the garment. These were the keys for the tin trunks in which every family stored its valuables – from a woman's wedding jewellery to the household's tea, sugar and boiled sweets. The latter especially had to be kept under lock and key out of children's reach. *Tawiz*, beads, fancy buttons, old silver coins and bells were added in great abundance to children's waistcoats.

Everyone wore their clothes until they almost literally fell apart, and few women, except new brides, had more than two outfits in their wardrobe.

There was another Nickbacht in the second group, whose small, pointed face and slanted eyes made her look like an attractive cat. 'Has Nickbacht nice eyebrows?' I asked Iqbal.

He looked hard at me for a moment before replying, 'What have you heard about me and Nickbacht?' Taken aback, I assured him I had heard nothing, but, curiosity aroused, asked, 'Why, what is there to hear?'

Iqbal at first would not be drawn but, finally, confessed that Nickbacht had been flirting with him. She had even suggested they meet one evening, at a certain place in a copse of trees near the clinic. Disbelievingly, I cried, 'But she's married!'

'Do married women in your country never have love affairs?' asked Iqbal.

'Well, yes, but they aren't going to be stoned to death if they are caught.'

Iqbal shrugged, 'In theory, yes, but you must remember that under Islamic law there must be four witnesses to the act. People who want to love each other do it in very secret places.' He explained further that if there were only three male witnesses, the evidence of two women was required to bring the numbers up to equal four men. 'And', he added, 'if only two men and four women witness the adultery, the offender would not be stoned, but only receive 100 lashes.'

'Oh, well,' I muttered sarcastically, 'that's all right then.'

Ignoring me, Iqbal continued, 'If a husband discovered that his wife was sleeping with another man, he would divorce her and she would lose her children and her home. Perhaps her own family would not accept her back because of the shame that would be on their heads.

'But remember we are talking about Hazara Jat. In Pushtoon areas it's different. A Pushtoon believes killing his wife and her lover restores his honour. Personally, I think that would be worse because everyone would know what she had done. Better to divorce her. Then the husband can say it was for some other reason. People might talk for a while, but never in front of the husband. So you see it is not so dangerous for Hazara women to have secret love affairs like you Western women do.'

Yes, I thought, if she doesn't mind risking the loss of her children and her home, and probably ending up destitute. Iqbal's reassurances that it was extremely unlikely that four male witnesses would pop up in what a couple had thought was their secret love nest did, however, alter my perception of the improbability of illicit sex in Hazara Jat.

'Why', I asked, 'is the evidence of a female witness only valued at half that of a man?'

Iqbal looked wary. 'I'll tell you what Islam says,' he said, 'so don't get angry with me, it's not my idea. Women are not reliable witnesses because their power of reasoning is not the same as men's. Women are more emotional and that makes them unreliable witnesses. Also, menstruation makes them less responsible for their behaviour.'

In mock terror, he cringed at my stone-faced expression. 'Don't start shouting,' he commanded. 'I was only answering your question, not giving my opinion. Though it is true that women are more emotional than men. Look how often they cry – when they are happy, when they are sad, when they are in love . . .'

Suddenly remembering how the conversation had started, I interrupted to ask, 'Did you ever go to meet Nickbacht?'

Iqbal shook his head, 'No, I didn't. I had a lesson planning meeting with you at the time she suggested.' I wasn't sure whether to believe him or not.

Smiling enigmatically, he said, 'There is always gossip. People sometimes joke about a man being too friendly with a woman who is not his wife, but love affairs are only a small part of life. Mostly people are too busy with their work to bother about such things.' As he was leaving the room, he turned, adding, 'You should talk to your friend – the other Nickbacht. She had lots of affairs when she was young.'

I didn't feel that I was on quite such an intimate footing with Nickbacht to start asking her about her extra-marital love life. I wasn't even sure if the women talked about their personal sex lives amongst themselves. In class, whenever anything connected with sex was mentioned, they giggled and made jokes of a general nature. Although when we visited each other, pregnancy, childbirth and birth spacing were all discussed at length, nothing personal was ever said about sex.

For the time being at least, Iqbal was my only source of information on that aspect of the women's lives. Like a dog with a bone, I worried him relentlessly for more information.

Where did people go to meet? I found it difficult enough to find a private place to pee, so how did they manage to escape prying eyes? How did such affairs begin? Who made the first moves? What if the woman became pregnant? What about unmarried girls?

Iqbal was amused by my constant questions. 'Did you think that sex was only for foreigners?' he asked.

'Of course, not.' I replied, then, slightly shame-faced, continued, 'Well, I suppose I hadn't expected to hear there was so much of it going on here. Whenever anyone talks to me about Islam, they always make it sound as though everyone in Afghanistan respects and obeys all the Islamic laws.'

I was constantly being told things like 'Muslims don't drink alcohol because Hazrati Mohammed said it was *haram*' [forbidden]. Or, 'Muslims must pray five times a day' as though, therefore, no Muslim would ever dream of touching alcohol or skipping a few prayers. By extension, if Islam prohibited adultery, sex before marriage, homosexuality – then they did not exist.

My would-be teachers seemed intent on making me believe that all Muslims were good Muslims, and followed the rules laid down and never strayed into that grey area that lurks between theory and practice.

I was expected to accept an image of Muslims as deeply religious people, all of whom adhered strictly to their faith. The men who talked to me about Islam were creating an Afghan Muslim stereotype. Added to my own, Western created, stereotype of repressed and passive Muslim women, the two together, I thought, amply justified my confusion and surprise at the extra-marital sexual freedom Iqbal was describing.

Iqbal, equally guilty of swallowing stereotyped images, pronounced, 'It is, of course, different in your country, where everyone accepts that married women will have many lovers.' His conclusions were drawn from watching 'sexy movies' he had seen in Karachi, leading him to believe that Western women spent their days and nights indulging in mammoth sex romps with a never-ending variety of partners.

'Hazara women would never do the sort of things European women do in bed,' he declared, his expression a comical mixture of prudery and envy.

Alarmed that Iqbal and other Afghan men thought that I was some sort of sex starved nymphomaniac, I asked if he really thought that all European women, including myself, behaved as he had seen on the films. He roared with laughter.

'You? You are OLD!' he finally managed to splutter, between guffaws. 'Old women don't have sex.' At thirty-nine and believing that I had several years of sexual activity still ahead of me, I found it strangely humiliating to be told that Afghan men considered me devoid of any sex appeal.

'So what won't Hazara women do?' I asked, for the pleasure of seeing him blush with embarrassment.

'Hazara women don't do *anything*,' he replied, in tones that suggested he was speaking, despairingly, from personal experience. 'When a man tries to touch or kiss a woman, she pushes him away, saying, *"Na koo! Na koo!"* [Don't! Don't!]

'We have to keep talking, holding her hand maybe, telling her how much we like her, how beautiful she is. Finally, maybe after several meetings, she allows a kiss.'

He mimed the sort of kiss on the cheek an elderly aunt might bestow, saying, 'They think kissing on the mouth is disgusting. On the cheek and the forehead is all right and maybe, finally, on the eyelids or the neck. But never on the mouth. If we try to touch them below the waist, they start the *"Na koo"* business again. They don't understand how difficult it is for men when they behave like that.'

I laughed at those familiar words, repeated, probably, by every man around the world, whenever his efforts to achieve his own sexual gratification is thwarted by a woman who does not understand HIS needs.

How could there be any understanding of either partner's needs when sex and sexual feelings were a taboo subject? Girls were not even told about menstruation until it started (Basma remembered her terror on waking one morning, convinced she was bleeding to death) They were, however, taught from an early age to feel shame. When little girls of two or three years old, lifted up their dresses, as little girls invariably do, their mothers angrily shout 'Shame! Shame!' at them until they cried in fear and bewilderment.

Islam decrees that a menstruating woman is so 'unclean' that sex with her is forbidden and Allah will not even hear her prayers. Girls have been conditioned to believe that everything in connection with their ability to give birth is dirty and shameful. At the same time, they have been given the contradictory message that their 'honour' – or, to be more exact, their father's honour – resides in this dirty place that bleeds.

With constant warnings to keep away from boys, who would immediately attempt to dishonour them, bringing shame on their fathers' heads, it is hardly surprising that girls grow into womanhood with very confused feelings about sex. Girls approach their wedding night with dread, having had their heads filled with horror stories whispered by other girls who knew no more than they did. Instead of married women explaining sex to their daughters, there appears to be a conspiracy of silence amongst them.

Iqbal assured me that the old custom of spreading a white sheet on the bed on the wedding night was dying out. In the morning the girl's mother, often accompanied by other women, would inspect the sheet for bloodstains. In some areas, the sheet was publicly displayed so everyone could see the evidence that the girl had truly been a virgin.

Her father, who had been responsible for ensuring his daughter's virginity remained intact prior to her wedding, could hold his head high. The boy's family would be reassured that their son had not been duped and the boy himself could delight in the fact that everyone knew he had proved his manhood. No-one considered how the bride felt about this degrading practice.

'I would like to see this custom finished everywhere,' said Iqbal. 'I know there can be many reasons for a girl not to bleed, even though she has never had sex. But while it is still the custom here, I would never try to sleep with an unmarried girl, even if she would allow it. I don't want to ruin someone's life by causing her a problem on her wedding night.'

One of the favourite meeting places was, according to Iqbal, the *assea* [the flour-mill]. In the early autumn, before the harvest, couples met in the fields, where the tall wheat gave them cover. Adultery may not be 'allowed' in the West in quite the way Iqbal supposed, but it is certainly easier to organise and arrange privacy.

Even for married couples in Hazara Jat there is no such thing as privacy. Once the babies start to arrive, a couple is never alone at night, since children and parents sleep together in one room. Sex has to be a hurried, silent performance.

Blushingly, Iqbal said, 'When a husband wants his wife, he just undoes the string of her *tunban*, rolls on top of her, and five minutes later he is asleep. She just lies there, without doing anything, until he is finished. No-one says anything or makes any sound. I don't think women get any pleasure from sex.'

If what Iqbal said was really true, I had to agree that sexual fulfilment for the women of Hazara Jat was unlikely. Surely, though, it could not be as bleak a picture as he was painting? And if all the men were such selfish, insensitive lovers, why did so many married women take such risks for a peck on the cheek and a five-minute furtive fumble with someone else's husband?

Or was it that since a woman can not discuss such intimate details with her women friends, she thinks only HER husband is useless in bed, and hopes that another man might prove to be a more skilled and sensitive lover?

Even knowing that what Iqbal had told me could not be the whole picture, it had added an extra dimension to what I knew of the women's lives. Unfortunately, it was almost time to return to Mazar-i-Sharif and I reluctantly accepted that there would be no opportunity to hear the women's views on the subject. I would have loved to ask Nickbacht, with her bewitching cat's eyes, what she found so attractive about Iqbal.

A constant stream of visitors invaded my room to say goodbye while I was trying to pack. Many of them brought small gifts of food for the journey or *nishani* [remembrances] in the form of embroidered handkerchiefs, and then they settled down to drink tea and gossip with each other.

While the women talked amongst themselves, I carried on packing, only half listening to their conversation. Catching the words, 'microbe' and 'diarrhoea', I realised they were discussing their work and paused to reflect on all they had achieved over the last three months.

One thing was clear, I could shelve the notion that women in Hazara Jat were passive creatures, mutely accepting whatever life handed out to them. These women were actively working towards improving the health of mothers and children in their communities. They had already gained tremendous respect in the area. Even husbands who, at first, had been condescendingly amused by the idea of their illiterate wives studying, were proud and supportive of what the women were doing.

Twenty years earlier, some of these same men had threatened to burn down the school and take up arms against a Government that wanted to enforce education for girls. Now, admitting the importance of that education, they were preparing to enrol girls in the school when it re-opened after the winter break.

Tuning in to the conversation again – Nickbacht was describing how she persuaded a mother to start feeding solids to her nine-month-old baby – I felt a huge surge of admiration for these women, regretting that I had to leave them.

Jon, who had been touring the clinics in the south, had arrived to collect us, and an ecstatic Basma, whose family had given permission for her to return to school in Pakistan.

On the morning of our departure many of the women gathered outside the clinic to bid us farewell, despite the early start. Although I had promised to return the following year I knew that in Afghanistan nothing could ever be so certain, and as we drove away, I had a huge lump in my throat. The lump became bigger when at almost every village en route Jon had to stop the jeep, while we women clambered out to embrace and kiss the women waiting on the roadside. Nickbacht, the wool-spinner, was at work in the fields but came running up, breathlessly, to hug me goodbye. Zohra was waiting with her children and neighbours on the roadside, tears streaming down her face.

We spent a night in the Oxfam office in Panjau, where Basma's mother, Aquila, said goodbye to the daughter she might not see for the next five years. For Aquila, Pakistan might as well be on another planet and she was grief-stricken at the thought of her daughter being so far away for so long.

She could have refused to allow Basma to go. She could have spared herself the anguish she would suffer, worrying about her daughter, alone amongst strangers in a distant land. She also understood that Basma's experiences in a foreign country, and her education would change her daughter forever. Giving her permission and her blessing for this venture was a brave and selfless thing to do.

Next day we headed for Sheikh Ali, where we met up with Naeem, who was completing his own tour, auditing clinic accounts. It was good to see him again and we trooped into the staff room, eagerly anticipating exchanging news over tea.

No sooner had we sat down than Ali Baba, the clinician in charge, turned to me, saying, 'Come, there is a separate room for you and Basma. I'll have tea sent there.'

We gaped at him, lost for words. Naeem laughed, saying, 'I don't think either Mary or Basma is going to accept being hidden away, Ali Baba.' Reluctantly, Ali Baba acquiesced, though he was clearly uncomfortable about our presence in the staff room.

The room in which he had hoped to keep us in purdah was our bedroom, and it was tiny. An examining couch took up the entire length of one wall. By putting Jon under the couch (he was afraid he would fall off if he slept on top) there was just room for Basma and me to lie down, David between us, on a couple of mattresses. We could manage to sleep in it, but there was no way we were going to be kept shut up in there all day.

The next day Basma remarked, 'If I stay here for three days, I shall become old.' No one spoke to us, although everyone stared hard at us the moment we stepped outside – something we were forced to do several times a day as there was no latrine in the building. Even the few women we saw in the street stared intently and remained silent.

Ali Baba pointed us in the direction of a small building a hundred yards down the road. It was a donkey house, which, for some reason that remained a mystery, contained a latrine. In the evenings, when the donkeys were in residence, we used the apple orchard opposite, and in the mornings we waited cross-legged for them to leave before we could use their facilities.

The evening before we left for Mazar a truck driver brought an emergency case to the clinic. The woman had delivered a baby three days earlier, the placenta had not been expelled and she was bleeding heavily. When he heard the story, Ali Baba refused to have anything to do with her, telling the driver to go to the Jamiat hospital, some four hours' drive away.

While the woman certainly needed a degree of medical intervention that he could not provide, I was angry that he did not even attempt to implement some basic emergency procedures that might keep her alive long enough to reach the hospital. He shrugged at my suggestions, not wanting to admit that he did not know what to do.

Climbing into the cab I persuaded the woman, who was sitting with her husband behind the driver, to lie as flat as possible. Trying to raise her legs was difficult in the cramped space, especially as her husband was reluctant to move. Describing how he should feel it become hard, like a ball, I showed him how to massage his wife's uterus. The man stared blankly at me. Thinking it was a language problem, I asked Ali Baba to translate and again demonstrated what he should do. The man nodded at Ali Baba's instructions, but made no attempt to touch his wife. In despair, I asked where the baby was. At least its suckling might help the uterus to contract.

The husband opened his mouth for the first time. 'The baby is at home.' Now it was my turn to stare. 'But . . . but, how can you feed it? What is it doing at home instead of with its mother?'

'Dr Ali Baba will send milk powder for him,' he murmured. I handed over a litre of rehydration, asking Ali Baba to persuade the man that he must make sure his wife kept drinking.

As I began to climb out of the cab, the other passenger

tugged at my sleeve. Her baby, she told me, was 'always sick.' He was only six months old but the expression in his enormous, sunken eyes told that he had already suffered a lot in a very short life. Watching her firmly shoving a filthy plastic soother in her son's mouth, I felt utterly frustrated and helpless.

I had begun to believe that my students were representative of all Hazara women, expecting to find the same degree of intelligence, strength, spirit and freedom throughout the region. My students had made me believe that we could really make a difference to the lives of women and children, not only in one district but also in other areas. What, I wondered, could be done in Sheikh Ali, and what made the women of Sheikh Ali so different from those I had been working with?

Basma said, 'The women are different because the men are different. In Waras, the men treat women like human beings. My father asks my mother's opinion and it isn't always the same as his, but at least they talk to each other. Here, the men treat the women the same way they treat their donkeys. If you are treated as though you are stupid all the time, you believe it. And if there is no reason to use your brain, it stops working.'

While accepting the point she was making, it still left the question – why were the men in Sheikh Ali so different? Basma shrugged, 'I don't know but I don't think you could start a Female Health Volunteer programme here.'

Sadly, I had to agree with her.

11

What's Wrong with Eating Potatoes?

We were relieved to leave Sheikh Ali at five o'clock next morning.

We had to stop, reluctantly, for petrol in a small bazaar with a reputation for periodic outbreaks of fighting between rival mujahideen groups. Ali Baba had warned us that several people had been killed in the most recent skirmish, only days before.

It was an ugly place, its few crumbling buildings displaying numerous bullet holes. A number of grim-faced men wandered around, shouldering Kalashnikovs and rocket-launchers. There was a tension about the place that made us uneasy and eager to be on our way. While Jon paid for the petrol, Naeem hurried into a nearby shop to buy cigarettes.

Returning empty-handed he shook his head in wonder, 'They don't sell cigarettes here. The local commander has banned them because they are dangerous.'

For a few moments, we stared at him. The, realising that he was not joking, the absurdity of it made us hoot with laughter. Soldiers turned to glare at us. As we headed out of the bazaar, Naeem murmured, 'That probably explains why they are so bad tempered around here.'

After a brief stop for lunch, the next stage of the journey took us through the famous Salang Tunnel. Cutting through the Hindu Kush at a spectacular height of 3,363 metres, the 2.6 kilometres took six years to complete, with financial and technical assistance from the Soviets. An additional 5.4 kilometres of galleries protected the roads at either side from snow drifting in from the fierce blizzards that frequently occur.

When the tunnel was opened in 1964, it reduced the previous route from Kabul to the Russian border by over 200 kilometres. When the Soviets invaded Afghanistan, it was their main communications and supply route and, therefore, the focus of many attacks by the mujahideen groups.

As we began the long, winding ascent up to the tunnel, ominous clouds were gathering. The sky was a kaleidoscope of constantly changing colour – from a benign blue to deep purple, then to an increasingly threatening black. Small villages clung here and there to the barren, rocky slopes.

With the towering mountain tops brooding above, it was a bleak though dramatic landscape, made more sinister by the rusting remnants of Russian tanks and armoured personnel carriers littering the roadside.

In the galleried sections of the tunnel huge columns of ice had formed. Snug in our well-heated vehicle, we had not realised until we saw the ice how bitterly cold it was at such a height. Huge cracks had appeared in the concrete as a result of the seasonal cycle of the ice freezing and melting. In the tunnel itself there was no other traffic, and it was eerie driving so completely alone in the dark.

We emerged into a blinding snowstorm. The road already lay thickly covered. With the exception of David, who was oblivious to the dangers, we were all terrified. With no snow chains for our descent, the jeep slipped and slithered alarmingly. The drivers of big, overloaded trucks coming up towards us set a determined course, never wavering from the middle of the road. It was we who had to move precariously near to the edge of the abyss to let them pass. At least the snow was falling so thickly we could not see the extent of the drop below us.

We barely spoke. The only sound in the vehicle was from our manic crunching as we devoured an entire packet of orange flavoured boiled sweets. Somehow, they helped.

It was already dark by the time we reached Pul-i-Khumri, with another three hours travel ahead of us. The town was feet deep in snow and none of us was eager to start searching for a room for the night. We drove on.

To our relief the snow turned to rain, and by the time we arrived in Mazar-i-Sharif, around nine o'clock, the roads were clear. After dropping Naeem at his house, we headed for the office, exhausted, longing for tea, food and our beds.

It took ten minutes of ringing the bell and hammering on the door before anyone let us in. Ismail, recently arrived from Pakistan, had been afraid to open the door so late at night in case we were thieves. There was no food. Although the staff had been expecting us that day, when it became dark they decided it was unlikely we would arrive and ate up all the food that was left.

Next morning, after a good night's sleep, things looked brighter. There were welcoming hugs and kisses and my favourite halwa for breakfast from a hugely pregnant Latifa, and Sharifa – still tearful – with more hugs and kisses.

There was hot water for showers – and an opportunity to deal with our maddeningly itchy heads. Basma was the only one of us not crawling with head lice. Jon even had them in his beard.

Sharifa was in her element. Every morning she sat me down to search my head with a nit comb. My head ached by the time she finished with me and I suspected she was more disappointed than pleased the day she announced I was clear of both nits and lice.

Latifa, despite continuing high blood pressure, looked remarkably well and was now looking forward to the arrival, in a few more weeks, of her third baby. 'It will be the very last, though,' she declared emphatically.

Reza had still not come to terms with Latifa working as the cook and had been trying to stir up trouble for her. Naeem told me, 'He came to me suggesting I search her bags when she leaves at night because he suspects her of stealing sugar and coffee.

'I told him I couldn't do that unless he had evidence against Latifa. I'm afraid that if he's spreading stories it will cause bad feeling and suspicion amongst everyone. Already Ismail is taking Reza's side, complaining about Latifa, and he has hardly been here five minutes.'

Sharifa, though happy in her new job in the office, still had problems with Jawad. 'He still hasn't found a job,' she grumbled, 'and he never will as long as he spends all day drinking tea and talking to his friends.'

She had a new list of health complaints, including daily headaches, caused, she believed, by the contraceptive pill. 'So', she declared, 'I've stopped taking it.'

Telling her that she would have more than a headache to complain about if she became pregnant again, I asked if I should bring condoms back from Pakistan. 'Oh, no,' she giggled, 'He'd never use them. I think, when I have enough money, I'll have the operation, you know . . . they tie the tubes. Then, there'll be no more worries.'

David and I flew with Basma to Pakistan to enrol her in school in Karachi.

Luxuriating in a hotel for a couple of days, we gorged ourselves on American soaps. Basma, greatly taken by 'Baywatch' caught me off guard by suddenly demanding, 'Why are they always kissing each other on the mouth? It's disgusting!' I mumbled vaguely about different cultures, different ways.

Basma was persistent. 'Do you mean that women in your country actually LIKE that kind of kissing?' When I nodded, she shook her head, announcing emphatically, 'Well, I hope my husband won't want to do anything so horrible.'

The subject was dropped, though I couldn't help smiling to myself at the memory of her brother's different view of the subject.

The brief interlude in Karachi's sunshine left me ill prepared for the intense cold of Mazar-i-Sharif's winter weather. When it rained – which it did with depressing frequency – the dust, which had plagued the city's residents throughout summer, turned to thick, squelchy mud.

A thin, treacherously slippery coating on which vehicles constantly slithered out of control and into each other covered the main roads. Side roads became quagmires, impassable for vehicles.

Mazar's mud, deep, glutinous stuff, had an evil life force of its own, reaching out to clutch and cling to passing legs. Every few yards, mud-spattered individuals seemed to be engaged in some crazy war dance as they tried to extricate a boot – held fast in the glue like substance – without putting a thickly-stockinged foot into the mud.

Icy winds swept across the plains to pierce our many layers of clothing. Everyone was so well padded it looked like the city had been taken over by a tribe of Michelin men. When crossing roads people had to rotate their entire bodies to check the traffic in each direction.

In the early morning, strange shapes loomed eerily out of freezing fog – camels and donkeys loaded high with firewood, horse-drawn carts full of vegetables for market. The stallholders, turban ends pulled tightly across noses and mouths, struggled to unload their boxes with fingers reddened and numbed. They lit fires in tin boxes or pails, over which they thawed frozen hands, making me think with a mental 'Ouch!' of the resulting painful chilblains.

It was the worst time to go house hunting, but with the arrival of Ismail and other colleagues from Pakistan, the office accommodation had become cramped. Over the past eight months, Jon, David and I had rarely lived together as a family, and the prospect of sharing one room in the same building in which we would also work during the winter months induced instant claustrophobia in us both.

Shivering in the icy rain, we headed through the mud to the property dealer's office. Inside was hardly any warmer. Three men, huddled under a huge quilt, were sprawled on a wooden platform, beneath which burned a charcoal brazier. Called a '*sandali*', this form of heating is useless if one is more than two feet away.

Perched on two sagging armchairs, through chattering teeth,

we described the kind of house we were hoping to rent. The agent nodded understandingly, 'No problem. I have many *'luxe'* houses – just what UN workers want.' Explaining that we were not on the UN payroll we said we wanted something simple.

The first house we were shown had twelve rooms, most of them incomplete – with no plumbing and no kitchen. When we indicated that these were fundamental drawbacks the agent replied, 'No problem. You pay a deposit and the landlord will fix everything. In one, maybe two weeks, you can move in.'

We soon learned that *'luxe'* described anything with a grand facade which would 'be wonderful when it is finished'. We were shown one *'luxe'* des. res. after another. It was clear that the architects and builders gave no thought to the women who might inhabit these lavishly designed houses.

Not one had a water supply other than a well in the garden, though occasionally there was a hand pump. All water would have to be fetched from the compound – women's work. None had a kitchen – the verandah or an outhouse would serve the purpose.

The owners of these unfinished follies, usually 'big' commanders, had discovered that building Hollywood-style palaces took more cash than they had. Building work had stopped. With the influx of dollar-rich staff with UN agencies looking for accommodation, the commanders thought they had found the answer to their problems. The building work would be completed provided the tenants paid out a handsome advance. We were not in a position to do this.

At this point, having heard on the city's impressively efficient grapevine that foreigners were looking for a house, Habiba entered my life, striding, unannounced, into the office one morning.

A proponent of power dressing in a style that would not have been out of place in 'Dallas' she wore an ultra-smart black suit with padded shoulders. Her *'tunban'*, usually worn baggy, were narrow, delicately edged with fine embroiderey. With her short hair and discreetly applied make up, she would have looked equally at home in a boardroom in London or New

York. Only her teeth, the most crooked of which invariably bore a smudge of lipstick, spoiled the image.

She was terrifyingly intimidating, wasting no time in small talk.

'I know of a suitable house for you. When would you like to see it?'

She waved aside Jon's tentative questions about water supply and toilet facilities. 'I know what foreigners want. In Kabul, I knew many foreigners and I am telling you this house is exactly what you need. It has a telephone.'

She quoted, without batting a lightly shadowed eye-lid, an exorbitant rent. Bravely, Jon and I managed to shake our heads. Habiba sighed at our foolishness, repeating, 'It has a telephone.'

Telephones in Mazar-i-Sharif could only be used within the city limits, and we did not know anyone who had one.

'All right,' Habiba shrugged, 'Without the telephone we can reduce the rent. When will you look at the house? Tomorrow? Three o'clock? I shall send my son to direct you.'

It seemed the interview was over. At the door Habiba paused, turning to Jon. 'Your Persian is very bad. If you would like to improve it, I could give you lessons. In Kabul I taught many foreigners to speak good Persian.'

Although we did not take the house Habiba recommended, we did soon afterwards find one we liked. Built in a traditional style of sun-dried mud bricks rather than hideous concrete, it had three spacious rooms, a long, shady veranda and a large compound, complete with mulberry trees.

I did contact Habiba later about Persian lessons – for myself, not Jon. Trying to reach an amicable agreement regarding tuition fees was difficult. Habiba wanted to charge what she would have charged a class of ten students in Kabul. When I pointed out that I was only one student, she replied that she would spend the same amount of time teaching whether there was one student or twenty. Embarrassed at haggling over my tuition fees, I accepted her final offer, ending up with the most expensive teacher in Mazar-i-Sharif.

Each morning Habiba spent an hour teaching me grammar and pronunciation from her conversational Dari manual – the one she had used in Kabul. As I had expected, she was a demanding teacher who made great efforts to iron out mistakes I had been making for years. She was also determined that I should speak the language as it is spoken in Kabul, and would pull me up sharply whenever I used a word in Hazaragi – the dialect of Hazara Jat.

I explained that I needed Hazaragi as well as her Kabuli Persian because much of my time would be spent with Hazara women.

'Oh, it is quite easy to understand them,' Habiba retorted, 'In Kabul, all my servants were Hazaras and we understood each other perfectly.' She sometimes reminded me of Margaret Thatcher.

Habiba loved to talk. While wearing her teacher's hat, she spoke slowly, but after class, over tea, she would revert to her normal speed, expecting me to keep up with her rapid-fire outpourings. It was excellent, if exhausting, practise.

Habiba, so different from Latifa and Sharifa, was a revelation. Like them, she was a refugee from Kabul – but there the similarities ended. Habiba, unlike Sharifa and Latifa, was educated. On the other hand, they had an unquenchable zest for life that seemed to have bypassed her.

Although Sharifa and Latifa sometimes looked back and cried for who and what they had lost, they mostly lived life in the present. The future, perhaps too scary to contemplate, they rarely contemplated except to express a wish for peace in Afghanistan. Habiba found the present unbearable and spent more time looking back regretfully.

Sharifa and Latifa complained about their menfolk, shrugged, and laughed about them. They told earthy jokes, could neither read nor write, spoke ungrammatical Persian and, in Habiba's eyes, were too common and crude for words. For Habiba was the most frightful snob.

The way in which standards of gracious living had slipped since the mujahideen came to power upset her. 'Look, see, now we are sitting on mattresses,' she complained, slapping disdainfully at the one on which we sat. 'In Kabul we had chairs in our house – we did not sit on the floor like peasants.

'My house was beautiful,' she sighed, 'I had a sofa set in the *mehmankhanna* [guest room] and a separate dining room with proper table and chairs. We did not use the common custom of bringing water in a jug for guests to wash their hands. We had a washbasin in the dining room. I think you have this custom in Europe?'

I shook my head in denial of washbasins in our dining rooms. Habiba, not at all abashed at being contradicted, shrugged, 'Oh, well it must be in America – they are more advanced aren't they?'

In Kabul she had worked as a ticket clerk for Arianna Airlines. She spoke so proudly of her position that it was weeks before I realised that she had not been in an executive position. This job, along with her degree in theology (taken because all the better courses such as medicine had been filled) from Kabul University and her lovely home had given Habiba status.

Giving language lessons to foreigners had brought additional kudos. As she reminisced about the various expatriates who had visited her home, she sounded like 'foreigner collecting' was a hobby, like stamp collecting.

Although Sharifa, Latifa and many other women had suffered as much, if not more, than Habiba over the last few years, I was never to meet anyone as deeply bitter about her changed life as she. She complained about every aspect of enforced exile in Mazar-i-Sharif, mourning her loss of status and her inability to find a job.

Whenever a new NGO opened an office, Habiba would be first in the queue of job seekers, and she regularly toured the UN offices asking about vacancies. Always unsuccessful, she complained, 'I have a degree. I don't understand, why won't they let me work?'

I tentatively suggested that she was aiming too high, expecting a managerial position, for which she had no experience. Perhaps she could apply for one of the support jobs – making tea, cleaning – which often came vacant? Many people in these posts had been teachers or civil servants in Kabul but were prepared to take any job they could find.

Habiba shook her head. 'I will not lower myself to work as a cleaner. My husband would never allow me to do such menial work.'

I never met her husband. According to Habiba he had been a successful businessman in Kabul, was educated (naturally) and had many important contacts in Mazar. Even so, he was also finding it difficult to find a suitable job.

Eventually I came to understand that her reticence about her husband's work was caused by a mixture of shame that he was now an employee rather than an employer, and her own ignorance as to what he actually did.

She admitted one day, 'My husband hardly discusses anything with me. He goes out in the morning and comes home in the evening, expecting his food to be ready. I never know where he has been all day, or what he has been doing, and I have learned not to ask. Since we came from Kabul he becomes angry quickly, especially when I have to ask for money for medicine for the twins.'

I did not tell her that her husband sounded very much like Sharifa's. She would have been horrified to think they had anything in common, but both husbands had undergone similar character transformations since becoming refugees. Habiba's loss of everything she had held dear, including her job, was a tremendous blow to her self esteem, yet it never seemed to occur to her that perhaps her husband was also experiencing difficulties in coming to terms with his change of circumstances.

Or maybe their relationship was so bad that she would not have particularly cared about his feelings – any more than he, seemingly, cared about hers.

Habiba was the only Afghan woman who admitted that she wished she had never had children. 'Of course, I love them,' she added hastily, 'but I have no patience with children, especially when they are little.

'Not that we can make that kind of choice here. We can take pills to have a rest in between babies, but not to prevent any from coming. Even amongst our class of people, it is important to produce sons. Well, my husband cannot complain – I have given him three, as well as two daughters.'

After her third child Habiba had wanted to be sterilised, but her husband, hoping for another son, had refused permission. Instead of one more, he got two at once. Habiba had not known she was expecting twins until she went into labour.

'I had not wanted even one more. It was a terrible shock. I insisted on being sterilised immediately after the delivery, and my husband accepted it. Children cost so much money, always needing clothes, food, medicines.'

When Habiba was not bemoaning the loss of her job, her beautiful house with its fine furniture and washbasins – and the indignity of living in such a provincial backwater as Mazar – she was holding forth on the subject of the twins' health. She may not have received her share of maternal feelings but she was sensitive as to what others might think of her mothering skills. The twins' refusal to thrive irked her – people might think it was her fault.

The twins, whose names I never remembered – their mother always referring to them as the *doganagi* – came to visit. They were promptly despatched to David's room to play while Habiba took tea with me, relentlessly querying the price of every item on which her gaze alighted.

Although critical that we sat and slept on mattresses on the floor, rather than proper chairs and beds, she was deeply impressed by our worldly goods – from the television in the living room to the gas bottle for our cooker in the kitchen. Having our possessions so openly admired – and coveted – was horribly embarrassing, made even worse when the *doganagi* joined in, hauling half David's toys in for their mother's inspection. This prompted another round of price queries, accompanied by asides like, 'It is so sad there is nothing like this for Afghan children.'

If it had not been for the fact that I would have been unable to live with the subsequent wrath of Jon and David, I would have gladly handed over the bulk of our belongings to quell the unending murmurs of admiration.

I was thankful when the teapot was empty. Collecting her boys, blatantly encouraging them in their screams of rage when told they must leave the lovely toys behind, her parting shot was, 'It is so good for David to have some little friends to play with, isn't it? I shall bring the *doganagi* round more often.'

David, sitting shell-shocked in his room, surrounded by a heap of broken toys, glared balefully at the departing twins, swiftly dodging Habiba's attempt to kiss him.

She was convinced the boys were too thin and weak, spending a fortune on tonics and syrups. 'What do you think is wrong with them?' she asked. 'Can you not give me medicine so they become strong and healthy, like your David?'

'Habiba, you shouldn't waste your money on those vitamin syrups. They are useless. Give the boys fruit and vegetables instead.'

'You are lucky, you have a good salary and can afford to buy fresh fruit and meat for David, but I have no money to feed my little *doganagi* properly. In Kabul, we ate fruit every day and meat twice a day. Now, we can only afford potatoes. Every day, we eat potatoes. You cannot imagine how awful it is.'

Habiba's voice would take on a plaintive whine which, instead of eliciting the sympathy she hoped for, irritated me. As a Scot, I saw nothing wrong with eating potatoes every day. They featured frequently in Sharifa's household too and we had been swopping potato recipes. I offered to tell Habiba some of the interesting ways of cooking them I had learned.

Heaving a sigh, she said, 'I really hate to think about cooking when I can't afford to buy meat.'

Once, when Habiba was complaining about being poor, Sharifa appeared to clear away the tea tray. She winked at me, nodding surreptitiously towards Habiba, who was checking her appearance in a small hand mirror. Immaculately dressed as usual, she had enough gold around her neck and at her wrists to buy fresh fruit for the twins for years to come.

She had lost much. When heavy fighting near their home forced them to flee, they had left everything behind. When her husband returned to Kabul, their house had been looted, their possessions gone.

Yet her discontent and self-centred unawareness that life had also become difficult for many others often made me lose sympathy for Habiba.

Sharifa's economic circumstances were far more precarious than Habiba's. Yet, her round, cheerful face streaked with black soot from the *bukhari* she had been cleaning, she was grinning broadly as she left the room.

— 12 —
Praying for a Husband

NAEEM HAD AT last found a house and moved his family to Mazar.

Latifa, Sharifa and Marzia soon included Maryam in their social activities and she and Sharifa became close friends. The older boys, Hassan and Hussain, and their sister Fatima were enrolled in schools that they liked. The youngest, Habib, was not yet ready for school.

Often on Fridays, Maryam would bring the boys to play with David – who found them much better company than Habiba's *doganagi* – while she, Fatima and I had tea together.

Maryam was a traditionalist, often dismayed by Naeem's attempts to modernise and 'free' her. He had taken her to a beauty parlour for a new hairstyle. Refusing adamantly to have her hair cut short she had allowed the stylist to perm it. The result – a mass of tight, frizzy curls – made it look as though she was wearing her chaddar on top of a woolly bobble hat. She was horrified. Eventually the perm subsided, but it had made her warier than ever of Naeem's modern ideas.

She was especially anxious when those ideas concerned Fatima's future. Although pleased that her daughter was able to continue her education and would go to college, Maryam felt that learning housewifely skills was of equal, if not greater, importance.

'Whenever I ask Fatima for help at home she says she has school work,' she complained, adding, 'I would never have spoken back to my mother like she does. And her father takes her side, saying that studying is more important than washing the dishes.

'Even if she does become a doctor, Fatima will get married some day. Does her father think a doctor's babies can feed themselves and change their own nappies? Men don't understand anything about what women need to know to survive in this world.'

Maryam was as proud as Naeem of Fatima's achievements – although I think she would have found it more fitting had her first born, and cleverest child, been a boy – but she was fearful about her future. In school the sexes were segregated, but in the medical faculty they were not. This already worried Maryam, who dreaded the prospect of her daughter falling in love with a co-student and wanting to marry him.

'Young girls are not able to choose their husbands sensibly. They don't think, but let their feelings control their actions. They don't know those feelings will change. I know my daughter, and I know the kind of boy she should marry. Of course, I would not force her to accept someone she did not like, but he should be Hazara, and from a similar background.'

Naeem too wanted Fatima to marry a Hazara, but had a different perspective on the subject. 'I know Maryam wants her to marry someone from our family in Jaghoray. I try to make her understand that it would be a difficult relationship if Shanaz is a doctor while her husband is an uneducated farmer, with no understanding of city ways.'

I wondered if Maryam was slightly jealous of her daughter. She was a clever woman and I suspected she sometimes felt left out when her husband and daughter discussed books they were reading, or when she had to wait for one or other of them to read letters to her.

Once Naeem put his foot in it, angering Maryam so much that she barely spoke to him for a month.

He had taken work home from the office and, spreading his papers on a table, remarked casually, 'If you were educated you could help me with this.' He had not intended it as a slight, only that he thought she might enjoy sharing in his working life, and was totally taken aback by Maryam's reaction.

Furiously she rounded on him, 'Oh, now you wish you had married an educated girl. I am not good enough now. Well, you knew how I was when you agreed to the marriage, so it is a bit too late to expect something different.'

Turning to Fatima, she continued, 'You had better study well and hard, daughter, you never know what things your husband may suddenly expect of you once you have married him.'

The Maryam I had known in Quetta would never have displayed anger towards her husband. There she had been a model of the traditional, docile Afghan wife. Living in Mazar-i-Sharif, meeting women like Sharifa and Latifa changed her outlook on life and, to some extent, marriage. As his docile, compliant wife began to disappear, Naeem's respect – and love – for Maryam grew.

Reza, as we had expected, did not encourage his wife to go out and about on her own when she came to Mazar. Fatima sometimes visited my house when other women friends were there, but was never a frequent visitor. When she did come, Reza always accompanied her, to Maryam's intense irritation.

Whenever Reza appeared, Maryam swiftly covered her head, pulling her chaddar across her face. Naeem explained, 'It is because he is from Jaghoray and Maryam is afraid he will spread stories at home about her behaviour here.'

Maryam added to Naeem's explanation. 'Reza's heart is not clean. If I did not cover myself, he would joke with me and then tell people at home that I am too free. His wife never appears in front of any man without her chaddar.

'Naeem does not behave like Reza. He speaks respectfully to women whether they wear a chaddar or not.'

Sharifa, meanwhile, was looking more than usually tired at work, often seeming preoccupied and distant. One day I found her in my office, studying the pictures in a reference book.

Before she snapped shut the book I had seen enough to understand the cause of her tiredness. 'Oh, no, Sharifa. It's happened, hasn't it? You're pregnant.'

Tearfully, she nodded. I could see how she felt about her situation but how, I wondered had Jawad reacted to the news?

Sharifa sniffed loudly, blinking back her tears. 'He is furious, acting like it is my fault, as though I did it deliberately. I told him I had to stop taking the pill because it gave me headaches but he wouldn't use anything himself. Then blames me for becoming pregnant.'

Remembering how Latifa's husband had refused his consent to terminate her pregnancy, Sharifa decided not to consult a hospital doctor. 'I know a doctor who does these things in her home,' she said

'Are you sure it is safe?' Visions of a dark, dirty room, wire coat hangers and blood filled my head.

'Yes,' replied Sharifa. 'She worked in a hospital in Kabul. She does this work because she doesn't get paid in the hospital here.'

The woman operated a sliding scale of fees that rose according to her client's social and economic position. A wife of a big commander had to find a much larger sum – especially if her husband was not to know that she was pregnant – than someone in Sharifa's impoverished situation. Even so, the lowest rate was almost as much as Sharifa earned in a month.

Looking drawn and anxious, Sharifa turned up for work the morning after she had seen the doctor, who had inserted some 'medicine' in the *batcha-dan* [uterus]. Steadily worsening stomach cramps started mid-morning. Next day she was in agony, but refused to go home.

'Who would do anything for me there?' she asked. 'Not Jawad. He wouldn't even make me a cup of tea last night, but complained because his dinner was late.'

Despite the agonizing pains, the expected bleeding did not start and Sharifa returned to the doctor, declaring she needed more medicine. The doctor demanded further payment and Sharifa wept and pleaded, begging her to believe she had no more money until, finally, she relented.

The bleeding started next morning. Naeem suggested I take Sharifa to his house, where Maryam greeted us calmly, as though it was a normal social visit. The pain worsened and the bleeding became heavier and Sharifa, by then convinced she was going to die, was petrified.

'The doctor warned me that no matter what happened, I must not go to the hospital,' she moaned through gritted teeth.

'She said they would see the medicine and know what I had done and I would be thrown in jail.'

While trying to reassure Sharifa that she was going to be all right, I began to wonder whom, within the expatriate community, I could call on for help. Then, Sharifa, who had run outside to the latrine, called us.

White faced, she beckoned us inside. 'Look,' she whispered. 'It doesn't look like a baby. Do you think it's still inside?'

'It's not supposed to look like a baby at this stage,' I replied. 'Anything else still inside will be the same as this.' The three of us peered at the bloody mess in the latrine. Sharifa started cleaning up, wrapping some blobs in newspaper to show the doctor. Suddenly she stopped, flung her arms around me, sobbing, 'Thank God, it is over. When I thought I was going to die, I kept thinking about my children. Who would look after them if I died?'

Some days later, as she hovered uncertainly round my desk, I urged her to say what was on her mind. 'In that book I was looking at, there was a picture of a baby inside the mother,' she whispered, her eyes filling with tears. 'It looked like a real baby, so why did mine just look like bits of meat and blood?' When I found the picture she had been studying, it was of a baby four weeks before birth.

Flipping pages, I found the illustrations of an embryo in the first few weeks of pregnancy. 'Oh, I am glad,' she commented softly. 'I would have felt much worse if it had looked like that other picture.'

Sharifa had imagined that, from the moment of conception, the baby in the womb looked like a full-formed baby, only tinier. She knew no more about what occurred during pregnancy than the students in Hazara Jat had done. The idea of running a similar teaching course in Mazar first crossed my mind then.

Sharifa bounced back remarkably quickly from her ordeal, though for some time our tea-break conversations tended to centre on abortion. Both Sharifa and Latifa had friends and acquaintances who had terminated pregnancies, usually illegally, although they claimed that in Kabul, before it was 'freed' by the mujahideen, it had been easier for a women to obtain a legal abortion.

They wanted to know how it was in my country – a Western country where, they knew *huqooq-i-zen* [women's rights] had been achieved. They were astounded when I explained that women in Britain also still required the permission of two doctors and that, although abortion had been made legal, women did not have the right to demand it.

If what they said about Kabul was true, then only a few years earlier, women in Afghanistan, although they had no legal framework supporting their right, had not been far behind women in Britain with regard to obtaining an abortion. The main problem had been in finding a sympathetic doctor who would confirm the mother's life was at risk if the pregnancy continued.

Neither Latifa nor Sharifa had any doubts on the question of moral issues. To bring an unwanted child into the world, especially when the family was too poor to care properly for existing children, was what was immoral.

Latifa's own baby – a son – was born in February.

Moosa, was tiny but strong, with a voracious appetite. Latifa, with none of the misconceptions of the village women about colostrum, had started breast feeding the day he was born.

Watching him feed, her expression was one of besotted motherhood. Looking up, she caught my eye and smiled self-consciously. 'Yes,' she said, as though I had asked the question, 'I love him.' Glancing down again at the contented baby, she added in a determined tone, 'But he is definitely the last, the very last.'

She was eager to return to work as soon as the forty day 'lying in' period was over. By then, it would be about 21 March, the Afghan New Year [*nau roz*] and the women were planning a special outing to the shrine.

Mazar-i-Sharif, translated as the 'shrine of the exalted or noble', was dedicated to Hazrat-i-Ali, the son-in-law and cousin of the Prophet Mohammed, whom the Shiah sect believe should have been the Prophet's true successor. Although Ali's remains lie buried in Najaf, in Iraq, Afghans believe that his final resting-place is in Mazar.

According to legend, when he was assassinated in 658 AD, Ali's followers were afraid that his enemies would take revenge on his body and devised a plan to remove it to safety. They loaded it onto a white she-camel, turning her free to roam. At the exact spot where the camel eventually dropped dead from exhaustion, they buried Ali's remains.

Almost five hundred years had passed, when, during the reign of Sultan Sanjar Seljuki in the early twelfth century, a man called Muhammad discovered evidence Ali's burial place. When Muhammad told the Governor of Balkh about his discovery, he was not believed. That night, however, the mullah who had poured the most scorn on the tale was visited by Hazrat-i-Ali himself and scolded for his refusal to believe the truth. The mullah hurried off to see the Governor, and together they went to open the grave, where they found Ali's body.

A shrine, completed in 1136, was built around the grave. Genghis Khan later destroyed it and it was not until 1481 that a new shrine was built. None of the original fifteenth-century decoration was left, as restoration work had been carried out over the years. The majestic shrine dominated the city centre, the glorious blue tiling of its twin domes sparkling in the sunshine.

In celebration of the New Year, Hazrat-i-Ali's standard or *janda* was raised in the courtyard of the shrine. General Dostum had, that year, officiated at the ceremony, watched by thousands of people, all anxious to be the first to touch the flagpole, believing this act will gain them religious merit.

Sharifa, Maryam, Marzia, Latifa and I, with the inevitable sprinkling of children, went on 'Ladies Day'. Habiba, torn between the kudos of being seen with a foreigner and the worry that anyone she knew might spot her socialising with the servant classes had, after a great deal of soul searching, finally turned down our invitation.

None of us had been in Mazar the previous *Nau Roz* and we were overawed by the vast crowds of women making their way along the beggar-lined paths towards the shrine. We struggled, in a small foyer, to remove our shoes without releasing our hold on the children, afraid they would be swept away in the midst of the jostling women. Bare-footed, we padded across the courtyard.

Gaining entry to the inner shrine required the super-human strength born of extreme piety, or, in Marzia's case, desperation. The rest of us sat in the warm spring sunshine and watched as, Shahnaz cradled protectively in her arms, Marzia determinedly shouldered her tiny frame through the crowds towards the inner chamber of the shrine in which lay Ali's tomb.

Convinced that she deserved more from life than trying to appease a brother-in-law – who still barely tolerated her existence in his house, despite the fact that she now contributed financially – Marzia had decided to take action. Not wanting to be a poor widow all her life, she was asking the sainted Ali to intervene on her behalf and find her a husband.

Soon she was lost from view, but I pictured her progress inside. She would pause, first, at the huge bronze cauldron on the right. It may once have been used as a drum, but in Mazar-i-Sharif it was commonly held to have been *Dik-i-Ali* – Ali's cooking pot.

To ensure her future fertility, Marzia would crawl under the pot, emerging dusty and dishevelled on the other side before moving towards the tomb, past the lines of turbaned mullahs, sitting cross-legged before their copies of the Quran.

These Mullahs were consulted by pilgrims and supplicants and – for a fee – offered prayers, readings from the Quran, or supplied a *tawiz*. Women asked them to wind thread around the railing surrounding the tomb, believing it would provide protection against all sorts of evil. People dropped small donations onto the little heaps of money beside each mullah.

Once, asking Habiba the Dari word for beggar, I described them as people who were often seen around the shrine asking passers-by for money. Overhearing the question, David piped up, in Dari, 'Everyone knows they are called mullahs.'

Concerned that she would take offence at his remark, I looked apprehensively at Habiba. Her shoulders were shaking with suppressed laughter. 'I should not laugh but really, he is quite right – many of them are no different from *gada*, which is the word you are looking for.'

Everyone to whom she told the story would ask David what the people in the shrine were called. Delighted at this response from grown-ups, David played on it for as long as possible. Whenever we were near the shrine he would point to the lame and the blind saying, 'Look, see, there are the mullahs.' It was a relief when the joke wore off.

Despite the money-grabbing and the superstitious beliefs, there was a feeling of deep spirituality at the shrine, making me believe that, maybe, prayers were answered.

I was watching the door when, at last, Marzia emerged. She looked dazed, as though under a spell. Whatever she had experienced, it had visibly moved her. Her face flushed with triumph, her eyes were bright and glittering with held back tears as she clutched Shahnaz in a tight embrace.

Too tight, for Shahnaz began to wail, breaking the spell and making Marzia laugh – her normal laugh, full of love for her precious daughter, mixed with the exasperation all mothers feel when their babies' demands intrude into their own space.

Leaving the courtyard, we purchased shallow tin plates of grain at a booth and took the children to feed the pigeons, thousands of which – all snowy white – lived within the shrine complex. It was believed that every seventh pigeon was a spirit, and people hoped to gain religious merit by feeding the birds.

Another local legend said that if a grey pigeon joined the flock, so holy was the place that within forty days it would turn white. Cynics joked that if it didn't, the mullahs would eat it to preserve the legend.

We were surrounded by a fascinating variety of ethnic groups in different colourful costumes. There were Hazaras and Pathans, Uzbeks and Tajiks. Tribal women wore heavily embroidered velvet dresses, their faces adorned with strange tattoos. Turkomen women could be seen wearing several caps, piled one on top of the other, under their chaddars. Each time a son was born another cap was added.

Groups of women were sitting passing round a water pipe. Young girls strolled by arm in arm, giggling. A great many women had discarded their chaddars, relaxing in the knowledge that there were no men around.

Everyone else, we noticed, had brought food. We had nothing, and were soon feeling hunger pangs as the aroma of pilau, kabuli and kebabs wafted past. Marzia disappeared again, returning laden with kebabs stuffed inside fresh nan. We cheered her, falling on the food with glee.

Feeling I should make a contribution towards the cost, I groped in my bag for my purse. Sharifa, noticing, shook her head at me, whispering, 'Don't offer. This is something Marzia wants to do – she hopes that by feeding us, she will gain merit and her prayers will be answered.'

While eating, we watched a party of young girls help their mothers throw ropes over tree branches. Then the laughing girls took turns to swing, looking, in their finery, like bright butterflies swooping heavenwards. From close by came the sounds of drumming from a group of women playing the *darieh* [a combination of a drum and tambourine, traditionally used at wedding celebrations].

Too soon, it was time to leave. Waiting at the entrance for Reza to arrive, I had a sudden feeling that I was being watched. Looking up, I found one of the soldiers by the gate staring intently at me. Catching his eye, I stared back at him, while slowly, ostentatiously pulling my chaddar across the lower half of my face. It was peculiarly satisfying to see him colour and drop his eyes in embarrassment at having been caught looking at a woman.

Latifa and the others had been watching with amusement, and, as Reza pulled up in the jeep, Latifa, with a laugh, said, 'I think you are close to becoming an Afghan woman now.'

— 13 —
Prudery and Penises

A MONTH LATER I attended another celebration, this time as the guest of the Foreign Ministry, when General Dostum was to take the salute at a military march-past commemorating the mujahideen victory.

The victory that had 'freed' Afghanistan, had resulted in thousands of refugees fleeing Kabul. Thousands more were killed in the capital when the various factions turned on each other in a vain effort to gain sufficient political power to control this 'free' Afghanistan.

Naeem and I were shown to VIP seats next to the podium from where General Dostum would take the salute.

The tanks that rolled past, spluttering and stalling, belching out filthy black smoke, did not inspire confidence. In every group of marching soldiers, some were out of step, and Naeem, becoming cynical all of a sudden, said he was sure the youngsters marching to represent the Military Academy had been picked up in the streets for the occasion. I thought that if I were Dostum, I would be rather depressed if this was representative of my military might. People around us were quick to assure us that the best tanks and equipment were in use in the fighting currently going on in Pul-i-Khumri and Kabul.

Wondering how much worse the war would become, I wished I had photographed the posters on the Darwaza-i-Balkh – one of the gates of the city – the year before. A triptych of Dostum, President Rabbani and ex-President Mojahdeedi had been on display, demonstrating that those three were united.

Rabbani, in those days, was calling Dostum his 'son' while Gulbedin Hekmatyar was calling him a communist infidel.

Less than a year later, Gulbedin was calling the communist infidel his brother and Rabbani was denouncing his erstwhile 'son' as an enemy of Islam.

It seemed that every round of fighting resulted in factions changing allegiances, but the balance of power remained much as before. Neither one alliance nor another could ever gain control. There were no winners, only losers – nearly always civilians.

Around this time, David's 'brother', my adopted son Daud, arrived from Pakistan. When we had moved to Mazar-i-Sharif, he had opted to remain in Quetta to continue his schooling. With the closure of that school Daud had decided to re-join his 'family' and enrol in a school in Mazar.

I was delighted when he arrived, not least because Jon had gone on tour and, although I admitted it to no one, I was nervous at night of being alone in the house with David. Foreigners in the next street had recently been robbed, something I found myself thinking about at bed-time. Quite what difference a seventeen-year old, unarmed youth would have made, had thieves broken in, I can't imagine, but his being in the next room was a comfort.

David was overjoyed to have Daud back in his life. Instead of coming to the office with me, he wanted to stay at home with his big brother. Sharifa agreed that Marzia, with Shahnaz, could spend the day in our house, helping out with housework and sharing the care of David with Daud, who would only be around for half the day once school started.

Sharifa's only words of warning were, 'You must promise never to allow Ismail to go to your house when Marzia is alone there.' I was amused at how swiftly Sharifa had summed up Ismail's character.

Ismail's family, like Ali Baba's, came from Sheikh Ali, and were very traditional. In the pre-Soviet days, when there had been a village school, Ismail had attended, but not his sisters. They never went out, unless covered up and well chaperoned.

In Pakistan, however, Ismail spent much of his time trying to find a girlfriend, and I often caught him ogling girls in the bazaar. 'What', I had demanded crossly one day, 'would you do if you were out with your sister and a man stared at her the way you are looking at that girl?'

Ismail's reply forced my blood pressure up further, 'If a girl is going to walk around without being covered up she has to accept that men will stare at her. Anyway, I would never take my sister out in the bazaar.'

I promised Sharifa that I would not allow Ismail anywhere near her little sister.

Now that David was happy with Marzia and Daud to keep him amused, I had more time to concentrate on my work. Before returning to Hazara Jat, I had to prepare new teaching materials.

I hoped Habiba could help improve my vocabulary on gynaecological subjects. But she was decidedly unhelpful, proving to be prudish about all bodily functions and anything concerning sex. She kept side-stepping the issue, making me practise verb endings so that there was no time for such embarrassing topics.

Scratch her, and under the veneer of sophistication was a woman as conditioned to feel shame about such subjects as any illiterate Hazara. She would have hidden her face in her chaddar, only, as she didn't wear one, she was left blushing, her embarrassment obvious. She also had as many misconceptions and superstitions about health matters as the village women in Waras.

One morning she complained of pain and stiffness in her shoulder and upper arm. Dismissing my suggestion that she had been lying awkwardly in the night, Habiba announced, 'It's because I ate too much chilli last night.' When Reza had the tip of a poisoned finger amputated she warned him against eating melon or cucumber – particularly dangerous foods for a person with a wound.

Having by then learned something about what education meant in Afghanistan, I should not have been surprised that someone even with a university degree should still cling to such 'uneducated' thinking.

Education was for the purpose of passing exams. Pupils were forced to commit to memory isolated and useless facts and figures. In Fatima's geography exam, for example, one of the questions asked for the exact number of people killed in an earthquake in Japan in the nineteenth century. There were no questions on the causes of earthquakes – which was fortunate, as she had not been taught anything about that.

I needed someone to translate a leaflet I wanted to use in the next training course. It had clear, easy-to-follow diagrams and simple text on how to use condoms. I suspected that one of the obstacles to condoms being accepted was that many men had no idea how to use them correctly, and were too embarrassed to ask for advice. Naeem said he would write the translation and I left the leaflet on his desk.

While waiting for me to appear for class one day, Habiba was chatting to Naeem when she suddenly let out a horrified gasp and ran out of the room. Grinning broadly, Naeem waved the leaflet at me.

Later, still reeling from the shock of being confronted by a picture of an erect penis, Habiba scolded me. 'Naeem is a man,' she pointed out, as if I might not have noticed. 'You mustn't discuss these things with a man. You should have brought it to me.' Covering her face with her hands, she shuddered, whimpering, 'Oh, it was so embarrassing.'

Habiba admitted that she had never derived any pleasure from sex. 'I don't think many Afghan women do,' she said. 'Afghan men are not like men from other countries. They want to have sex all the time. In other countries, men have a drink or smoke a cigarette when they need to relax. Afghan men only want sex – even when they are old.'

She looked down at her lap for a few moments, before continuing in a barely audible whisper, 'Since I was sterilised I have had problems, you know, down there. It is always dry and sex is very painful. But my husband thinks it is wonderful – he says it is like having a virgin every time.'

Poor Habiba, she talked about sex like a character from a Les Dawson sketch – silently mouthing the 'rude' words, exaggerating her facial expressions and rolling her eyes. It would have been funny had it not been so tragic.

The only time I did laugh aloud at Habiba's consternation was the day Naeem managed to cover his spotless white *tunban* in mud. Habiba, arriving for class, was just in time to see Sharifa and Naeem emerge, laughing together, from the bathroom. Naeem, sporting only his kameez, one sock and a pair of scarlet longjohns, explained briefly to a slack-jawed Habiba, 'I had to wash them, my wife would kill me if she saw the state of those clothes.' With great dignity, he disappeared into his office.

For the first time since I met her, I saw Habiba completely speechless. I am still not sure if it was the shock of the scarlet longjohns or that an Afghan man, admitting his terror of going home to his wife with dirty clothes, would wash them himself.

She invited David and me to a wedding reception. Actually, Habiba being Habiba, it was more of a royal command. I accepted, asking if I could bring Maryam, who had never experienced a Mazar-style wedding. Habiba instructed us to be ready by ten o'clock.

By twelve o'clock David and Habib were tired, hungry and grumpy about hanging around in their best clothes. At twelve thirty, as Maryam was about to go home, Habiba arrived.

When I explained that as the children were now thoroughly bad-tempered, we had decided not to go, she became distraught. She pleaded, 'Everyone wants to meet you and David, they have heard so much about you. They will be so disappointed if you don't come.' Realising that she would lose face if her foreign friend did not turn up, I reluctantly agreed we would go, but only for a short time.

Arriving at the home of the bride's family, Habiba led us through a small door into a high-walled compound. I barely had time to take in the decorated pavilion and the enormous number of women who were descending on us before David began to scream.

They were screams of terror, reserved for the merest glimpse of something that frightened him more than anything in the

world. As far as David was concerned the painted faces of the
ladies of Mazar-i-Sharif resembled circus clowns.

As the women pressed closer, attempting – like the real
clown he had once seen – to soothe and reassure him, he
became almost hysterical. I begged Habiba to find us a quiet
place to sit until he calmed down.

In an empty room I held him tightly until the screams
turned to sobs. Habiba, shooing away the curious onlookers
trying to press into the room, brought him a Coke. Thanking
her, I murmured, 'He is very nervous in big crowds.' It sounded
a feeble excuse even to me.

Maryam suggested we call Naeem to take us home, but I
couldn't do that to Habiba. Eventually, his attention caught by
the sound of a band playing outside, David left the safety of my
arms to peep, somewhat fearfully, out of the window.

Maryam was almost as shocked – though less vocal about
it – as David by the sight of the women. Most wore outfits
in garish colours with a large preponderance of lurid pinks
and greens and midnight blues, all shimmering with gold and
silver Lurex. Faces were heavily made up, and, unlike Habiba's
discreet and skilful application of powder and paint, it appeared
that the majority of women had been determined to use every
shade and colour combination in their make-up boxes.

Hairstyles were equally flamboyant. Many of the women
wore their hair up in a sort of beehive, bouffant style, teased
and lacquered and glittering with thickly sprayed gold and
silver. But it was neither the hairstyles – or the make-up –
nor even the clashing colour schemes, that caused the shocked
murmurs from Maryam as she knelt, gazing out at the scene:
it was the display of legs. Many of the wedding guests were
wearing knee-length Western (seventies era) dresses and suits –
without the customary trousers worn underneath. Although
this was a women-only party, there were still a number of men
present, including the musicians and small groups of boys who,
not of an age to leave their mothers for the men only party,
were quite old enough to giggle at the girls.

Maryam grabbed my arm, 'Look!' she commanded, 'They're

dancing without *tunban*. They have no shame.' In a whisper I
told her what had upset David earlier, immediately wishing I
hadn't, as she began to giggle, hiding her face in her chaddar. I
calmed her as Habiba entered our sanctuary.

When David felt brave enough, we ventured outside to pay
our respects to the bride. She was in her early twenties, though
it was difficult to be sure with the amount of make-up she
wore. She wore a white, Western wedding dress with about
half a ton of gold hung about her neck, wrists, ears and nose.

A few women danced in front of the band. Some giggled
self-consciously, but others clearly revelled in the limelight,
competing with each other in provocative, sinuous movements
and gestures. From time to time the other dancers would
stand back to allow one woman the floor to herself, holding
Afghani notes above her head to indicate their approval of her
dancing.

I was disappointed to find that there was no traditional
Afghan music or dances – the musicians played modern popular
songs and the dances were a mixture of traditional steps,
heavily overlaid by Indian film dancing.

By the time the food appeared, both David and Habib were
fast asleep. Maryam and I became restless, waiting for Naeem
who was by then very late. When I finally went to investigate
I discovered that he had arrived on time but been intercepted
by Habiba, sent a plate of food and told we were having a
wonderful time. She then 'forgot' to tell us that he was waiting
outside the gate to collect us.

For days afterwards the wedding was the main topic of
after-class conversation, which, tedious though it was, made a
change from the twins' health. Soon, though, Habiba was back
to asking if there was not some special medicine in my country
which would help her *doganagi* grow big and strong.

One day I discovered that she had persuaded Sharifa to
part with the UNICEF biscuits her children were given in the
camp. These high-energy biscuits were designed to provide
malnourished children with an easily absorbed combination of
protein and vitamins.

As with most UN supplies, stocks had found their way into the local shops. But Habiba – fearing that the biscuits in the shops might not be of the same quality – wanted Sharifa's.

'But don't you think her children need them?' I asked.

Shaking her head, she replied, 'Her children are quite healthy, not like my little *doganagi*.'

Sharifa's children were reasonably healthy, but, like the twins, they were small for their age. Her five-year old son, Nabi, was smaller than David and not much bigger than the twins. Yet Habiba was blind to the fact that other children were in need of nutritional supplements.

To my pointed query as to why she didn't buy her own biscuits instead of taking them from children who needed them, she replied with a disdainful sniff, 'The children of these kind of people thrive, regardless of what they are given.'

Why, I wondered, had I been anxious not to hurt her by not attending the wedding? The woman had skin as thick as a rhinoceros and it was becoming increasingly difficult to feel sympathy or affection for her.

A few days after the wedding reception, Marzia arrived at work with red-rimmed eyes. 'Did you have a bad night with Shahnaz? Is she sick?' I asked, indicating the child, fast asleep, her arms round one of David's teddies.

Marzia shook her head. 'No, Shahnaz is fine,' she replied, sudden tears welling in her eyes. 'It's because I am going to be m– m– married.' Her voice rose, thin and quavering, before ending in a flood of tears.

Between sobs she explained that Sharifa had accepted a proposal from a businessman recently returned from Iran. 'He buys blankets and shoes there to sell here. He has a house in Mazar but he lives in Iran and he will take me to live there. Sharifa says he is rich and will look after Shahnaz and me, but I don't want to go to Iran.

'It is all because of Jawad. He hates me and wants me out of his house even though I don't ask him for anything for us. I pay for our food. I pay for his cigarettes and I even bought him a bicycle. Sharifa says Jawad will blame her if I say no again.' Her sobs grew louder, making Shahnaz move restlessly in her sleep.

'A few months ago you were asking Hazrat-i-Ali to help you find a husband. Don't you like this man?' I asked.

'Yes, I like him . . . I suppose. I didn't expect to go so far away from my family. But Sharifa has never before pushed me to accept anyone so I can't refuse.' Waking, Shahnaz promptly added her own wails to those of her mother, who scooped her into her arms, hugging her tightly. She looked at me pleadingly, 'Could you speak to Sharifa? Persuade her to let me wait a little longer – at least until Shahnaz is weaned.'

Naeem and Maryam, anxious about Marzia, also offered to help try to persuade Sharifa to postpone Marzia's marriage. Everyone gathered, in an uneasy silence, in our living room.

Sharifa looked defensive while Marzia, keeping her head lowered, refused to look at her sister. Suddenly tongue-tied, wondering if I had any right to interfere in Sharifa's arrangements for her sister's future, I glanced round for help.

Naeem took the plunge, explaining to Sharifa that Marzia had told us she did not want to get married until Shahnaz was a little older. 'Couldn't you wait a year, or at least a few more months,' he suggested.

Sharifa burst out angrily, 'Do you think I am happy to force my sister into marriage? You have no idea how horrible life is at home. Since we went to the camp, men have been coming to our house like bees to a flower. They all want to marry Marzia – young men with no money and no jobs; married men who want Marzia because she is young and pretty and they want someone different to sleep with; men old enough to be her grandfather.

'It never stops, and every time I refuse someone Jawad shouts and yells at me, beats me. He says his name is being blackened because of the men seen coming and going from our house. I can't cope any more. I don't know what else I can do but accept this man. Jawad is determined to get rid of Marzia this time.'

Naeem offered to give a room in his house to Marzia and Shahnaz. 'We could tell Jawad that Maryam needs help in the house and wants Marzia, because she knows her.' Maryam nodded her head in agreement, though I knew she hated the idea of sharing her home with other people, enjoying for the first time in her married life the novelty of living in her own house without in-laws or relatives.

Marzia's face lit up at this suggestion, then, glancing towards Sharifa, who was anxiously biting her lip, her face clouded. 'It's the money, isn't it? You've already accepted, haven't you?'

Her sister, looking deeply unhappy, shrugged helplessly. A gloomy silence settled on the room, which was eventually broken by Sharifa, 'All right. You talk to Ghulam Ali, ask him how the future will be for you and Shahnaz if you marry him. If, after that, you still don't want to marry him, then I'll tell Jawad that we must cancel the marriage.' She shivered, 'He won't like it.'

Three days later, Marzia, her eyes lowered, told me she had agreed to marry Ghulam Ali. 'He is not so bad,' she assured me. 'He is handsome, and he promises to look on Shahnaz as his own daughter.'

'Oh, Marzia, are you sure this is what you really want to do?'

Marzia, forcing a smile, replied, 'I think he is a good man. He has promised he will bring me to visit whenever I want, and we shall have our own house, a real *luxe* house, in Iran.' Despite her attempts to reassure herself that she was happy, she went about her work quietly, sometimes tearfully for several days.

Once, when I was about to enter the kitchen, I noticed through the screen door Marzia and Daud standing close together, gazing wordlessly at each other. If I hadn't been in Afghanistan I might have thought they were lovers about to be torn apart and would have tiptoed away. This being Afghanistan, however, it could not be, so I opened the door. They both jumped, then Marzia giggled. I was so relieved to hear her bubbly laugh for the first time in days that I thought no more of how I had found them.

Marzia did genuinely seem to be happy again and began to

talk about her forthcoming wedding and Ghulam Ali's plans for their future. He was filling her head with promises of new dresses, gold jewellery and a beautiful house in Iran. Her eyes glowing, she described the jewellery set she hoped he would buy for her wedding gift.

As she talked, I realised I had forgotten how young Marzia was. Few girls of seventeen could fail to be bowled over about such riches becoming theirs and of being the wife of a handsome, successful businessman.

I did wonder why this supposedly wealthy and successful businessman was so anxious to marry Marzia. I could imagine men easily falling in love with her. She was beautiful and intelligent, with a keen sense of humour. But I had been in Afghanistan long enough to know that these qualities were minor considerations in marriage arrangements.

Why were there not families queuing up to secure this wonderful catch for one of their daughters? Why did he not look for a single girl instead of a widow, however young, with another man's child? I voiced my doubts to Maryam, who replied, 'I've been asking Naeem the same questions. It sounds very strange to me. But Marzia has made her decision.'

Marzia asked if I would employ her sister, Chaman, in her place. 'I won't be working after the wedding,' she explained. 'My husband would not like it. People might think he could not support me and he would feel shame.'

'But won't Chaman's husband feel shame if people think he cannot support his wife and children?' I asked.

'Oh, no,' replied Marzia, 'he is a nice man.' Realising the implications of what she had said, she blushed. Pretending I had not noticed her embarrassment, I agreed to her suggestion that Chaman replace her.

I still tried, unsuccessfully, to persuade her to carry on working for as long as possible while she saved her money for any emergency that might arise in the future. I had visions of her in Iran, alone, penniless and in distress, unable to make her way back to Afghanistan.

Jawad, anxious to be rid of Marzia and to get his hands

on the dowry, decided the wedding should take place almost immediately after the engagement had been announced. Sharifa was increasingly preoccupied – though not in the normal, excited, 'mother of the bride' sort of way, and I guessed there were problems.

She confided that Ghulam Ali had not yet paid any money to Jawad, saying that his dollars, which had been hidden in a friend's house, had been stolen. She sighed, 'Life is never smooth for us. Still,' she added with attempted brightness, 'his stock from Iran should arrive soon. He says he will make a lot of money selling that.'

The awaited stock of blankets, clothing and shoes never arrived. 'Ghulam Ali says there is some problem with customs at the border,' reported Sharifa, miserably, three days before the wedding.

I hoped that Marzia would realise that she was about to marry a liar, a crook and a womaniser (we had learned by then that he had not one but two wives already in Iran) and call the whole thing off. But it was too late; there was no turning back.

I couldn't face going to the wedding. Maryam also did not want to go but Sharifa begged her until, reluctantly, she agreed.

She reported back, 'Marzia looked beautiful and Ghulam Ali is a handsome man. But it was all wrong. She had new clothes but the only gold he gave her was a pair of earrings. Jawad had a very sour face and Latifa told me that Ghulam Ali has still not paid any *gala* [dowry].'

She sighed heavily, 'Well, it is done. We can only pray that Allah will protect her and keep her safe when she has to leave her family and her country.'

Sharifa was miserable. The marriage did not make her home life any easier with Jawad, who, angry that the dowry had not been paid, constantly picked fights with her. Making matters worse, the newly married couple had not moved into Ghulam Ali's house in the city. Sharifa shrugged, 'He says there is a problem getting the tenants out.'

Poor Sharifa got little sympathy from Latifa, who had been

critical about the match from the beginning. 'She should have ignored Jawad's complaints and waited until Marzia was ready to marry again,' she remarked, adding, 'Selling her sister was a bad thing to do – no happiness will come of it for anyone.'

'Don't tell her that,' I pleaded, 'she feels bad enough as it is.' Latifa shook her head. 'She knows it herself.'

— 14 —
Trouble with the
Government Bread

I FELT BAD about leaving Sharifa when she was so unhappy, but it was time to return to Hazara Jat.

Once again, as our jeep pulled out of the office compound, it was a tearful Sharifa who waved goodbye.

The road we had travelled the previous year had been closed for months because of inter-party fighting and the little-used route we were to take, via Dar-i-Suf, was over some notoriously difficult, high passes.

Out of the city, the metalled road ended abruptly and we hit a bumpy dirt track which forced us, as we hurtled over ridges and potholes, to grab desperately for whatever might provide some support. 'It is like being at the funfair,' commented David cheerfully, safely strapped into his car seat between Daud and me in the back of the jeep.

Delays caused by the engine going on fire and the inevitable punctures meant that by nightfall we had only reached the bazaar of Dar-i-Suf. We spent a sleepless night, disturbed by barking dogs, the firing of Kalashnikovs, and things that bit us.

Next morning we breakfasted perched atop a carpet-covered table in a hotel, the dirt-encrusted walls of which were decorated with a menacing display of AK 47s and pistols. As we chewed on dry nan, washed down with copious quantities of heavily sugared tea, the other customers stared silently at us with hostile eyes. Glad to be leaving Dar-i-Suf and its unfriendly atmosphere, we needed no urging from Reza to drink up quickly.

As we climbed higher, towards Yakolang, the scenery – bleak mountain ranges stretching to infinity – became ever more spectacular. Even though we closed the windows, the dust that blew in through every crack and crevice of the jeep clogged our throats, ears and noses, and coated us in a grey film.

Some of the passes were so steep that we had to bail out and walk up, slipping and sliding in the ankle-deep dust. Daud carried David over the steepest places for which I, struggling to keep on my feet and to gulp air into my protesting lungs, was eternally grateful. Naeem's job was to run behind, ready to throw a boulder under the back wheels should the jeep start slipping down the mountain.

At the top of Zard-i-Sang pass, waiting for the jeep to reach the summit, Daud, David and I stood awe-struck, enraptured by the view of desolate mountains, dust and rocks. Nothing moved in that bleak, starkly beautiful landscape, which might never have changed since the world was created. Silence, so complete, settled on us like a heavy cloak until the jeep's groaning engine shattered the stillness.

'The worst is over,' declared Reza happily as we climbed aboard again. At the bottom of the pass, however, we discovered about forty trucks and their morose drivers. No one was going anywhere. A truck coming down the other side had broken down, blocking the road.

Resigning ourselves to a night on the open mountain, we began, in the little daylight left, hastily collecting whatever fuel we could find with which to make a fire. In such a barren, treeless environment this was no task for the squeamish.

When David realised what we were gathering, he was aghast. 'Mummy,' he cried in horror, 'that's donkey pooh!'

We huddled round the fire to eat our supper, wrapped against the bitterly cold night air in all the spare clothing and blankets we could find (the winter woollies were, of course, out of reach at the bottom of the trunk). With bread and *busrock* [a fried biscuit, traditionally taken on long journeys] provided by Sharifa, Latifa and Maryam, enlivened by a carton of cream and a pot of home-made apricot jam, we dined well.

When I had seen the mountain of food the women had prepared heaped on the kitchen table before we left, I had wondered if they expected us to be on the road for a month. However, as we had only passed one makeshift *samovad* serving tea and one truck stop that had food since leaving Dar-i-Suf, we were grateful for their foresight.

Later, lying in my sleeping bag, listening to the silence, I gazed in wonder at the sky. Never have I seen such stars, stars that really did blaze in the heavens brighter than any diamonds.

Around three in the morning drivers started revving their engines. At a word from Reza, we bundled ourselves and our belongings into the jeep so that he could be first on the road. The remainder of the journey was anti-climactic – a brief stop in Yakolang for petrol and tyre repairs and one more night on the road; this time, under cover.

When we pulled up outside the clinic, Daud and his father, Hassan, meeting after almost three years, hugged and shook hands formally. I pretended not to notice that they both appeared a little watery-eyed and were trying to hide large handkerchiefs. Only women cry in Afghanistan.

David, delighted to be back amongst his old friends, kept up a non-stop stream of chatter until, barely able to keep my own eyes open, I dragged him off to bed. Next morning, I wandered into the staff room, surprised to find Daud sitting there.

'I thought you went home to see your mother and family?'

He nodded, saying, 'I couldn't stand the crying any longer. I knew my mother would cry when she first saw me, but she kept on crying. So did all the other women. I couldn't cope with it. I thought they would be happy to see me.'

I was trying to persuade Daud that his mother was truly happy to see him and that after a day or two the tears would stop, when the cook, Ibrahim, interrupted to say some of my students had arrived to greet me. Without waiting to finish my tea, I hurried to my room.

That was at eight o'clock in the morning, and from then until almost six in the evening, a stream of women came to welcome me back. Even at lunchtime my room was full of guests and Ibrahim had to come and rescue me so that I could eat something.

In the late afternoon, popping his head round the door, he shooed out the half dozen women sitting chatting to me. Taken aback by this surprisingly inhospitable behaviour, I started to remonstrate when he explained, 'The old ones from the village are coming now.'

'But they came this morning,' I pointed out.

'No,' he replied, 'I mean the really old ones.' I had no idea what he meant until, moments later, four stooped ancients hobbled into the room. One looked vaguely familiar but the others were total strangers. They were clearly the village worthies and I stepped forward to greet them respectfully.

The previous year I had had to learn the Hazara greeting rituals between women. If the woman was older, she kissed me on both cheeks while I grabbed and kissed the back of her hand, reversing the procedure if I were the elder. I did not like having my hand kissed, and at first would pull it away, but when I realised this bewildered people, causing hurt feelings, I accepted the custom. Confusion still arose when I judged the woman to be my equal in age while she assumed I was the elder.

I urged my guests to sit in the position of honour (at the top end of the room, furthest from the door), murmuring, 'Balla bishi, balla bishi.' Translated as 'Sit up, sit up', it sounded more like an order given to a slouching child! As the women drank their tea, their toothless gums worked noisily on the accompanying hard boiled sweets.

They were almost totally deaf, so, after we had one by one repeated the formulaic greetings, conversation rather lapsed. Fortunately, in Afghanistan, a sociable silence is perfectly acceptable, and in any case a few more 'How are you-s?' filled any conversational gap which threatened to become uncomfortable. After the ritual of offering and refusing of more tea three times, the visit came to an end and the women shuffled out, calling blessings on me as they went.

When a grinning Ibrahim returned to collect the empty glasses, he said, 'They are so old now, they hardly ever leave their houses. But they know everything that is going on. They wanted to show their approval about the work you did with the women last year.' I felt honoured by their visit and touched that they had made such an effort.

More guests appeared, excitedly chattering about the visit from the worthies. By the time the last of them had gone I was exhausted, still in my travel-stained clothes and no nearer to having the bath I'd been hoping for since morning. Ibrahim, who had spent the day boiling water for my guests' tea, was in no mood to boil up more for bath water.

The overwhelming welcome from the women had delighted me so much that I didn't mind going to bed filthy, a second night running. David, to avoid all the kissing he knew he would have been in for, had spent most of the day with Daud playing with the village children, and was even filthier.

We had been showered with gifts of eggs and chickens – enough to feed the clinic staff for the next week or so (which was just as well as there proved to be very little else to eat). For days after our arrival we ate chicken twice a day and eggs for breakfast. I begged Ibrahim to let some of the chickens live a little longer so that we could have something else for our evening meal.

'There isn't anything,' he said bluntly. I looked blankly at him, 'What do you mean? What about that spicy potato and onion dish or the vegetable stew?'

He shook his head, 'There are no vegetables at this time of year. You are too early.' The previous year we had been there at harvest time when carrots, turnips, potatoes and radishes were plentiful.

Children used to creep into the field next to the clinic and pull up young sweet carrots, devouring them immediately, cool and damp from the earth. Two months before the new crops were ready, the previous year's supply had run out.

For us well-nourished, temporary visitors the only problem was a lack of variety. When our supply of chickens ran out, we ate plain rice with a dollop of yoghurt on top, occasionally enlivened with a handful of dried apricots.

How could mothers wean their infants, I wondered? This

was a question the health volunteers were anxiously debating. Unless people kept their own poultry (which not everyone did), they had no access to eggs or chicken. The local shops stocked no beans or lentils, although rice, dried apricots and raisins were available. Many people throughout Hazara Jat survived this season on dry bread and tea alone.

Sitting on the clinic's flat roof (a favourite gathering place in the late afternoon for both my women friends and the clinic staff), it was difficult to believe there was such scarcity. The wheat in the surrounding fields grew tall and green, the *shaftal* [a pink flowering plant for fodder] filled the air with its sweet perfume, and, down by the river, there was a great swathe of more lush greenery for the cattle. It was beautiful – it looked like a land of plenty, but there was nothing edible.

None of my teaching manuals and books on childcare and nutrition had prepared me for this. I wished I could bring those experts to live with us for a week and see how they managed to put their advice into practice. Nickbacht said, 'We tell mothers weaning their babies to make *halwa* by cooking wheat or rice flour in oil and sugar. There really isn't anything else.'

The health volunteers were proud of their achievements over the winter. Antenatal care in their villages had, according to Iqbal's statistics, increased dramatically. Almost every pregnant woman from around a dozen villages had been reporting regularly for check-ups. 'And they've been taking iron supplements,' said Jemila. 'The new babies born this winter have been strong and healthy.'

Having been successful in spreading the word about the importance of rehydration and nourishment when children had diarrhoea, the health volunteers wanted to do more to prevent the problem. Jemila expressed their feelings of frustration, 'We know there should be latrines in the villages, and wells so that people can have clean water, but we need the men to build them. Our husbands say, "Yes, yes, you are right," but they don't do anything.'

Nickbacht added, 'We though maybe you could talk to them, persuade them to give more active support.' When

Iqbal suggested inviting the village leaders to lunch, I agreed, providing chicken wasn't on the menu. We killed a sheep instead.

About sixty *bozorg* came to the feast – double the number we had expected, considering we only had health volunteers in a dozen villages. Once they were full of food, they lounged under the shade of the trees, contentedly sipping tea. Iqbal, waving some impressive lists of statistics, explained that episodes of diarrhoea in children living in those villages with access to clean water and a latrine had dropped in number. 'If you want YOUR children to be healthy,' he declared, 'you must take some responsibility and not leave everything to the women.'

The chief guest was a well-respected mullah, a son of the 'King' (one of the leading political figures) and, to my delight, he was clearly on our side. He spoke eloquently – and at great length – on the need for participation throughout the community. Slowly at first, but with gathering momentum, men raised their hands to pledge support for the programme, promising to build at least one latrine and a well in every village.

There was only one dissenter – old Moh'd Ali, from Zohra's village. He had ridiculed the project a year ago, and was still adamant that it was all an unnecessary waste of time and money. 'This talk of microbes causing sickness is utter rubbish. I see no need to spend money on latrines,' he shouted angrily. The others laughed at him, telling him he was old-fashioned.

When I reported back on the meeting, the women, were jubilant. Nickbacht said happily, 'If the men made promises in front of the "King's" son then they have to keep their word.'

They begged for more details of the *mehmani*, crowing with pleasure when I repeated the mullah's final words. He had said, 'I always knew the women here were strong, now I believe they are stronger than the men.'

How they loved hearing that – and how I loved them, those strong women who were trying so hard to bring about change in the lives of the women and children in the community.

When they heard that some women in a village in the next valley were pregnant, they decided to encourage them to attend the antenatal clinic. 'But it's such a long way to walk,' I said, 'how could you do the return trip in a day?'

'Oh, we didn't,' replied Jemila. 'We stayed there for two days so that we could talk to all the women. We told them about the importance of having check-ups and taking iron and we helped them organise the things they would need at the time of delivery. We've promised that we'll go every two months to give health education.'

'What did your husbands say about you going away?'

Jemila shrugged, 'Suraya's husband was all right because she has a relative in the village, but mine was not very happy. He doesn't mind now because the *mooie-safeed* met him afterwards and told him what good work we are doing.' She grinned, highly delighted with herself.

The twins that Suraya had worked so hard to save the year before came for a visit. At a year old, they were bright, healthy, happy boys. Their mother, Nickbacht, was overjoyed, though she still looked exhausted. She sang Suraya's praises, until the woman was blushing in embarrassment.

'And', continued Nickbacht, 'I hope one day there will be classes in my village because there are other women who need to learn about caring for their children.

'My mother-in-law used to be so angry with Suraya always coming to our house, especially when she started to give the babies potatoes to eat. Now the boys are stronger, Mash 'Allah, she doesn't interfere so much.'

Suraya, delighted at how well 'her' twins were thriving, was eager to take on more work with malnourished infants. She could read and write a little, a skill she had been taught as a child, and was now improving with the help of a local teacher. 'Are there health training courses for women in Mazar-i-Sharif?' she asked.

'I can ask around,' I replied doubtfully, 'but would Hassan agree to you going away to the city?'

'Oh, yes,' she assured me, 'he would be happy for me to be a proper health worker.'

Her husband confirmed that he supported Suraya in her ambition. Surprised, but delighted that he had no objections to his wife deserting him to attend a course in the city, I agreed to find out if there were any suitable training programmes.

In the meantime, Iqbal left to attend a teaching camp for paramedics in another district. From now on I would be without a translator, and I wasn't sure about coping with teaching a class of ten. The women dismissed my doubts. 'When we visit you and you come to our homes we understand each other. What is so different about class?' asked Zohra.

I pointed out that there were still many words I did not know. 'Don't worry,' said Nickbacht, 'We'll help you.'

The women were delighted to be without the presence of a man. Not that they objected to Iqbal personally – they were all very fond of him – but they wanted to discuss gynaecological problems which they still could not do in front of him.

On the first day that I took class alone, using diagrams depicting the ovaries, fallopian tubes and uterus, I started to explain where these organs were situated in the female body. Aware of a movement just out of my line of vision, I turned, to find Nickbacht apparently taking her clothes off.

'What are you doing?' I shrieked.

'I said we would help you,' replied Nickbacht, straight-faced. 'It will be easier if you can point on a real body.'

'But anyone could walk in,' I protested. Nickbacht, her dress hauled up round her neck, pushed her breasts impatiently to one side and pointed in the general direction of her womb, '*Batchadan*', she said.

The class dissolved into gales of laughter that increased when Ibrahim, arriving at that moment with the tea, opened the door. I cast a swift glance in Nickbacht's direction. She must have dropped her dress like lightning, for she was once more decently clothed. She greeted Ibrahim demurely, and began to help pour the tea.

Classes invariably overran the allotted two hours despite

the women's remarks on my arrival that at this time of year they were too busy to spend time studying. There was so much they wanted to know and they asked me to teach them how to diagnose some of the more common complaints.

'If we know what the problem is, and how it should be treated, we can go with the patient and tell Iqbal ourselves,' said Nickbacht. 'The woman will not feel so embarrassed if we can describe her symptoms for her.'

This was easier said than done. I did not know how to translate medical terms such as fallopian tubes, or the names of particular infections. We simply invented our own vocabulary. I knew the *batchadan* was the 'baby's place', so we translated the ovaries as the *tochamdan* [the eggs' place]. The fallopian tubes became 'the road for the eggs'.

Explaining that thrush is a yeast infection stumped us when I didn't know the word for yeast, which was not an ingredient in the local flat bread. Itching and the curd-like appearance of the discharge were easy, but I was stuck when trying to describe the yeasty odour. My mime of baking bread, including a loaf rising was worthy of an Oscar – especially when Nickbacht called out excitedly, 'She means *nan-i-silo*.' (In Mazar-i-Sharif the government made a type of bread, with yeast, which was sold cheaply or distributed freely as part of low waged workers' rations. It was kept in a huge store called the silo. Nickbacht knew of it from her son who had lived in Kabul.)

We gave ourselves a round of applause. From then on, we called thrush '*taglif-i-nan-i-silo*' – translated as 'trouble with the government bread'. After that, trichomoniasis, although unpronounceable, was easy – I knew the words needed to describe the smell of rotten fish.

With spending so much time teaching and preparing for classes, I was worried that David might be feeling neglected. I needn't have – he was blissfully happy. Daud organised a kindergarten for the local pre-school age children, which proved popular. The teachers provided an empty classroom three mornings a week and on the other mornings they met in the mosque in Daud's village. We had to cut the pencils in half so that each child had a piece, and when they painted they sat in circles, happily sharing the brushes between them. As well as paper, pencils and paints, I had brought a stack of magazines, bought in Pakistan, where the censor had been busy with a black marker pen, obliterating bare bottoms and breasts. In every home – and in the mosque – samples of their artwork decorated the walls.

The teachers from the village school were intrigued by what Daud was doing, amazed that children could learn while playing and having fun, rather than sitting in straight rows repeating their lessons like parrots.

Daud taught the children to identify colours, something that few adults could do. One colour was often used to describe many things. The women would tell me the grass, the sky, and the deep blue dress someone was wearing was *subz rang* [green colour] not seeming to realise how different all these colours actually were. Or, if they noticed, they maybe did not think it was necessary to learn different words to show the difference. Similarly all cats, other than black ones, were described as yellow.

— 15 —
The Village of Love

IT WASN'T ONLY the children who enjoyed the magazines I'd brought for them to cut up: the women spent hours poring over them. I could feel them eyeing me speculatively as they studied the fashion pages, trying to imagine how I would look in such outrageous outfits. I was acutely embarrassed when asked the cost of things. The prices stunned them, and even when I explained that very few women bought the type of designer fashions illustrated, they found it unbelievable that anyone could and would spend so much money on clothes.

Thoughts of eating meat more than once every couple of months, having new clothes more than once a year, building latrines and wells and adding extra rooms to their houses, floated in the air between us.

As for the cosmetic adverts – they laughed pityingly as they contemplated women in far-off lands slapping night and day creams and special treatments onto their faces.

'I thought people in your country were educated,' remarked Nickbacht, one day, after I had translated the advertising blurb on something that fed and watered the skin. 'Do they believe these things work? What is the point, anyway? Everyone grows old. At least when a woman becomes old, people give her more respect.'

My explanation that in the West the reverse was more often true, led to a great deal of head shaking and 'tut-tutting'. They were shocked that my mother-in-law, a widow, lived completely alone, miles from her daughter and her family.

'But that is terrible!' exclaimed Jemila. 'If her son is living in Afghanistan then it is her daughter's duty to look after her. Why doesn't she live with her daughter?'

They were dismissive of my explanation that old people in

Britain valued their independence and that many did not wish
to become a burden on their families. When describing nursing
and residential homes for the elderly, my words about enjoying
independence sounded hollow even to my ears. Appalled by the
selfish, thankless way Westerners treat their ageing parents the
women's belief that Western countries were a kind of Utopia
started to crumble.

One grim full-page advertisement by Greenpeace caught
their attention. It showed a dying baby, its head grotesquely
swollen by radiation. I found it difficult to translate.

The women, who had never heard of nuclear power or
radiation, were disbelieving when I explained what the
advertisement was about. Feeling that they should be aware
that there are two sides to every debate I also put forward
the pro-nuclear point of view. But, for them, to whom their
children meant the world, there could be no counter-argument.
They were moved to tears by the deathbed quote from a child
in the advertisement, a victim of radiation, 'Hush mother,
do not cry. I am filled with angels.' They found it totally
incomprehensible that anyone could knowingly put children's
lives at risk to make cheap electricity, a commodity they were
quite able to live without.

I explained that the pro-nuclear side would argue that
the Greenpeace advertisement overstated the dangers and
oversimplified the arguments surrounding nuclear power.
But they would have none of it; they were unanimous in
their condemnation of nuclear power and hoped that these
Greenpeace people would be successful in doing something to
stop it.

Their response was a gut reaction. They had neither read
books and articles, nor listened to experts debate the subject.
Their view was simple – if there were doubts about the dangers,
if even one child's life could be destroyed, then this *chiz-i-
nuclear* [nuclear thing] was wrong.

Nickbacht said, 'We can't even read and write and there are
lots of things in the world we don't know about, but it seems to
me that people in your country don't understand what is right

and what is wrong. Why should we bother to send our children to school if education means learning how to kill children?

'Our mujahideen have been fighting and killing for years. I used to think that if our country were like yours, where everyone was educated, there would be peace in Afghanistan. Your country is at peace but the people still make life dangerous for others. What is the point of us learning how to keep our children healthy when other people might kill us with this nuclear thing? What other dangerous things do your people want to make?'

Despite being put on the spot with such difficult questions, I enjoyed the way the women were becoming more outspoken with me. If I had still been regarded as a guest, they would not have said anything that might offend me, and I was pleased the barriers were finally coming down.

They were coming down in other, much less expected ways, too.

I had been surprised that Daud rarely spent a night in his own home, except for when I was there at weekends. Then I discovered the reason for this was a young woman called Najiba, whose path he found every opportunity to cross 'accidentally'.

The only time I ever saw Daud cross with David was when the latter unwrapped and submerged a fancy bar of soap in a bucket of water before Daud caught him. The soap had been intended as a gift for Najiba.

Although I knew he was attracted to the girl I was incredulous when Daud announced his intention of visiting her in the middle of the night. 'How can you do that?' I asked, 'Doesn't she sleep with her family?'

'It is easy,' he replied, nonchalantly. 'She and her sister sleep in a room by themselves. She will leave the window open for me. I can reach it by climbing onto the roof of the outhouse.'

'It sounds dangerous,' I replied. 'What if her sister wakes up, or her father? He would kill you.'

'No, he might beat me and insist that I marry Najiba, but he wouldn't kill me. Don't worry, I know what I am doing,'

Daud grinned, as though he made such nocturnal visits to his girlfriends all the time.

'I hope you are taking condoms with you,' I remarked. He blushed, a deep rosy red, answering in a shocked voice, 'I won't need them. She won't let me do anything like that. I'll just lie next to her, holding her hand. If I'm lucky, she might allow a kiss before I leave.'

'I think you are crazy to take such risks,' I repeated. 'And even though you say Najiba won't let you do anything, you are hoping for more than that. If things get out of hand you are not going to stop because you don't have a condom with you. Do you know how to use them?'

Hoping he was not going to ask for instructions, I watched his embarrassed blush deepen. After a long pause, he nodded. 'I used them in Mazar-i-Sharif – with Marzia. She insisted.'

Stunned, I could only gasp, 'Marzia? *My* Marzia?' I suddenly remembered how I had found them, silently gazing into each other's eyes the day Marzia had agreed to marry Ghulam Ali. I had ignored my intuitive feeling that they were lovers saying goodbye, because such things, I had thought then, did not happen in Afghanistan.

I remembered too my promise to Sharifa that I would never allow Abdul Ali to go to the house when Marzia was there alone – and all the time it was my quiet, innocent 'son' who should have aroused her suspicions.

Daud's seduction of Marzia had begun one day as she was dusting our living room. He told me, 'There was an American drama on television and I made a comment about how the people on it were always kissing. From the way she giggled and looked at me I understood she was interested, so I kept trying.

'It took a long time, because we didn't have many chances to be alone. Sometimes though, when I came back from school, you and Jon had taken David out and Shahnaz was asleep. The day that she agreed to sleep with me was terrible, because that was when she said I must use a condom. Of course, I didn't have any.'

Daud smiled ruefully at the memory before continuing, 'I ran to the bazaar. But I was afraid the shopkeeper might ask questions about my age or demand to see a paper showing I was married. Finally, I plucked up courage and bought a packet. I ran all the way home – and you were sitting on the veranda, drinking tea with Marzia!'

The affair had ended when Marzia agreed to marry Ghulam Ali. 'She came once to the house with Sharifa after her marriage. She said we had to stop, now that she was married. I missed her very much. I wish I could have talked to you then. It is hard always pretending to be happy when you feel sad. If I looked miserable, people would have asked what was wrong and I wouldn't have been able to tell them the truth.'

Over the next few nights I learned a great deal about Daud's love life. Still reeling from the shock of learning about Daud and Marzia's fling, I barely registered surprise that Daud had not been Marzia's first lover – until I learned that he had been one of our drivers, and it had happened in Kabul. 'I didn't know they knew each other before they came to work with us in Mazar,' I commented.

Daud shrugged. 'There is a lot you don't know,' he said with a cheeky grin.

In the end, Daud did not risk visiting Najiba in her room at night. Despite his earlier bravado, I think he was secretly terrified of being caught by her parents. Much as he liked Najiba, he did not want her father to catch him and beat him and possibly force him to marry the girl.

His attraction to Najiba did not, to Daud's surprise and embarrassment, go unnoticed. From our vantage point on the roof, some of us watched Daud's courtship. The first *mushoong* [peas] of the season were ripening and Daud convinced David that the most delicious in the district belonged to Najiba's father. Every day Daud and Najiba accompanied by a willing David would disappear into the greenery.

My women friends often joined me in the early evening for tea on our rooftop perch. Nickbacht, watching Daud approach, asked if I had noticed that he had been in a bad mood or unusually sulky recently. I shook my head. 'Ah, well, he is not ready yet,' she said. With a laugh, Jemila added, 'He may not be, but Najiba hopes he is.'

Nickbacht continued, 'You see, when a boy feels it is time to marry he can't tell his parents directly, so he starts acting bad tempered and moody with everyone, until his parents get the message.'

She and Jemila explained how the boy's parents would discuss between themselves, and with the *mooie-safeed*, which girl their son should marry.

'Does the boy never say who he wants to marry?' I asked.

'Sometimes – but usually the parents decide,' said Jemila. 'If the boy is happy with their choice he will change his mood and work hard to show he is happy. If he doesn't want that girl, he will sulk. Though that doesn't mean his parents will change their decision.'

It wasn't only girls who were pushed into marrying someone they didn't want, I realised.

Nickbacht explained how the boy's parents visit the girl's family, indicating that they have come with a marriage proposal by saying, on arrival: 'We have come for a cup of water.'

Jemila picked up the story, 'When the tea is served, the boy's parents will ask what happened to their cup of water. The girl's father will promise to talk to the women in the house, saying that if they agree to the proposal, he will send a message. They go home to wait for news.

'If the women like the boy and his family, the next step is to fix the *gala*. This is becoming more and more expensive, and apart from money they will ask for sheep, cloth, rice, sugar, tea – maybe a horse.

'But don't forget that although the girl's family receives all this, they have to spend a lot of money too. They must provide everything for the couple: two sets of gilims and bedding as well as cups and teapots and other kitchen utensils. Everything is packed in boxes to be carried to the boy's home by donkey. If the boxes are not heavy, everyone will talk and say the girl's family is mean.'

As Nickbacht and Jemila were ending their explanation of local wedding customs, Daud and David arrived. David's pockets were stuffed with pea-pods and Daud was grinning like a cat that had just had the cream or, more likely, a snatched kiss.

At the sight of his beaming face, Nickbacht burst out laughing, 'He is definitely not bad-tempered enough yet!' she exclaimed.

Listening to Daud's confessions – and Iqbal's the previous year – made me feel vaguely voyeuristic. Also, although I had no reason to disbelieve what they told me, I still felt that I was hearing only one side of the story. I was pleased, therefore, when the friendship between Nickbacht and I deepened enough to allow more personal conversations than we had had the year before.

I had become a regular visitor to Nickbacht's house, and once I ventured to ask what it was like to live in a village that was referred to as the 'village of love' throughout the district.

Laughingly, she replied, 'I don't know when it started but for as long as I can remember it's had that name. If it was because the young girls living here years ago were free with their loving, those girls must be grandmothers now.'

'That's not too old for love, Nickbacht. You are a grandmother yourself,' I pointed out. She laughed uproariously, saying, 'I think the boys are after something younger nowadays. Someone like Sharifa maybe.'

Sharifa was a young married woman with a reputation for being 'too free', as most of the women described her. One of the reasons I liked Nickbacht so much was that I never heard her attach such judgmental labels to people. There was always a lot of talk around the villages, and although, like the rest of the women, Nickbacht enjoyed a gossip, with her it was never malicious.

Perhaps gossip, with its unpleasant connotations of slander and character assassination, is not the correct word to describe everyone's fascination with what everyone else said and did.

Amongst the women – and, just as often, the men – it was more in the nature of telling and listening to oral news bulletins.

Apart from the men's habit of listening to the BBC Persian news broadcast every day, knowledge of events in the outside world were almost unknown. Khulsom and Latif's cow's new calf or Agha's engagement excited far more discussion around the district than anything happening in Kabul, or in other countries.

The community was currently divided over the matter of Latif's freshwater spring. In the next village the people were suffering from a shortage of water and had asked him for permission to dig out his spring, which would increase the flow of water in the tiny stream that trickled through both villages. Latif's refusal – he maintained they would want to start planting trees around his spring next – and the many meetings between him, the villagers and the elders were discussed daily by everyone.

Such 'gossip' was, in fact, a substitute for the best kind of local community newspaper. There were, of course, many stories that would never have been published in such a newspaper.

'There is the other Fatima,' said Nickbacht, still musing on the 'village of love' title. 'You know, Moosa's wife. She is looking for love.' She glanced at me, adding, 'With good reason.'

'Yes,' I nodded in acknowledgement of Nickbacht's last comment, 'but more than love, it's a baby she wants.'

Fatima's husband, Moosa, had suffered since childhood from untreated epilepsy. By the time the clinic had opened, he was suffering from seizures every day and had suffered considerable brain damage – although the seizures were now controlled by medication. The childless Fatima confided to Iqbal that since the start of their marriage, her husband had been totally disinterested in sex.

Nickbacht's next comment startled me: 'I hear she has even been after Iqbal?' I gaped at her, finally managing to splutter, 'I thought that was a big secret. How did you know?'

'Nothing is secret round here,' Nickbacht grinned. 'What happened?'

I shrugged. 'I don't think he felt he could help.'

Iqbal had confessed that Fatima had, after dropping many hints, openly invited him to father a child for her. It wasn't from any particular moral standpoint that he had not attempted to help Fatima conceive. He was more concerned about being laughed at if he were not able to rise to the challenge.

Admitting that this was sometimes a problem, he confessed, 'It is not easy to perform, when you've only a few minutes snatched in secret, with the fear of being caught always in your mind. Women think we can make it stand up to order, and are very cruel if it doesn't happen.'

Impotency, whether occasional or permanent, was a problem about which our paramedical staff was often consulted. Young men complained that they were unable to make love to their wives, though they had never experienced any difficulty when they had visited prostitutes while working in Iran or Pakistan.

Brought up in rural Afghanistan, under the powerful influence of illiterate mullahs, they had been taught as boys that sex before marriage was sinful. They were warned that if they went with prostitutes they would be unable to make love to the good, unsullied girls they married. Such brainwashing proved effective and, unfortunately, none of our Afghan staff had the counselling skills required to do anything much about it. Most of them probably believed the mullahs themselves, anyway.

From what I was learning from Daud – and from Iqbal – it seemed that Afghan men suffered as much as the women from sexual repression and ignorance.

Traditional values and social conventions governed the lives of the men as much as they did the women, and it was no easier for them to break free from those bonds. There were two sides to the coin of sexual repression. And the double standards of sexual behaviour that applied to men and women in Afghanistan were not so different from those in Britain until recent years which, some might argue, still exist. I could not, however, imagine a situation such as that of Malika and Abdul Wali occurring in the West today.

Malika was the sister of Miriam, who had eloped when her parents refused to allow her to marry Ghulam Ali. They also refused to let Malika marry Wali, who was Ghulam Ali's brother. Afraid that if she too eloped, the shame would kill her mother, she refused to run away with him.

However, she steadfastly rejected every man her parents suggested. If she could not have Wali, she would have none of them, though it was common knowledge that their love affair had continued. Already in her early thirties, too old to be married off to anyone else, Malika was likely to endure a lonely future. Abdul Wali was bowing to his family's pressure and had recently agreed that he would marry a girl of their choosing.

I had heard that Malika had given birth to two children during the years of their affair, both of whom she had drowned. Yet again I found myself confronting yet another cultural barrier too high to cross. That Malika did not want to add to her mother's misery and bring further shame on the family by eloping, as her sister had done, I could understand. Girls are under intense pressure to uphold family honour, to be dutiful, obedient daughters. That her mother could be less heart broken by the murder of her grandchildren than by her daughter marrying the man she loved, I could not even begin to comprehend. Maybe the story about the babies wasn't true?

Nickbacht replied, 'Most people accept that she drowned a baby some years ago. It would be strange for them to be lovers for so long without her ever becoming pregnant.'

'Does Abdul Wali really love her?' I asked.

She shrugged. 'If the family agreed tomorrow, I think he would still marry her, but he will not think about her feelings when he marries someone else.

'She loves him – but what has love to do with life? It is only something in songs that makes you sad. I'd rather have a cup of tea.'

I laughed in agreement, asking why so many married women bothered to have affairs. 'From what I have heard sex is not so wonderful even between husbands and wives. It doesn't seem that Afghan men are the world's best lovers, so why do women risk being beaten, divorced, losing their children, for ten minutes in the *assea*?'

'Oh, they are not all that bad!' replied Nickbacht with a grin. 'Besides,' she continued with a hint of wistful smile, 'the ten minutes in the *assea* is not the point.

'You have seen the boys at the well – teasing the girls, trying to splash them with water. Girls enjoy having so much attention.

'When they marry, her husband wants to spend a lot of time with her at first, but that changes. There is always so much work, and then the children start arriving, and we begin to feel old and tired.'

As though conscious that she had slipped from generalisation to the particular, Nickbacht paused for a moment, pouring tea, pushing the sweets towards me. She shrugged, 'When a man shows he is interested – you know, little jokes, the way he looks at you – it makes a woman feel special again. That is why women take the risk, though they like it better if they can keep the man interested without having to do anything more dangerous than flirt with him. But men are never satisfied – they want everything.

'And you should hear how a boy goes on when a girl won't give in! He says she is responsible for the way he feels about her, says it is dangerous for a man to become aroused and not find any relief. "Do you want to kill me!" they cry. "You are twisting a dagger in my heart!"'

'Sounds like men are the same everywhere,' I said. 'What happens when a girl becomes pregnant – surely they don't all drown their babies?'

'No, not always,' replied Nickbacht, grimly. 'Sometimes they leave them on the mountain to die – it doesn't take long in the winter.' She shrugged helplessly, then said, 'Some are luckier. Two years ago a girl in the village became pregnant and her

father took her to the *Shura* [the local Government]. They
asked her to name the boy. They beat him and sentenced her
to be beaten after she had her baby. Then they made them
get married.

'Was the girl beaten after she had her baby?' I asked.

Nickbacht shook her head, 'No. The *Shura* was acting tough
as a warning, and I think they had forgotten about it by the
time the baby arrived.'

I must by then have started to look depressed because
Nickbacht suddenly laughed, 'Don't think so deeply about
everything. There are problems for women everywhere – not
only here. You have talked about things in your country that
should not happen to women. At least now our girls are going
to school. Maybe some will go to college in the city and learn
new ideas, new ways. Perhaps my granddaughters' lives will be
different, or the generation after.'

Nickbacht paused for a moment before continuing, 'The
thing that stops us from changing is shame, and the fear
of what other people will say. That's why I try not to say
bad things about people, whatever others say they might
have done.'

Sharm, translated as shame, has many more connotations
and shades of meaning than in English. It can mean the
shyness a child might feel when meeting unknown adults, or
the embarrassment women feel when discussing anything to
do with their reproductive systems, even with a doctor.

However this is not the same embarrassment or shyness many
women in the West feel when undergoing undignified, personal
procedures such as internal gynaecological examinations or
smear tests – it is something that goes much deeper. Nickbacht's
friend, Fatima, had suffered from a prolapsed uterus for *five*
years because she felt too much shame to mention it to
a doctor.

Then there was the shame that came from a member of a
family being talked about because she (it was nearly always
a she who brought shame on a family) was known to have
stepped outside the rigid code of the community's ethical

conduct. 'What would the neighbours say?' was a fear so deeply entrenched in Afghan society it seemed impossible that it might ever change.

Was it not the same less than a hundred years ago, in Britain? Divorce, illegitimacy and adultery were scandals that ruined peoples' social standing, brought shame on families and destroyed lives.

There were Homes for 'fallen girls' where they could hide their shame and disgrace until after the birth of their babies who were immediately taken from them. Infanticide happened too. Young girls, terrified of their family's reaction and society's disgusted rebukes, disposed of their newborn babies after giving birth alone and unaided. Yet, we conveniently forget our recent past, forget our once deep-rooted sense of *sharm* and our fear of what the neighbours would say.

Nickbacht walked part of the way home with me, reluctant to end the conversation. As we parted, she said, 'One day, life will be better for women in Afghanistan, but it will never be the same as in your country. We have to find our own way.'

— 16 —
No Smoke!

JEMILA ARRIVED ONE afternoon to report that men had actually started digging latrines in three of the villages. 'Now we know our work is being taken seriously at last,' she said, delightedly. 'We are moving forward, although it will still take time for people to accept that they should use the latrines.'

Many people, even, I suspected, some of the health volunteers, still preferred to use the fields rather than a latrine, claiming that the latter were smelly. Properly built, with a deep enough pit and well-ventilated, latrines should, I knew, be odour-free, especially if the urine was kept separate from the faeces – but I had to agree some of them did tend to smell a bit.

The health volunteers were steadily gaining in confidence in their own skills and abilities. Most had been asked to act as birth attendants in their own villages. This was a huge break with the custom that prevented outsiders going anywhere near a new baby for forty days. The women were pleased that, at least in the villages where they had some influence, some horrific procedures once used in emergencies had been stopped.

At one of our coffee and shop-talk sessions the women discussed what used to happen – and which they knew probably still *did* in places outside the catchment area. It was customary, when labour had been going on for too long, to apply pressure on the abdomen, or, in cases of a retained placenta, to pull on the umbilical cord. Jemila told me of a custom which thankfully had ended some years earlier. People thought (some still did) that the body's organs – heart, liver and kidneys – were all connected to each other and to the tongue. The belief was that when a woman strained to give birth, there was a danger of the heart being dislodged. To counteract this, the 'midwife' would jab a large threaded needle through the tongue of the labouring woman, pulling hard on it to ensure that all connecting organs remained in their rightful places.

By the time Jemila had completed her graphic description, I had turned quite green – much to the women's amusement. Back in Mazar, when I told Maryam about this barbaric custom she said, 'It was still happening in Jaghoray when I had Fatima. By chance, Naeem saw the woman with the needle in her hand going into the room where I was lying. He stopped her. There was a row between him and my aunt, who was really frightened I would die if they didn't do it.'

Deciding they had told me enough horror stories for one day, the women prepared to leave, rummaging in the pile of shoes at the doorway to find matching pairs. Every one of them wore identical, Russian rubber shoes, and it was not uncommon for people to slip on the wrong pair or even a mismatched pair from the jumble left outside the door.

Kulsom turned back to ask if I would look at a woman, pregnant with her first baby. 'She is so small.' Not much over five feet herself, she indicated a place level with her shoulder, before continuing, 'and she has a limp. As it is her first baby it could mean problems.'

A group of volunteers brought Aziza to the clinic – as though producing a prize exhibit for inspection. She was indeed tiny, barely over four feet six, and her limp was caused by a curvature of the spine. The women were right to be concerned and I explained to Aziza that, as it was her first pregnancy, I would like her to be examined by the midwife in the Oxfam clinic in Panjau. I offered to arrange transport for the five-hour journey and Aziza said she would talk to her husband. Although I estimated she had maybe six weeks before the baby was due, I did not want her to delay her decision too long.

A few days later, her husband, Hussain, appeared at the classroom door. 'Aziza's in terrible pain. Come quickly!' he urged. I hurried after him, the students' anxious twittering echoing my own concern.

Telling Hussain to pack a bag, I called for Abdul Ali, the

clinic driver, to take them to Panjau. Hussain, looking shaken, said, 'Aziza is in a lot of pain. Maybe we should wait until she feels better.'

I shook my head, 'If these are real labour pains, they won't stop, and if there are complications there is nothing we can do for her here. If it is a false alarm, the midwife will send Aziza right back.'

The next day I called Panjau on the radio – a frustrating piece of equipment with which I was supposed to keep in touch with Mazar and with Jon, who was on tour. The previous year I had enjoyed the feeling of being completely out of touch with office concerns and hated having to bring it with me. It involved me in an inordinate amount of running up and down to the roof to adjust the frequencies on the antenna in the hope of finding a clear signal. When it did work, it was certainly less frustrating than trying to use the telephone system. This involved a trip to Waras bazaar – two hours by jeep – where the nearest telephone was situated. Every hour, on the hour, the operator picked up the receiver and yelled into it at the top of his voice in the hope that someone at the other end would hear him. Telephone operators in Lal, Panjau, Bamiyan, and wherever else there was an instrument and a line, were usually also yelling at full volume so that in the resulting chaos, messages were invariably garbled or lost.

Admitting to myself that in such an emergency, the codan had its uses, I talked to the midwife at the Oxfam clinic. She said the pains were a false alarm and estimated another four weeks to delivery. Then she dropped her bombshell – Aziza would need a Caesarean section for which she would have to go to Kabul or Mazar-i-Sharif.

I translated only the first part of the message to the three ancients – amongst whom was Aziza's mother-in-law – gathered round the radio, thankful that they could not understand English. I dreaded having to cope with the mass hysteria that would break out when everyone heard Aziza required surgery. The place would be awash with dire tales of women dying under surgeon's knives in far away city hospitals.

I contacted Jon asking him to come sooner than arranged to collect me, explaining that we would have to take Aziza with us to Mazar.

Aquila, who had accompanied Aziza and Hussain, returned next day with Abdul Ali and wasted no time in spreading the news. In class there were a few tear-streaked faces. Abandoning the day's scheduled topic, I had to spend the lesson time reassuring them that Aziza would be all right.

'The midwife says the pelvic canal is too narrow to allow the baby's head to pass. Without the operation Aziza would spend many hours in a lot of pain when the baby tried to come out. The baby would probably die and Aziza might also die too.

'But, you know all this. You brought her to the clinic because you were afraid something might go wrong. You did well to recognise the danger and take action and you should be feeling proud. Aziza will come back with a new baby that might not have lived.'

As I displayed my own caesarean scar for the umpteenth time and described what I could remember of David's delivery, I tried hard not to think of the nightmarish journey ahead of us. I could not share my fears with the already worried students that the horrendously bumpy roads might cause Aziza to go into early labour when we were still two days from Mazar.

Jon arrived two days later. Anxious not to delay our departure, I had already started packing. The three ancients who had sat in front of the radio waiting for news of Aziza horrified me by declaring that one of them must go to Mazar with Aziza and Hussain.

I doubted if any of them – one nursing a broken arm, one almost blind from cataracts, the third, in her late eighties, suffering from high blood pressure – would survive the journey, never mind be of any use if things went wrong on the road. I explained as diplomatically as possible that it would be better if one of the health volunteers came as a companion and helper for Aziza. Aquila was fortunately related to Hussain by marriage, and was an acceptable alternative.

She was more than willing – her trip to Panjau the previous

year had whetted her appetite for further travel and adventure –
though worried about her husband's reaction to the idea. When
asked, Ewaz simply replied, 'If Mary has asked you to go then
I know there is no point in my trying to stop you.'

Aquila packed her one spare outfit and was ready, making
me feel ashamed of my trunks – one of which I had to leave
behind to make room for the extra passengers – containing
clothes, books and David's toys.

In Panjau, I was pleased to find Aziza looking well and
relaxed, undaunted by the prospect of the next morning's early
start on a journey that might take several days. She, Hussain
and Aquila travelled in the clinic jeep driven by Abdul Ali,
while Reza drove David, Jon, Daud and myself.

The journey – tough at the best of times – was absolute
torture for Aziza. From the outset, she was constantly car sick,
throwing up into a rapidly dwindling supply of plastic bags.
However, at the roadside hotel where we spent the first night,
she managed to eat a little and was still remarkably cheerful
when we settled to sleep.

Only Jon and Aquila slept soundly, their synchronised
snoring ensuring that the rest of us tossed and turned all night.
It was actually a relief when Reza called us shortly before four
o'clock to start the day's journey.

Aziza's vomiting started less than half an hour after setting
off. Exhausted by her painful retching, she refused to eat or
drink anything. On the mountain passes the jeeps struggled
on the tortuous gradients and passengers had to walk – except
Aziza, who was allowed to sit in the back of Abdul Ali's jeep.
Poor Hussain, understanding the need to lighten the load to
get the vehicle to the top of a pass hated leaving Aziza facing
the prospect of hurtling back down the mountain if the jeep
slipped.

We became increasingly worried about Aziza's rapidly
deteriorating condition. At one stop we persuaded her to drink
some water, but after only a few sips she began a further
bout of retching so painful she crawled back into the jeep and
sobbed convulsively in Hussain's arms. This frightened Reza so

much that he refused to contemplate another night on the road. Driving like the proverbial bat we reached Mazar-i-Sharif at seven-thirty in the evening. We had never accomplished the journey in such a short time and, battered and bruised, we hoped never to have to attempt it again.

Aided by Hussain, Aziza barely had the strength to walk across the compound and into the house. However, after drinking a full litre of oral rehydration salts she looked, amazingly, much brighter, and went to have a bath. Although still unable to face food, she declared that she felt fine and the family settled down to sleep. Dizzy with fatigue, I collapsed gratefully into my own bed.

Around three o'clock a tentative tapping on the door awakened me and I staggered out to find Aziza standing on the veranda, bleeding heavily, worrying about the bedding. Aquila and Hussain, hanging the newly washed sheets on the line, were discussing how to tackle the bloodstains on the mattress.

'Aquila,' I yelled, 'are you a health volunteer or what? What did you learn about bleeding in pregnancy?'

Shamefaced, she sprang into action. Spreading out the plastic sheet, she made Aziza lie down with her legs propped high on a pile of cushions. It was still too early for the nightly curfew to be lifted so, while I made tea for everyone, Jon went to ask the soldiers for permission to drive Aziza to the hospital.

There she was examined by a woman doctor – which started the bleeding again – who scribbled a hasty note to be taken to the home of the chief obstetrician. Jon was despatched to deliver it. The doctor disappeared and we were left alone. Aziza, lying on the filthy, blood-stained examining couch, discussed with Aquila how to scrub the veranda clean before any men came to my house.

When the chief obstetrician, Dr Jemil, arrived I heard Aquila's sharp intake of breath as she realised a man was going to examine Aziza. The doctor, pulling on the bloodied glove the previous doctor had used (asking first on which patient it had been used) approached Aziza. Aquila, unconcerned about matters of hygiene, was only worried that a man was about to fiddle around in Aziza's private parts.

Deciding that even if this was strictly necessary, he was certainly not to be allowed to look at anything down there, she began a tug of war with him over Aziza's clothing. The doctor won, and Aquila stood by, wringing her hands in anguish. Announcing that the Caesarean section had to be done immediately, he wrote a list of everything required for the operation.

There were no supplies in the hospital, so Jon was sent to buy the anaesthetic, needles, sutures, antibiotics, and everything else needed before surgery could begin. Someone else was sent to find the anaesthetist.

After escorting Aziza as far as the door to the theatre, Aquila, Hussain and I returned to wait in the corridor. Someone from the office turned up with welcome thermoses of tea and coffee. Hussain and I chain-smoked in silence.

Eventually, a disembodied voice from the hatch announced the birth of a son. We congratulated Hussain, but he was much too terrified about what was happening to Aziza to take in the fact that he had become a father.

The doors suddenly banged open and the theatre nurse rushed along the corridor, a bundle in her arms. I had only time to catch sight of a tiny blue foot protruding from the blanket before the nurse beckoned to Aquila and me to follow her.

She uncovered Aziza's son, laying him, limp and terribly blue, on a table. Aquila moaned, 'He's dead.' The nurse shook her head, frantically massaging the tiny form. It looked like she was attempting to beat him back into life. 'He's not dead. He cried when he was born. Where are his clothes?'

Aquila and I stood helplessly, neither of us believing the nurse, not even bothering to find the bundle of clothing. 'Get his clothes,' she snapped. 'He is alive. Look at his heart!' We looked at the tiny chest, seeing for the first time how it throbbed with life, and rushed for the clothes, tears blinding us.

As Aquila nervously began to wrap up the tiny baby, the nurse sank down on a chair, begging a cigarette. As I handed her the packet I noticed she too had tears glistening in her eyes, which set us all off again. Poor Hussain, fearfully peeking around the door, seeing three sobbing women, assumed the worst and rapidly retreated.

Dragging deeply on her cigarette the nurse called him back. Hussain, his thoughts entirely on what might be happening to Aziza, peered silently at his son.

The doors of the theatre opened again, and Aziza, deathly pale, was wheeled on a trolley to the ward. Shivering violently, despite the heat, she looked dreadful.

The ward was indescribably dirty, suffocatingly hot and smelled strongly of the latrines, which were only several yards away. Aziza opened her eyes long enough to register that she had a real live baby to show for all her troubles, smiled, and sank back into a deep sleep.

The occupants of the other beds eyed our strange little group with excited curiosity. Hussain, oblivious to the stares and whispered comments from the other occupants of the ward, was determined to remain glued to Aziza's side. The staff soon gave up trying to evict him, agreeing he could sleep outside on the veranda.

We brought bedding for them – the hospital had no clean sheets – as well as food, tea and everything else we could think of to make the stay less horrendous, including a bedpan. It was stolen less than an hour later.

Apart from Dr Jemil and the theatre nurse who had fought so hard to keep the baby alive, it was clear that the staff cared little about their patients. The female doctors, disdainful expressions on their made-up faces, drifted around in their white coats, left open to show off their fashionable clothes. The nurses sat in their station rooms chatting over endless glasses of tea, or slept away their duty hours, while the cleaning staff roamed around gossiping to each other.

None of them was paid a proper wage. Sometimes they might have to wait six months or more before receiving a salary that was so meagre it would not keep one person alive for a month, never mind provide food and shelter for a family.

Small wonder there was no sign of vocation or motivation amongst the medical profession.

The doctors relied on their private, after hours, clinic work to provide their income. Nurses, who had very little status, often eked out their incomes by offering private services from their homes – giving injections and changing dressings. They also supplemented their income by charging hospital patients for services that should be provided freely – putting in a drip (which the patients had to buy) or changing dressings. The cleaning staff, who had no status at all – neither within the hospital hierarchy nor outside it – relied on extracting *baksheesh* from patients for bringing a bed pan, or finding a sheet for the bed.

When Aziza was at last groggily conscious, at least enough to look at her son for a few moments, I suggested that next time she awoke she might like to try putting him on the breast.

Dr Jemil agreed that Aziza could come to our house rather than stay another ten days in the hospital. He smiled at Aziza, who was nursing her son. 'Well done. I wish more mothers did that on the first day. The *pila* is the best protection for babies – a wonderful gift from Allah.' Aquila swelled with pride and shot a look of triumph towards the other women in the room, who had been aghast when she had put the baby on to the breast.

The family was installed in Daud's room, and within a few days we were all totally besotted by the tiny infant. Aziza was a wonderful advert for motherhood – she positively bloomed. Her skin glowed, her eyes sparkled, and her long, dark hair shone with a healthy gleam as it rippled down her back. Safe from prying eyes in the privacy of the house and compound she cheerfully abandoned her chaddar.

Loved and petted by everyone, Sultan was a contented baby who rarely cried. We were convinced that he was smiling by the time he was three weeks old – and no one was going to tell us it was wind.

Satisfied that Aziza and Sultan were no longer in any danger, Aquila relaxed and began to enjoy herself. Everything in the house fascinated her. Whenever I was preparing meals she joined me in the kitchen where she sat, spellbound, by the process of cooking on a gas flame. 'No smoke!' she would exclaim in wonder. She loved what she called the *sanduq safeed* [the white box] as she referred to the fridge. The washing machine was another source of wonder and she was very quickly persuaded to abandon her original plan of washing the family's clothes by hand.

She loved the television, especially motorbike racing. As the huge, powerful machines zoomed round the track she would edge excitedly forward, her eyes blinking owlishly behind her spectacles. An accident would have her gasping in horror, mopping her brow with her chaddar, then, when the adverts interrupted her viewing, she would shuffle back to her place, waiting to begin the whole performance again.

All too soon, Aziza and Sultan were strong enough to face the rigours of the journey home. The family's last few days in Mazar were spent visiting the shrine and shopping. All we had been through together had formed a close bond between us, so our goodbyes were painfully emotional and tearful. The most difficult thing about friendships in Afghanistan was the uncertainty of when – if ever – we would meet again.

There was, fortunately, little time for sitting around brooding about missing friends. We were going home on leave – the first in two years – and it was a welcome prospect.

— 17 —
Who are these Taliban?

'WHO ARE THESE TALIBAN?' I asked, after reading a couple of small stories in the Pakistani press about the hitherto unknown fundamentalist group.

Afghan friends in Karachi, where we were spending a few days soaking up sunshine before facing winter in Scotland, knew no more than I did. It was December 1994 and Taliban (the name, an Arabic word, means students – in this context, of Islam) were critical of all the mujahideen groups still fighting for supremacy in Afghanistan, accusing them of being un-Islamic and guilty of corruption and lawlessness.

They had already, according to newspaper reports, launched a clean-up operation to rid those areas of the country under their control of illegal roadblocks. Travellers had to pay heavy tolls to be allowed safely through, the money going to line the pockets of crooked commanders. Taliban had summarily executed those highway robbers they captured.

Around Kandahar and the routes leading to and from the Pakistani border, it was reputedly now safe for people to travel. None of the people I questioned about Taliban were particularly concerned. Most seemed to think they were too few in numbers and without sufficient resources, both in terms of military hardware and money, to be relevant to the political situation in Afghanistan.

We returned to Mazar-i-Sharif in March 1995, shortly after the Afghan New Year. The day before our arrival, the city had witnessed the funeral of Mazari, who had been the leader of the Hazara Hisb-i-Wadhat Party. He had been captured by Taliban, tortured and murdered. Within a couple of weeks of the funeral gruesome photographs were circulating in the bazaar of Mazari being tortured by his grinning captors.

Less than four months after I had first read about them, they were no longer a political irrelevance in Afghanistan.

With the Quran in one hand, Kalashnikov in the other, these students of Islam, who had spent years as refugees in Pakistan, studying in their own Madrassahs, were storming through Afghanistan. Their declared intent was to install what they described a true Islamic government in Kabul. The ultra-conservative Pushtoon majority around Kandahar had shown little resistance as the militant students began to sweep through the country. Many rival fighting groups simply switched sides, strengthening Taliban's numbers as they rolled on towards their ultimate goal – Kabul.

Most of Afghanistan's major political figures had attended Mazari's funeral, condemning, in their speeches, Taliban's murder of the Hazara leader. Even Gulbedin Hekmatyar, who had in the past been anti-Hazara because of their Shia faith, allied himself with them (at least publicly) against Taliban. Hisb-i-Wadhat swore publicly to take revenge on Mazari's assassins. Whatever implications the appearance of Taliban might have on Afghanistan's political arena, an end to the war was clearly not on anyone's agenda.

In the days following the funeral, talk centred on Taliban and how their assassination of Mazari might tip the balance of power. The Uzbek, Hazara and those Pushtoon Parties, like Hisb-i-Islami, who were anti-Taliban, were loosely united in a coalition to oust the Tajik President Rabbani from Kabul. Taliban shared the same immediate aim but, if they were successful in taking Kabul, it seemed unlikely they would consent to any power sharing with the other political groups. For the time being there seemed to be a stalemate, with each protagonist studying the next moves in this deadly game.

Perhaps if the main players had stopped their internal fighting long enough, they might have understood the danger from Taliban, but it seemed each group's thirst for power made them blind to anything else.

Soon, however, for the people of Mazar, other events in their daily lives began to reassert their precedence over the national upheavals caused by Taliban. The crowds of mourners going to pay their last respects at Mazari's grave-side began to lessen – except when, from time to time, there came news of someone experiencing a miraculous cure after praying by the grave. Life, once again, resumed normality.

Our house had been burgled while we were away and the thieves had stolen the television, video and other, easily sold electrical equipment. The police had wanted to take Daud in for questioning, but Naeem, knowing we would not allow that, persuaded them not to. Denied the chance to beat a confession out of their suspect, the police abandoned the investigation.

Jon spent days rigging up alarm systems which would trigger a floodlight if anyone tried to come over the roof in the night. Yards of cables festooned the house, attached to push button switches in every room, which were connected to a battery-operated alarm. Everyone took it for granted that the thieves would return once they knew we had replaced the stolen goods. On the advice of the police and friends, we reluctantly appointed a night *chowkidar* [watchman].

Chaman, when taking over Marzia's work in our house, had omitted to mention the fact that she was expecting a baby and was by now hugely pregnant. We persuaded her to take maternity leave and welcomed Sharifa temporarily back into our household.

Latifa and family had moved into the house immediately in front of ours. David was delighted to find that Farid and his old sparring partner, Rukshana, were living right at the bottom of the garden, and the three children spent a lot of time together either in our compound or at Latifa's.

Latifa arrived one evening, with half an uncooked chicken on a plate, saying, 'We can't eat a whole one so you can have this and next week you can buy a chicken and give us half.'

Next day, she appeared with another half chicken on a plate. 'One of my hens crowed this morning so we had to kill it. It brings bad luck on a house when a hen starts crowing,' she announced by way of explanation. A few days later another of Latifa's chickens found its way rather abruptly into our respective cooking pots. It broke a leg falling of its perch in a tree.

We ate rather a lot of chickens in our first weeks back in Mazar but I was not prepared to join in Latifa's next culinary venture – boiled sheep' heads. I tried. Jon and Daud tried, but we hated them. David refused point blank. The smell as they cooked was vile and the taste was not any better – very, very sheepish. And, no, I did not try the eyeballs.

Once again, we organised an outing to the shrine during the forty days after Nau Roz – seven women and an assortment of children and babies. We met at the gate to the shrine, each of us laden with bags and bundles containing blankets to sit on and things to contribute to our communal picnic. Finding one of the few unoccupied places in the shade of some trees, we spread our blankets.

I found myself thinking back to the previous year when the young and giggly Marzia had been with us. Confident that Hazrat-i-Ali would intercede on her behalf and help her to find a husband, she had been convinced the future held happiness and fulfilment for her and her daughter. I had hoped she would join us but Ghulam Ali had refused permission.

Sharifa had lost no time in updating me on the situation as soon as I had returned from leave. 'You know they were staying with us after their marriage?' she asked. 'Well, you can imagine how furious Jawad was and to make it worse Ghulam Ali never paid the *gala*. There were always excuses – his stock had been delayed, he couldn't get his tenants out. Then he said there were problems sorting out Marzia's passport and visa for Iran.'

Incensed that he was clearly not going to get any money, Jawad finally told Ghulam Ali to take Marzia and get out of his house. The couple moved into a mean, poorly furnished two-roomed house in town.

'By then,' continued Sharifa, 'Marzia was afraid to ask any questions. Ghulam Ali's temper is worse than Jawad's and he is a liar. No one can believe anything he says.'

'One day, Marzia heard Ghulam Ali arguing with someone about the rent, but he did not tell her what the problem was. A

few days later, they came back from the bazaar to find thieves
had stolen everything from the house – even the light bulbs.
Reza has agreed they can live in his house until Marzia's visa is
ready. Ghulam Ali told him it would take a few days, but that
was weeks ago.'

I wondered how Marzia was feeling. Could she still believe
what her husband told her about their rosy future in Iran?
Did she convince herself that things would be better? Did
the respect and increase in status she gained from having a
husband make up for such a miserable start to her marriage?
Did she regret praying so fervently for a husband?

Latifa laughingly shook me out of my reflections on Marzia's
problems to demand that I take some photographs. I had taken
the first when an angry shout came from a neighbouring group
of women.

While Sharifa yelled back at them, Latifa explained, 'That
is Rasool Pahlwan's new wife and she is annoyed that you are
taking her photograph.' As I began to protest my innocence,
Latifa laughed at Sharifa's final retort in the angry exchange.

'The silly cow', she said, 'said you were going to send her
picture to the foreign newspapers. Sharifa's just told her that,
outside of Mazar-i-Sharif no-one has even heard of her, and
the foreign newspapers would not want her picture anyway.'

Sharifa, the light of battle in her eye, would have continued
the slanging match, but Maryam and Fatima calmed her,
pulling her down beside them. The other group, still muttering
to themselves, then subsided, and I allowed myself to glance
over in their direction.

Rasool Pahlwan was a powerful commander, so powerful
it was said that even General Dostum was afraid of him.
Peace initiatives between President Rabbani and Dostum had
reputedly failed because it was in Rasool Pahlwan's financial
interests to have the war continue. He was labelled a cruel man
(quite a condemnation in a country where cruelty – in Western
eyes – often seemed to be the norm) who ordered the disposal
of all who crossed him – including girls who did not want to
be numbered amongst his many wives.

The new wife – 'his eleventh' confided Latifa, though Sharifa contradicted her, saying she was only wife number nine – was decked out in her wedding gold. Vast quantities of it gleamed at her throat, ears, wrists and fingers. Her clothes – part of her wedding trousseau – of synthetic shiny material, were loud and garish. Her small face was hard and she chewed gum and smoked cigarettes, as did several of her companions.

I remembered being frightened of girls like that at school – *teuchters* we called them. As I watched them, fascinated, the expression 'gangsters' molls' seemed the most apt description.

One young woman stood out in stark contrast. She was dressed in denim jeans, the rolled-up sleeves of her jacket showing tattooed forearms. Her hair was cut very short and she wore neither make up nor jewellery. Latifa noticed the direction of my gaze and grinned. 'She's the bodyguard. Do you have women like her in your country?'

'What do you mean?' I asked cautiously.

'You know, women who like women the way men do.' She laughed, rolling her eyes expressively. I wanted to say that even if the woman was a lesbian, as Latifa was suggesting, there was nothing wrong with that but, while I was still struggling with the complexities of Western political correctness and Afghan culture, Maryam suggested we move.

'These are not good people,' she said primly. 'What nice girl would want to marry Rasool Pahlwan?'

Gathering our belongings together, we wandered off in search of a less dangerous spot where I could take photos of our party without fear of suddenly being attacked.

The women sprawled on the ground, relaxed and happy. We watched the other groups of women surrounding us, spotting one or two other foreign women wandering amongst the crowds. They did not notice me, and, not wanting to hear their remarks about 'how colourful' it all was and 'how friendly' Afghan women were, I made no move to greet them.

After the previous year's *mela* one woman told me she had been to the shrine but, though it had been 'quite interesting', had soon become bored 'sitting around doing nothing'. This, from a woman whose organisation expected her to teach expatriate staff about the culture of Afghanistan.

When it was time to go I felt a lump in my throat: while on leave I had decided not to extend my contract beyond the following March, and I realised that although my friends and I would see each other almost every day, we would never again attend the spring *mela* together.

David was four years old and would soon need to start school. I knew I could not devote sufficient time to 'home schooling' as some of the other expatriate families did, and was not convinced that this would be the best option for David anyway. Also, after almost ten years of working in Asia, I needed to go back home before it became too late to make the transition successfully. I did not want to be like those expatriates who, having worked overseas for years, neither fitted in to their own culture, nor belonged in the countries where they had been working.

Colleagues and friends were touchingly dismayed when I told them I was leaving after a year. But, as Naeem pointed out, next year was a long way off and I did not often dwell on the thought. There was too much to do.

Now that we had opened the clinic in Mazar, which had only slightly mollified the Minster of Foreign Affairs (who still urged us to open more), the clinic in-charge Mustafa wanted to establish a team of female health volunteers in the district as well. We ran a trial teaching programme, inviting female staff and wives of other staff to be guinea pigs to help us see what adaptations to the course material would be needed for an urban setting.

Sharifa, Latifa, Maryam and Fatima were enthusiastic about the idea. To my surprise, Marzia appeared for class. Normally, Ghulam Ali never allowed her to go anywhere without him. Sharifa explained his change of heart, 'Marzia is pregnant. I persuaded Ghulam Ali that it would be a good idea for her to join the classes, to learn how to be a good mother to his son. He is sure the baby will be a boy, of course.'

I was delighted to be able to see Marzia regularly again,

though I was disturbed by the change in Shahnaz. The chubby, happy little toddler had become so thin and silent and withdrawn that she could have been a different child. Sharifa, with tears in her eyes, said that Ghulam Ali – the man who had promised to love and treat Shahnaz as his own daughter – beat the child with an electric flex.

Before the end of the course, Marzia arrived unexpectedly, with Sharifa, at our house one Friday afternoon. My delight was short lived when I understood the reason for the visit. Her visa for Iran had been granted. Ghulam Ali had given permission for Marzia to accompany Sharifa to the shrine, where the two sisters had been praying for a safe journey. They had called for a fleeting visit before going home.

I hurried off to the kitchen to make tea, blinking back tears. I had almost begun to hope that Ghulam Ali would have to leave Marzia and Shahnaz behind. A very subdued Daud joined me in the kitchen to help with the tea and carry the loaded tray to the living room.

Conversation was strained at first until a giggle from the garden made us look out. David and Shahnaz were playing happily together, splashing about in the paddling pool. At the sound of her daughter's laughter, Marzia commented, 'She really misses David. She loved being here with him every day.' I suggested she bring her over a few more times before she left Mazar, but she admitted Ghulam Ali would not allow it.

'He is too *badguman* [suspicious].' She shrugged, adding, 'Men are all the same. Before we married, I wore lipstick and nail polish but now he objects. They think that once we are married we spend all our lives trying to attract other men. Not that other men will want to look at me soon.' She patted her stomach.

'I thought you didn't want another baby until Shahnaz was older?' I asked.

Marzia shrugged again. 'What I want doesn't matter if it is not what he wants. He wouldn't wait, wanted everyone to know that he was a real man.' With a huge sigh, she said, 'I think my kismet is not good. Nothing has gone right since we married.'

Daud, who had been sitting quietly, suddenly slammed his glass down and walked out. I ached for him, knowing how much Marzia's unhappiness hurt and angered him.

After the months of waiting and worrying about when she would finally leave Mazar-i-Sharif, her departure was unexpectedly abrupt. One day at the end of class she told me quietly that she would not be coming again. 'We leave tomorrow, at six o'clock in the morning, Insh 'Allah.'

Knowing that the chances of us ever meeting again were almost non-existent, I could think of nothing to say and we embraced tightly as tears ran down both our faces. I hugged Shahnaz, hoping that her future would not be as bleak as I feared.

Sharifa was inconsolable. Not only did she weep incessantly for days at the loss of her sister, she was also tormented with guilt at allowing the marriage in the first place. 'Marzia is strong,' I said, 'and her sense of humour will help her to make the best of a bad job.' But she deserved so much more from life than that.

My biggest fears – and Sharifa's – were for Shahnaz. Sharifa had even offered to keep her in Mazar, but Marzia had been horrified at the thought of losing her daughter.

Daud was miserable and angry. When I heard him speaking sharply to a tearful Sharifa one day, I pointed out that she was feeling even worse than he was. 'I don't see why,' he snapped. 'She is the one who sold her sister.'

As after most traumatic events, normal life eventually returned. Marzia and Shahnaz were not forgotten, but the acute pain of their departure whenever we thought of their future, finally eased to a dull ache.

Although Sharifa was still far from happy, the birth of Chaman's son helped stop her brooding about her little sister and niece.

The first training session at the clinic had ended and Mustafa and I, already inundated with requests to join the class from women living nearby, were planning the next course. The donors had agreed funding for the project, including a salary for a local woman to take over from me, and we had discovered Benazir. She was Reza's landlady. When Reza's wife had asked to come to the first course, he had persuaded Benazir to accompany her. If he thought his wife required a chaperone, he need not have worried. Fatima had spent half the time hiding her face in her chaddar, too well indoctrinated by Reza to cope with either contact with other men or hearing anything mentioned about procreation.

Unlike Fatima, Benazir was at ease with Mustafa and the other male staff in the clinic. She was eager and quick to learn and to put into practice what she heard in class.

When we talked about weaning and nutrition, she happily tried out mashed potatoes and vegetables on Malika. After discussing how dirty soothers were one of the prime causes of diarrhoea, she threw Malika's away. When Malika had diarrhoea, Benazir mixed up oral rehydration salts for her and tried, tirelessly, to persuade her neighbours to do the same.

Towards the end of the training session, I asked Mustafa what he thought about offering Benazir the job of female field assistant in the clinic. I thought she was an ideal candidate as, with her warm, down-to-earth manner, she would be able to gain the confidence of the mothers we hoped to reach.

Mustafa nodded, 'Good, I'm glad you think so. I have already asked her. She said she would like to do it, but we have to talk to her husband first. Shall we go together?'

Benazir's husband, Murad, was a tall, good looking man with a luxuriant black moustache and gleaming white smile. Benazir, with her short dark hair framing a creamy complexioned face and her dimpled smile was a beauty, and together they made a handsome couple.

Murad was a civil servant in the Traffic Department, and, like everyone else in Government service, earned barely enough to feed the children. That was why Benazir had split their small house, renting out a portion to Reza. She was clearly the dynamic force in the family, taking responsibility for everything from running the home and managing the finances to organising the older children's schooling.

Despite his friendly manner towards me, five minutes in Murad's company was as much as I could bear. And his insistence on explaining things about Afghanistan and its culture as though I had arrived from another planet only five minutes earlier was extremely irritating.

When he understood that Benazir would be based in Mazar-i-Sharif and not have to make field trips outside the city, he agreed to her working with us. 'Although I know that I can trust *mudder-i-Malika* [Malika's mother] I could not allow her to travel away from home,' he explained. 'People would say bad things about her or laugh at me for allowing it.'

Leaning towards me and speaking slowly and loudly (I thought only the British were supposed to do that!), he said, 'In Afghanistan, many husbands would never allow their wives to go out to work. It is not in our culture, you see. I, myself, don't mind. I am not a country peasant, and I know my wife is a good woman. Do you understand?'

I nodded and smiled, resisting the temptation to say something rude in case he changed his mind about 'allowing' Benazir to join our team. Although I felt sure she would take the job and that asking Murad's permission was a courtesy, I was afraid he might make things difficult.

Now, to complete that team, we needed someone who would take over from me, ensuring that the female health volunteer project would continue in both Mazar and in Hazara Jat when I left.

There was no shortage of women anxious to work for an NGO, even a small one such as ours. Many were nurses, midwives or teachers, but none were prepared to travel outside the city. Mustafa and I also found it depressing at interviews when we heard prospective health educators, referring to the people we hoped to train as health volunteers, use phrases like: 'the trouble is, these people don't know anything' or 'these people cannot learn such things – they are not educated'.

When I heard Nauroz, a friend from Quetta days, had come to Mazar to establish an Afghan NGO, I went to see him. He was an extraordinary man, one of very few who not only talked about women's rights but actually believed in them. His sister, Jemila, had recently completed a two-year midwifery course in Pakistan.

When I asked Nauroz if Jemila would be interested in coming to Mazar to work with us, he replied, 'You must ask her. That's for Jemila to decide.' When I mentioned the need to travel to Hazara Jat, however, his bushy black eyebrows suddenly knit together alarmingly as he frowned.

'Alone?' he demanded. 'You are thinking of sending my sister alone to work in Hazara Jat? She is not a *kharijee* [foreigner] you know.'

When I explained that we could not expect funding for a project that only addressed the needs of city women, Nauroz, a Hazara, readily accepted the point. 'I know how important this work is for the women of Hazara Jat, and I believe Jemila would be excellent in the job. Maybe we can find ways to make it possible?'

After much discussion it was agreed that if Jemila accepted the post she could travel outside the city as long as someone went with her as chaperone, and the driver was a member of Nauroz's family. He left me to contact Jemila myself.

Not only did she agree, with reassuring alacrity, to accept the post, she promised to be in Mazar within a few weeks. Mustafa and I did a gleeful little jig around the staff room when we received this news.

We had the staff we wanted, we had students queuing up to join the course and we had secured funding for the next two to three years. The Female Health Volunteer project was no longer just an experiment – it was a concrete reality and set to continue and expand. We were jubilant.

18

Burnt Macaroni

TRUE TO HER WORD, Jemila arrived, breezing in on a waft of perfume, two weeks later. In her early twenties, she was a strikingly attractive young woman. Taller than the average Hazara women, her movements were full of grace and confidence. A ready smile lit up her eyes, which often crinkled with mischief, and I knew her light skin colouring would make her irresistible to men – and be the envy of women.

She was thrilled to be back in Afghanistan, which she had left as a refugee when still a small child. As it would be a few months before her mother joined her in Mazar, Jemila was especially pleased by the prospect of being free to enjoy city life – knowing she could twist her brother Nauroz around her little finger.

Before setting the course material for the next group of students, we carried out a house-to-house health survey to learn as much as possible about the existing health status of women and children in the area. The questionnaire covered diarrhoea, children's other illnesses, infant mortality and antenatal care.

An appeal for volunteers to join the survey team produced a wonderful mix of women, some of whom were literate and able to team up with those unable to read and write. Mustafa's field assistant, Sharif, brought his wife, Chaman, who brought her sister-in-law, Aliya. Benazir found two stunningly beautiful girls from the university. Mustafa, Sharif and Hussain immediately volunteered to accompany any women who felt shy about knocking on doors. To their intense disappointment, neither of the students, Shoguffa nor Shafika, felt they needed a chaperone.

We spent many days acting out role-plays on conducting interviews and completing the questionnaires. Knowing they would be entering houses which might be dirty, and would meet mothers who were ignorant about hygiene or how to feed their children properly, I wanted to be sure the interview team would not display disgust or pity – a response guaranteed to put any mother on the defensive.

The survey results were much as we had expected. The total population surveyed was just over 5000, of whom 1400 were children under the age of five. Over 25 per cent of those children had suffered from at least one episode of diarrhoea in the previous two weeks while 13 per cent had had diarrhoea in the last twenty-four hours.

Six per cent of children under five had died within a year, the majority of those deaths (38 per cent) caused by diarrhoeal diseases. As a child killer, respiratory infections came a close second at almost 23 per cent.

The figures did not make encouraging reading, particularly as the area was by no means one of the poorest in the city. Most of the men were working; they had access to clean drinking water and the population was young with the majority of the mothers interviewed still under thirty-five.

Jemila and Benazir pored over the statistics with Mustafa, Sharif and Hussain. Jemila, her midwifery training coming to the fore, was particularly troubled by the number of miscarriages that had been reported. 'Do you realise', she demanded angrily of the room at large, 'one in ten pregnancies ends in miscarriage? And, look at that,' her finger stabbed at another row of figures, 'almost every mother questioned said they had taken medicines during pregnancy, though not *one* of them had ever had an antenatal check-up!'

Benazir, who had suffered two miscarriages as well as losing a baby in infancy, blushed as she spoke up, 'I never went for an antenatal check during any of my pregnancies. I didn't know such things were important before I came to class, nor that it can be dangerous to take drugs during pregnancy.

'There's no point in getting angry, Sharifa. That won't make people change. It only makes them feel guilty. I don't like to think that maybe it was my fault I lost my babies.'

Jemila nodded. 'I'm sorry. You are right,' she said, putting her arm round Benazir's shoulder. 'We have a big challenge in front of us, but at least we know now what topics we need to teach.' She gave Benazir a quick hug, saying, 'Come on teacher, let's get the timetable worked out.'

I loved working with the clinic staff, whose enthusiasm for everything they did generated an air of excitement and fun throughout the day. Best of all, they worked together as a real team.

The men in the clinic were so different from men like Reza and Ismail: they gave me hope for the future of Afghanistan and for the women. Mustafa had grown up a refugee in Pakistan. After finishing school he had worked for a foreign health NGO before doing his own two-year paramedic training.

Unlike Reza, Mustafa was used to women's presence in the work place and he treated them no differently from his male colleagues – even to the extent of forgetting we were women and slapping whichever of us was next to him heartily on the back when he told a joke.

At lunchtimes there was always much laughter, and although there was a great deal of joking and banter, it never had the sexual innuendo of many of the things said amongst some of the office staff.

The clinic cook, Habibullah, was teased about his unadventurous style of cooking. Once, when I had suggested using the wonderfully sweet dried apricots – *kishta* – he, not understanding I had meant as a dessert, had turned them into a savoury stew. Desperate for a change from the monotonous diet of rice and red kidney beans, the staff presented him with a packet of macaroni. He boiled it, added a couple of tomatoes and served it up with dry bread.

He served this unappetising meal once a week until one day he burnt it. To his astonishment, instead of being told off, everyone fought over the crunchy burnt bits, which were the tastiest thing in the dish. From then on he was expected to burn the dish every week. The poor man had a terrible job cleaning the enormous cooking pot afterwards.

It wasn't that there were never any disagreements between the staff. Benazir complained that Jemila looked down on her because she was not properly qualified. 'I have asked her many times to show me how to hear a baby's heartbeat, but she never has. Maybe she doesn't want me to know as much as she does?'

When I mentioned this to Mustafa, he suggested inviting everyone to a meeting at which grievances could be discussed. I agreed, though I doubted if Benazir, or anyone else, would speak openly in front of colleagues. To my surprise, she did, and was able to explain how she felt without becoming angry or upset.

Jemila hadn't realised how she was undermining Benazir's confidence and was apologetic. The two women organised a timetable of teaching sessions so that Jemila could share her knowledge with Benazir. Then together they accused Mustafa of making arbitrary decisions concerning the clinic opening times without consulting anyone.

In the summer, because of the fierce heat, Mustafa decided to start the clinic work earlier in the morning, when it was a little cooler. He had sent the driver to collect Jemila and Benazir without telling them they were expected to begin work an hour earlier than usual.

The meetings did not take place every week. There was often too much work, and sometimes no-one had anything they particularly wanted to raise, but at least everyone knew there was a way of sitting down and solving problems through open discussion and negotiation.

If only problems between Latifa and Reza could be solved so sensibly. Unfortunately, the situation between them had worsened too much to be put right. Naeem had tried to achieve this over *Eid* – a time when old enmities are traditionally forgiven and forgotten when everyone shakes hands and swears everlasting friendship. The uneasy truce, pledged over a plate of sweetmeats, had lasted about five days.

The situation was only finally resolved when Reza 'accidentally' bumped into Latifa, causing her to drop a tray of tomatoes she had just washed. The clatter and shrieks from the kitchen had everyone rushing from their desks to find Latifa, amidst the squashed tomatoes, brandishing a knife at Reza, who was standing with his arms wide in a gesture of injured innocence.

Naeem gave up at that point. 'All right, I accept you two can't be friends and I don't care if you hate each other – just stop fighting at work. Next time anything like this happens, I'll deduct two weeks' wages from you both.' That threat kept them quiet for a while but the tension was ever present.

One evening I saw Latifa marching up our path. From the determined set of her shoulders I guessed there was trouble ahead. By the time she was sitting down, tea in front of her, she seemed less resolute. 'Come on, Latifa,' I urged, 'just say it, whatever it is.'

Drawing a deep breath, she began, 'There is no easy way to say this. I have come to complain about Ismail's behaviour.'

This was a surprise. I had supposed there was going to be a tirade against Reza. Not expecting to hear anything particularly heinous, I nodded encouragingly.

'This afternoon, he tried to kiss me.'

Choking on a mouthful of tea, I spluttered, 'Where?' Pointing to the corner of her mouth, she replied, 'Here.'

'I meant,' I tried again, 'where did it happen?'

'In the *dalrez* [hallway] at the office. He said he loved my mole.' She pointed to the beauty spot above her top lip. 'Then he said he loved me, and tried to kiss me.'

The conversation, unexpected in the first place, suddenly seemed so utterly bizarre that I had to smother the laughter that threatened to explode. Latifa was not remotely amused.

I said I would have to speak to Naeem in the morning, though I expected her to tell me not to say anything to anyone. Often people bringing complaints against someone backed down when told their name would have to be mentioned in an investigation of the situation. She nodded agreement, 'Yes, you ask him. Ask what game he is playing? You know this is a very bad thing to do in Afghanistan. I haven't told anyone because if my husband hears, he might kill Abdul Ali.'

'Has this anything to do with Reza?' I asked. 'Is he encouraging Ismail to make trouble?'

Latifa shook her head. 'I don't know. He hates me, but he wasn't there today. You know that Reza also tried this with me?'

'I knew something had happened to stop all the joking between you.'

'Yes, I used to be happy at work, when we all had fun together. But he didn't know when to stop. He thought I was offering something else.

'One day when you and Naeem had gone to the bazaar, Reza came into the kitchen and put his arms round me. He asked directly if I would have sex with him. I told him I was married and I loved my husband. But he thought I was teasing him and wouldn't accept it. When I finally made him understand that I was not interested in him, he became angry. That's why he hates me.'

Next morning I called Ismail into my office. Like Latifa the evening before, I suddenly found it was not an easy subject to raise. Drawing a deep breath I repeated what Latifa had said. He turned white. I never saw anyone change colour so dramatically before – his face, even his lips went as white as paper and he shook, literally, from head to foot. I have never been sure, either then or now, if it was with fear or rage.

'Call her in here,' he hissed, through trembling lips.

Latifa came in, eyes flashing with the light of battle. They raged and roared, too fast for me to follow – though I caught enough to understand each was calling the other a liar, plus hurling a few choice obscenities at each other.

Naeem and Jon became involved, questioning them both together and separately. We discussed the problem over and over, going round in circles, but it was an impossible situation. There were no witnesses. Latifa could not prove that Ismail had tried to kiss her; he could not prove he had not.

While I knew Ismail was a sexually frustrated young man who would almost certainly leap at any opportunity offered for a sexual liaison, I also felt that he would be too afraid to take the chance with a married woman, especially so close to home.

He was deeply hurt that I did not believe that Latifa was lying, simply to cause trouble for him. For her part, Latifa felt badly let down when I explained we could not dismiss Ismail for something that could not be proved. I don't think either of them ever quite forgave me for not being able to come down firmly for or against one of them.

Reza went around looking smug with an 'I told you so' expression. The incident proved his point entirely that allowing women out of their houses led to trouble.

I thought of the struggle Western women had faced – were still facing – in their fight to be treated as respected, equal partners in the work place. It was sad to realise that Afghan women – and men – were going to have to repeat the mistakes and face the same problems in the process as we did. There seemed no way to circumvent the 'growing pains' arising from such dramatic upheavals within a society.

At least the young men and women in the clinic, showing each other mutual respect, gave me hope that, one day in Afghanistan, the dinosaur thinking of people like Reza and Ismail would become extinct.

We were still reeling from the shock waves of Ismail being accused of kissing Latifa when Sharifa announced that Jawad had left her. She had no idea where he had gone or when, indeed if, he would come back.

Their marriage had continued to deteriorate, even after Marzia's departure. Jawad, still without a job and increasingly short-tempered, had continued to provoke endless arguments. 'Whether I try to keep the peace by saying nothing or try to reason with him, it makes no difference,' she once explained. 'He gets more and more *jiggerkhon* [angry – a wonderfully descriptive word more appropriately translated as 'choleric', since *jigger* means liver and *khon* is blood] until he lashes out with his fists, threatening that he will leave me. Then he storms out of the house. When he comes back he is sulky.'

This time, she feared he really meant to leave her. 'I don't know where he is,' she wept. 'He went out as usual after an argument . . . said he was leaving . . . but I didn't believe him. He always comes home . . . but not last night.' Convulsed with sobs, she suddenly wailed, 'My life is over, all because of a shirt button not sewn on.'

'Perhaps', I suggested, 'he meant to return but was caught by the curfew and stayed with friends. Or maybe he stayed out to give you a fright. He'll probably be home tonight or tomorrow, expecting you to be sorry.'

I was wrong. Jawad did not come home. A few days later, Sharifa received a message from one of his friends that he had gone to Hazara Jat to join Hisb-i-Wadhat in Bamiyan. There were more tears. 'He might get killed if they send him where the fighting is! What shall I do? How can I manage without him?' she wailed.

'I expect you'll manage an awful lot better without him than with him,' I replied, perhaps insensitively. 'He spent most of what you earned. Now you will have more money and one less mouth to feed. You won't have to be afraid of going home to arguments and beatings.'

Sharifa shook her head mournfully, saying, 'In your country it is all right for women to be alone, but here a woman's life is nothing if she has no husband. No one respects a woman on her own.'

She had practical concerns too. 'I am afraid at night. Thieves will come to rob us if they know there is only a woman and children in our tent.' Knowing how small and weedy Jawad was, I could not imagine him doing much in the way of protecting his wife and children.

'You don't have anything worth stealing,' I pointed out, hoping to reassure Sharifa that a visit from thieves was unlikely.

'That makes it even worse. They would probably kill us if they didn't find any money.'

Sharifa's neighbours rallied round. They offered their sons as watchmen and a series of young men were despatched to sleep on her rooftop each night. Other women offered to watch the children until she came home from work. When Jawad was supposed to be watching over them, the little ones sometimes wandered off so that, when she came home in the evening, Sharifa had to search the camp to find them.

I told her to bring her clothes to our house and wash them in the machine while she was working. I would return from work some days to find the washing lines full of her children's clothes and Sharifa locked in the bathroom enjoying the last of the hot water for her shower.

She had days when she was really down, especially after a night trying to reassure crying children that their father was going to come back. 'It makes me mad', she remarked, 'that they cry for him and miss him so much. I always did everything for them. He did nothing. All the little ones remember is that he bought them sweets on Fridays. The big ones know he gave me a terrible life, and they don't talk much about him, but the babies cry at night.'

In time, the children stopped asking about their father. Sharifa began to start appreciating that she no longer had to go home worrying about what might trigger off an abusive outburst from Jawad. 'Neighbours and friends have been good,' she said one day. 'I couldn't have coped without them. Maybe because everyone has so many problems in their lives nowadays they want to help each other,'

Whenever I saw her sunny smile, I privately hoped that Jawad would never come back, and wished that he had gone away before Marzia had married Ghulam Ali. The two sisters would have had easier, more contented lives without their respective husbands. But, maybe not – being a wife was still so important to Afghan women.

Sharifa announced that she wanted to be sterilized. Mustafa, when asked to make the necessary arrangements at the hospital, was reluctant to do so. When I asked why he was being uncooperative, he replied, 'This is the third time she has sent me to arrange her operation. I go to a lot of trouble fixing the date and time and asking the doctor for a reduced fee – then she changes her mind. I don't want to do it again because I need to keep a good friendship with this doctor for the sake of my other patients.'

I knew that after her abortion, Sharifa had talked about it but had abruptly changed her mind. She had not kept the appointment Mustafa had made for her with the surgeon. I had not known there had been a second appointment.

Mustafa said, 'It was last winter, while you were away, and it was very embarrassing. It was all arranged and she had even reached the operating theatre when she changed her mind.'

A slightly sheepish Sharifa explained, 'I was lying on the table looking at some dirty instruments in a metal bowl thinking that they needed cleaning. The doctor came in and I suddenly became afraid. I knew if they used those dirty instruments on me, I would die.' She giggled at the memory. 'I leaped off the table and ran. The doctor and nurses were too surprised to do anything until I was out the door.'

Now I understood why Mustafa was not enthusiastic about making a third appointment for Sharifa. We pleaded with him and, being Mustafa, a thoroughly nice person, he agreed. This time, Sharifa saw it through.

'What I don't understand', I said to Mustafa after we had visited her – very much alive and complaining about the pain – the next day, 'is why now? When Jawad was here and she risked becoming pregnant again, she ran away. Now that he's gone, she doesn't need to worry about becoming pregnant. Or has she heard he is coming back?'

Mustafa shrugged, but I was puzzled by his obvious struggle to hide a smile. It was several days before the penny dropped.

I didn't know whether to be amused or angry with myself. After more than two years in Afghanistan I was still so lacking in perception that it had never crossed my mind Sharifa might have found someone to cheer herself up in Jawad's absence.

When I hesitantly asked Benazir if she had heard any rumours about Sharifa, she roared with laughter at my innocence. 'Everyone has known for weeks,' she said. 'It was so funny when you were talking the other day about it being unfair on Farid always being late finishing work after dropping Sharifa at home. Everyone in the staff room had the giggles about that.'

I stared at Benazir in open-mouthed astonishment. 'You

mean, it's . . . Sharifa's . . .' I spluttered, 'Sharifa and Farid?'
Wiping away her tears of laughter, Benazir nodded. Farid
was a driver, a young bachelor, and some eight to ten years
Sharifa's junior.

Once I knew about the affair, I looked for tell-tale signals.
Once, when Sharifa decided, in an unusual fit of domestic
enthusiasm, to clean the carpets in our house, she requested
that Farid be sent from the office to help her lift them. It was
late afternoon before he returned, although we only had two
carpets. On another occasion, I glimpsed Farid and Sharifa in
the office jeep in the bazaar, long after Farid had supposedly
gone home.

But they were very discreet and Sharifa never mentioned her
affair to me. Nor, as far as I knew, did she confide in anyone
else. It was one of those open secrets that everyone knew about
but ignored in front of the people concerned. I could even have
believed that it was no more than speculation and gossip until
the day Farid's mother arrived in the clinic, asking to speak
privately to me.

Barely waiting until the usual pleasantries were over, she
made her plea, 'I want you to stop this thing between Sharifa
and my son. He is supposed to be saving to marry his fiancée
but he gives all his money to that woman.'

When I asked why she could not speak to her son, or Sharifa,
she replied, wearily, 'I have tried. He just gets angry. He
threatened to beat his sister if he ever heard Sharifa's name
in her mouth again. That is why I want you to talk with that
woman before she destroys my son's life.'

I didn't see what I could do. Latifa was in no doubt: 'Tell her
you will throw her out of her job if she doesn't leave him alone.'

'I can't do that. I have no right to interfere in the staff's
private lives.'

Latifa, shaking her head despondently, refused tea and left.
I talked it over with Maryam, a frequent visitor to our house
now that it was the mulberry season.

We had two mulberry trees, laden with fruit, in our
compound. Spreading a huge plastic sheet on the ground we

sent an obliging child up the tree to shake the branches. Down tumbled vast quantities of berries, ranging in colour from white through dark red, deep purple to shiny, luscious black – our favourites. Waiting just long enough to rinse them in icy cold water, we fell on the sticky fruit, cramming handfuls at a time into our juice stained mouths.

We were not the only ones to enjoy the harvest: David's tortoise adored them. At four o'clock every day, he reversed out of the cool hole he had dug in the mud boundary wall and made his way to the mulberry trees. For half an hour he hoovered up the fruit on the ground, ambled round the compound and returned to his hole.

Maryam advised me to say nothing to Sharifa. 'She will deny it and tell Farid who will be furious with his mother. Naeem told Farid that people were talking but it is difficult when no one can say anything directly.'

I was happy to let the matter drop thinking that it was about time Sharifa had some fun in her life for a change.

19

Wandering Navels

ALTHOUGH I HAD long since become accustomed to the staff foraging for anything useful I had thrown out, I felt Sharifa was taking re-cycling too far the day she asked if I had thrown away any used gum.

I offered her a fresh piece from the packet but she shook her head. 'It has to be already chewed,' she explained. 'It's good for joint pains. Ah, here's some,' she cried in triumph.

After softening it slightly by working it between thumb and finger, she stuck it to the underside of her afflicted toe joint.

I wondered if Wrigley would be interested in an advertising campaign featuring the unusual curative properties of pre-chewed gum. But then, I don't suppose toothpaste makers or battery manufacturers had ever considered the medical uses to which Afghans put their products.

Knowing my fascination with local folk remedies, people took a delight in telling me about the many and varied 'cures' they knew. Reza told me that Kabul people used toothpaste as a substitute for an egg poultice, traditionally used for chest complaints.

'Kabul people like to think they are being very modern so they try out new things,' he said. 'For instance, for toothache, instead of a hot nail applied to the painful tooth, the filter from a cigarette is packed against it.'

Jemila had laughed. 'Surely no one believes that will work! Worms in the tooth cause toothache.'

Mustafa hooted with derision. 'Some health worker, you are, Jemila, if you believe that.' She bridled.

'I have used a special herb that had to be put in boiling water. When I covered my head with a towel and breathed in the steam I saw little white worms drop into the water.' She looked at our disbelieving expressions. 'It's true. I saw them with my own eyes, I tell you.'

Reza, swiftly changing the subject from toothache, interrupted. 'Kabul people also believe that a battery tied to the navel will cure *'naf raft'*.'

This gave everyone pause for thought. *Naf raft*, literally translated as 'lost belly button', was a strange complaint that afflicted many Hazaras.

Presenting in the form of unexplained abdominal pain, it was sometimes accompanied by nausea, vomiting or diarrhoea. Everyone knew a variety of cures, designed to encourage the belly button to return to its proper place.

The simplest method was to lay the patient down, insert the handle of a large spoon in the navel and turn it, as though winding the belly button back into place. If that didn't work, the patient could be suspended from a tree branch or house rafter, while someone pulled sharply on his/her legs.

The most dramatic cure was administered while the patient was asleep. Some dry earth was placed in a piece of cloth, the ends gathered and tied together with thread. Jemila described the next stage, 'You soak the bundle in kerosene. Then you set it alight inside a tea glass and tip the glass upside down over the *naf.*'

The flame would be extinguished as soon as the oxygen in the glass was used up but not, however, before the patient was thoroughly and painfully awoken. There was general agreement that the battery cure sounded a lot more pleasant.

No one could explain exactly what caused the navel to disappear in the first place. I wondered if it was a pulled abdominal muscle, which could, at times be sufficiently painful to cause nausea, but Mustafa shook his head. 'A pulled muscle would not get better so quickly,' he said.

'Mustafa, if anyone tried hanging me from a tree and yanking on my legs, I'd be pretty quick to say that I was better. Especially if I thought they might try setting my belly button alight next!'

Feeling I should contribute something to the collection of

strange cures, I told them that some people in my country believed you could cure warts by tying a thread tightly round it and burying a second thread in the earth. By the time the buried thread had rotted, the wart would have gone.

'Oh,' said Jemila, delightedly, 'that sounds better than our cure. I went to a mullah when I had warts on my hand. He told me to go to the grave of a very holy man and sweep it clean every night for a month, then find a frog and put a big stone on top of it. He said when the frog had rotted, my warts would have disappeared.'

'Did it work?' we wanted to know.

'No, my frog escaped,' laughed Jemila, 'after I'd done all that sweeping.'

By then, Jemila was doing most of the teaching on the training course by herself and was preparing to start a weekly clinic for pregnant women and children under three years and under.

We had hoped to spend time in Lal at a teaching camp, organised for the paramedics. Reluctantly, we had had to cancel this when fighting between factions of Hisb-i-Wadhat had erupted in the area. Rumours that it was likely to continue throughout the summer months made it too risky to go ahead. For a time, I even feared I would not be able to go to Waras. Then came a lull in the hostilities, too late for us to call together the staff for the camp, but providing me with an opportunity to make a brief, final visit. The thought of leaving Afghanistan without saying goodbye to friends in Waras was unbearable.

Once again, my room at the clinic was the scene of a non-stop tea party. The joy of being back was, however, tempered by sadness that it was for the last time. When they heard that I was leaving Afghanistan, the women harangued me for what they considered an unforgivable defection. They made it difficult for me to justify my decision.

'David needs to go to school,' I said.

'There are schools in Mazar,' they said. 'Why, does he have to go so far away for his education?' As far as they were concerned, schooling meant learning to read and write, which must surely be learned in the same way everywhere.

They could understand that after being away from my own country and my family for so long I had a need to go back. But they thought a few months would be sufficient. 'After all,' said Jemila, 'you have family here too. Does your Waras family not mean anything to you, that you can go away and leave us?'

Nickbacht burst out, 'We never thought you would leave us when we still have so much to learn. Can't you still come once a year to teach?'

To the women, as a foreigner, I was wealthy beyond their dreams, and telling them I could not afford the airfare to return only made them laugh. 'Even if I was staying in Afghanistan I could not spend every summer here. Already the other clinic in-charges are angry because I have been here so often instead of going to their clinics. They also want a health volunteer project.'

I explained about Jemila taking over from me in Mazar and assured them she would come to run a refresher course. 'Please,' I begged, 'let's enjoy the time we have left together and not think about saying goodbye yet. Tell me the news about your work and everything that has happened since I was last here.'

Thoughts of my departure were pushed resolutely away while the women vied with each other to bring me up to date on news of births, deaths, marriages, grasshopper infestations, crop yields and other important things. Aziza proudly showed off Sultan, who at a year old was a plump, cheerful little boy.

Although I had not found a training course for Suraya in Mazar, I had heard that the new doctor at Oxfam's Panjau clinic was going to run courses. I promised I would ask her to give a place to Suraya.

When I asked after the twins, Suraya's eyes filled with tears. 'Did no one tell you?' she whispered. I shook my head sadly, realising from her anguished expression that the twins had died.

Suraya had continued to visit them regularly, though less frequently, and when they continued to thrive, surviving their second winter, she had felt able to discontinue the visits when her own baby (another daughter) was born. In the spring, the boys had contracted pneumonia, but their father had not sought help until it was too late.

I dreaded to think how the boys' mother, that exhausted, unhappy woman, was coping. For Suraya, who had given so much of herself to keeping them alive, it was almost as though her own children had died. She looked at me beseechingly, 'The mothers and children here desperately need more qualified women health workers. There is so much to be done.'

I went to see Dr Aziza, who had requested we meet to discuss how our two organisations could work together more. We met at the Oxfam office in Waras' main bazaar. It was a non-productive meeting. In her mid to late twenties, Shaghlah was an attractive but haughty single woman. Afghans would describe her as too proud. Her idea of mutual co-operation was to suggest that we send a worker once a month from our clinic to her clinic (five hours by road) to treat their tuberculosis patients with our medicines.

I asked about her health-worker training course for women. Dr Aziza became quite animated for a few moments as she explained how she trained young girls from villages around Panjau. However, when I suggested Suraya as a possible candidate, Aziza promptly rejected her.

'*Married* ladies can't do this work,' she explained kindly, as though talking to a simpleton. 'Their husbands won't allow them to attend classes or go out to work. Besides, they have to look after their own families.'

Pointing out that the women I had trained were all married with children, I made a last plea that an exception was made for someone as highly motivated as Suraya, whose husband was also eager for her to do the training. Aziza seemed to be considering when I blew it by mentioning that Suraya would have to bring her baby along. 'It won't be a problem,' I added hastily, 'because her older daughter will take care of her while Suraya is in class.'

Aziza shook her head, emphatically. 'I can't allow it. A baby in the dormitory would disturb the others and prevent them studying.'

Miserably, I reported back to an indignant Suraya. 'Why does she say married women can't work?' she demanded. 'What does she, coming from Kabul, know about the people here? Teaching young girls about pregnancy and deliveries is important. But she should realise they will not be able to teach older women, nor help at the time of delivery, especially not in Panjau, where the women do not have the freedom we have.' Next day I used the hated radio to contact Rob, the British volunteer who was about to leave for home after acting as programme manager in Panjau. I explained the problem about the baby and Aziza's reaction. Although positive Suraya would not allow the class to be interrupted, I could see that a baby in the dormitory might be a problem.

Rob immediately offered the use of his room, saying, 'I'll be leaving soon and can kip down on someone's floor for a night or two. We should be doing all we can to encourage women who want to work in the health field. That's the whole point of the project. I can't understand Aziza's attitude but don't worry, I'll sort it out.'

The course was due to start in three days and I agreed to send Suraya and her children to Panjau on time. An ecstatic Suraya rushed home to make preparations for her departure.

The day before leaving for Panjau, Suraya arrived mid-morning at the clinic. We had two male guests for lunch, foreigners who were accompanying a UN delegation on a tour of Hazara Jat. As we sat down to lunch, the men could not hide their surprise at seeing Suraya join us. 'Is she a patient? Doesn't she mind sitting in mixed company? Is there not another room where she can eat?' they asked.

Laughingly, I explained that Suraya would be mortally offended if told to sit in a room by herself.

This was not what they expected. After all, women in Afghanistan are kept in purdah. They cover their faces in front of strangers, don't eat with men who are not their relatives, and certainly don't go off to residential training courses. One of the men tried again, 'Does she feel she must eat here because you are here? Isn't she embarrassed by such a situation?'

Remembering my own confusion on arriving in Mazar, I bit back a rude retort about development workers being so full of prejudices and misconceptions that they refuse to accept the evidence of their own eyes when it contradicted their preconceived ideas. Instead I explained that Suraya would eat with the staff whether or not I was here, and the only embarrassment she might feel was caused by their neglecting to greet her.

In the morning, half the village turned out to say goodbye. To our dismay, Suraya was home again by evening. Dr Aziza had won – Suraya had been refused a place on the course. She handed me a note from Hussain, Rob's successor, which apologised for the disappointment, reiterated that there was no place on the course for married women with children, and hoped that we would enjoy better co-operation in the future.

Bewildered and bitterly disappointed, Suraya could not understand Aziza's attitude towards her. 'This woman doesn't even know me. How can she be so against me? What did I do to her? I thought Oxfam's programme was to help women go forward, not to push us back.'

Later, I heard from Rob that when he explained that he had sanctioned Suraya's place on the course, Aziza had immediately burst into tears and stormed off to see Hussain. Presumably unable to cope with Aziza's tears he had immediately reversed the decision.

Did Aziza, a professional woman unable to find a husband, resent Suraya – a self taught village woman – having the audacity to believe she could have both family and career? Had it been Suraya's husband, father or brothers who were opposed to her attending the training course and working outside her home, there would have been an almighty fuss about men's oppression of women. Aziza's attitude crushed Suraya's spirit far more effectively than any man could ever have done.

Despite the bad feelings Shaghlah's behaviour engendered, my last weeks in Waras were not all gloomy. David was enjoying life and, at the grown-up age of four, he had become very independent, spending whole days on the mountainside with his friends Afzal or Iqbal helping to herd their flocks.

In the evenings, desperately tired but glowing with health and ecstatically happy, he returned, ravenously hungry, to the clinic. He enjoyed in those days a freedom that he would probably never know again. I was glad that I did not always know what he got up to when not under my supervision, especially when I heard that he had climbed onto the back of a sleeping cow notorious for her cantankerous behaviour. Evenings at home in Daud's village were filled with fun and games and laughter – supposedly for the children, but equally enjoyed by the adults. The younger children always demanded an appearance by the *khooroo* [chicken in Hazaragi dialect]. A blanket was spread on the ground, the two top corners folded into the centre as though making a giant paper aeroplane. Qurban lay down, fitting his arms into the folds and was neatly rolled up in the rest of the blanket. This was the chicken, complete with a pointed beak, and the children vied with each other to feed it, holding outstretched, cupped hands while Qurban pecked away.

The young girls danced. The more self-assured could perform the entire routine, complete with words, without pausing; others, overcome by shyness, collapsed in giggling heaps on the floor.

There was a wonderful game called *cor jangi* [blind fighting]. Two blindfolded contestants knelt on the floor, facing each other. Each held a cloth wound into a soft rope while in the other hand they clutched a corner of a cushion, which they were not allowed to drop. At a signal from Uncle Abdullah, always the master of ceremonies for the evening's entertainment, battle commenced. Neither of the boys (girls don't play such wild games) was allowed take more than one swipe at a time.

The contestants were never sure if they had scored a hit – they simply thumped a cushion as they circled round each other, straining their ears for a sound to betray their opponent's precise position. Some were patient players, others became quickly frustrated, the temptation to get in an extra blow too much to resist. The audience was invariably reduced to rolling on the floor, eyes streaming with tears of laughter at the antics of the boys.

The *haiwan* [animal] was a wondrous creature that rampaged around the room, provoking shrieks of laughter from everyone. It was made with great ingenuity from a couple of blankets with two men's caps for pointed ears. David would beg Daud to lift him onto the creature's back so that he could ride it around the room.

Even he, however, was not brave enough to face down the *dehyo* [an ugly giant]. But then he was not the only one to be afraid of this creature. Marzia was utterly petrified. I thought at first she was play acting but soon realised that when she crouched down, burying her head in her hands at the approach of the *dehyo*, her frightened whimpers and moans were for real.

This creature, which inspired such fear, was one of the boys dressed up wearing a crudely made, two-horned cardboard mask. Eyes glittered devilishly through the cut-out holes, a large belly was created by placing a cushion under the boy's jacket, and a twisted chaddar formed the tail. When he spoke, the *dehyo*'s voice was hoarse and rasping.

The braver children reached out to tug at his tail, making him rush, growling horribly, at them, whereupon with shrieks of half frightened laughter they sought refuge on parents' laps.

I wondered at Marzia being so afraid of a young boy she knew well, a cushion and a cardboard mask. Certainly, the dim lighting of the room (for by then the lamps would be burning low) helped create a spooky atmosphere and the children's shrieks, oscillating between delight and fear, generated an air of near hysteria. To Marzia – and to the other women who, though they laughed at her, would not go outside alone in the dark – the *dehyo* represented a fearful reminder that horrors such as *djinn*, the evil eye and Al Khatoon were lurking, waiting to pounce.

After hearing about the wonders of the city from Aquila, Hassan's wife, Fatima, had been scheming to return with me to Mazar to have false teeth made.

She prodded me into asking permission from Hassan. Hassan's only question about Fatima's visit to Mazar was 'How will she come back?' Luckily, Abdul Ali, the clinic driver, had some work in Mazar a few weeks after my return and could bring Fatima back to Waras with him. Satisfied, Hassan gave his consent.

It was impossible not to become emotional at saying goodbye. I was glad Fatima was coming back to Mazar-i-Sharif with us – and so too, was Chaman, her niece. And when Kulsom's husband told me he would be coming to Mazar to collect books for the schools, I immediately suggested he bring Kulsom with him. If I had been returning by truck, rather than jeep, I would have filled it with friends from Waras – anything to postpone the final farewell.

Tears blinded me when the women gathered to say goodbye with hugs and kisses and I stumbled down the steep path trying to pretend that I would come back to see them all again in the not too distant future.

Travelling was not going to be comfortable – as well as Fatima, little Leila and Chaman, Qurban, had also at the last minute joined the party. He had looked so dejected as we climbed into the jeep that I impulsively told him to jump in. David was ecstatic to have his best friend with him and couldn't understand why I was crying as we moved off slowly through the village.

From Yakolang we spoke on the radio to Jon in Mazar. There had been fighting in the vicinity of Dar-i-Suf and a large-scale build up of troops was taking place. Renewed fighting between the Kabul Government troops and the Dostum/Wadhat opposition was expected after three days, but for now, the road was, in theory, still open to traffic. Reza reckoned we had a twenty four-hour safety margin in case of mechanical problems and we decided against taking a detour that would have added several days to the journey.

20

Drunk Chickens

As NIGHT FELL we still had some miles to go before reaching our stopping place. We were travelling on one of the few stretches of flat road, and from time to time in the distance lights flickered in the darkness. Everyone – even Reza – was becoming increasingly tense and it was a relief when we came within sight of our destination.

Suddenly, from out of the darkness a soldier leapt in front of the vehicle pointing a Kalashnikov. Swearing, Reza slammed on the brakes, switched off the headlights and put on the interior light. The soldier approached, closely followed by several others, all armed. They were, however, friendly – Hisb-i-Wadhat men – billeted in the *chaikhanna* for the night before moving on towards Dar-i-Suf the next day.

They invited us to join them. Reza explained we would prefer to move on, find somewhere less crowded, if the road ahead was safe and we had their permission to proceed. Assuring us that the road was safe all the way to Mazar-i-Sharif, we were waved on our way.

The lights of the *chaikhanna* were still visible behind us when another *mujahid* leapt in front of the jeep. He was pointing a rocket launcher at us. Reza swore again as he skidded to a halt. 'Thank God the brakes are good,' he commented, when we had been waved on, 'If it had taken too long to stop he might have fired that thing. He should have known we had permission to travel or we would have been stopped at the first place.'

As he spoke we heard shots being fired. Reza pulled up. He was becoming irritated now – a bad sign. When Reza became bad tempered he became rude to people, and it is not wise to be rude to people who are pointing Kalashnikovs – firing them even – in one's direction. The soldier would not allow us to continue. Reza demanded that he bring the commander out to speak to him. The soldier said the commander would be angry if he was disturbed. Reza started to climb out of the jeep, using a lot of bad language. The commander was summoned.

While he and Reza were arguing about whether we could continue our journey, one of the soldiers began pacing round the jeep, peering in the windows. As he pulled open the passenger door, Chaman pulled it shut, shouting, 'Ijazat nist!' – 'You have no permission.' The soldier angrily began to tug open the door, just as the commander gave us the go ahead to continue. As we drove away I asked Daud to explain to Chaman that if a *mujahid* pointing a loaded Kalashnikov, wants to open the door he has permission to do so.

'I'm stopping at the next *chaikhanna* we find,' said Reza. 'It's too dangerous to go on in the dark.' After a few more tense but mercifully incident free miles, we trooped wearily into the welcoming light and warmth of a roadside 'hotel'. The place was packed.

The other travellers were refugees returning from Iran. They had suddenly been ordered by the Iranian Government to go home. Thousands had been forcibly transported across the border. The people we met that night had been in trucks going from Yakolang towards Mazar when news of the fighting in Dar-i-Suf had panicked the drivers into returning to Yakolang, abandoning their human cargo on the roadside. During the day's journey we had passed several groups sitting by the roadside or travelling by foot, their small children and few belongings on donkeys they had hired.

While we prepared for bed Chaman became fascinated by the travel alarm clock which I placed near my pillow. When the alarm buzzed in my ear I groped sleepily, not feeling like I had enjoyed a good night's rest, to switch it off. The luminous dial showed two o'clock. Chaman must have moved the alarm setting when she was admiring it earlier.

I snuggled down in my sleeping bag. 'Sister, sister. Is it time to pray?' one of the refugees asked me. Telling her it was too early, I tried again to sleep but it was useless. The woman anxious about her prayers asked every five minutes until she had succeeded in waking almost everyone else – with the exception of Chaman.

By the time the sun came up we were well on our way. The jeep was running well although on the steep passes Daud had to run behind with a heavy rock to throw under the back tyre whenever it stalled. Once Reza had it going he daren't stop again and Daud had to leap and scramble in as best he could. Normally, someone in the front seat would hold open the door to make this acrobatic feat slightly easier to achieve.

Not Chaman, however. Every time Reza started up the pass, she grabbed for the handle, pulling the door shut, instead of opening it. Daud, running as fast as he could, had to first wrestle with the handle to tug the door open enough to allow him to claw his way in. Reza would yell at her to open the door but she would sit, stony faced, ignoring him. I realised that if Daud was not by her side, she refused to acknowledge Reza's existence. I tried yelling at her but she seemed incapable of understanding that Daud was not running alongside the vehicle for the good of his health.

However, it was a beautiful sunny day, we were making good progress and by the time we had breakfasted everyone was in a more cheerful, relaxed mood.

Suddenly, spurts of dust were jumping up in front of the jeep as bullets came zinging around us. Reza stopped and we sat without speaking, scarcely breathing. The firing stopped. Slowly we stepped out of the vehicle. High above us we could just make out two figures on the mountain top. As we stood in the dust, gazing upwards, we heard the drone of a plane.

In a panic, Fatima and Chaman dragging the children, ran to the bottom of the mountain where they huddled fearfully. Having once been in a bombing raid and seen the mountainside being hit more often than the intended target, I stayed where I was. The plane flew over the mountain and we heard the distant crump of a bomb being dropped. The plane circled lazily and flew off.

Reza began shouting up to the soldiers, telling them we were

UN workers and asking permission to proceed. But the wind swept away his words as the soldiers' words went unheard by us. Suspecting that we were not being given permission to carry on, Reza and Daud took turns screaming into the wind. The soldiers screamed back, then we saw them begin to descend towards us.

Chaman was almost hysterical, convinced she was about to be raped – a possibility which had not even entered my head. Fatima was silent but obviously terrified. I was busy removing film from my camera – they could have the camera if they must, but not my precious pictures. I also stashed some cigarettes out of sight, leaving the remainder in the pocket in the door.

One soldier stood above us, his Kalashnikov covering us while his companion approached. Immediately Chaman started sobbing and moaning, 'I am sick, very sick. Please don't touch me. I am sick.' The soldier, ignoring her, demanded that Reza unload the jeep.

Hissing at Chaman to shut up, I moved nearer the soldier and Reza who was assuring him that we were not carrying weapons. The soldier wandered around, peering in the windows. Opening the rear door, he demanded, 'Whose are the cigarettes?' Reza nodded in my direction. 'She has a lot, doesn't she?' remarked the soldier.

Removing two packets from the carton, he glanced at me questioningly. I nodded vigorously. Of course he had permission. When I heard him mention money, I hastily explained that I had none with me. The soldier looked insulted. 'I did not ask you for money. I asked how much money do you want for the cigarettes.' Laughing with relief, I refused his offer of payment. If I had been stuck on top of that mountain with no cigarettes, I would be stopping any vehicle on the road as well.

He explained that having been ordered to halt all traffic, they had stopped us but had no idea what to do next. Calling their commander on a walkie-talkie, they were ordered to check the vehicle for weapons and let us pass. The soldier assured us we would have no more problems as his commander had informed everyone that we were coming through. These soldiers, from the Dostum/Wadhat alliance, were in control of the road all the way to Mazar.

Mazar-i-Sharif had never looked so welcoming as we drove into the city. Even Chaman stopped snivelling and complaining about the dangers of travelling long enough to start gawping at the city sights.

Fatima, as her sister-in-law Aquila had been the previous year, was an easy guest to have around. Chaman took longer to settle in and relax. Her cousin, Daud, sometimes found her difficult to cope with.

Daud returned from taking her on her first outing to the bazaar, absolutely furious, vowing never to go shopping with her again. She had been looking for the rubber sandals everyone wore in the bathroom and about the compound. Daud had taken her to place where such sandals were on sale. 'She tried on hundreds of pairs, but couldn't find any that she liked. Not one pair, out of thousands,' he grumbled.

Even worse, she had been rude to the shopkeepers. 'How', he wondered, 'did she learn to be so insulting to people – she has never been in a bazaar before? I was so ashamed, and then my mother made it even worse.'

He shuddered at the memory, continuing, 'While Chaman was throwing slippers and insults around, my mother was looking at hair combs on another stall. When Chaman decided there was nothing she liked, we started to walk away. The shopkeeper came running after us, shouting. He said my mother was trying to steal from him. She still had a comb in her hand! Everyone was looking at us. I am never, ever taking them shopping again.'

Our house, which had previously seemed large and roomy, shrank when the second batch of guests arrived.

Driver Abdul Ali, his wife Yasmin and their son Iqbal were installed in David's room – in which he never slept anyway in case thieves came again in the night. Hassan, Fatima, Farid, Leila and Chaman slept in Daud's room. Habib, Kulsom and their baby occupied the living room. It was a glorious muddle of a house-party and the weeks that followed, though often chaotic, were wonderfully happy.

If anyone had told me I would spend a month cooking for around fifteen people, I would have laughed, or had hysterics. At home, a dinner party for four had been a major occasion. In my delight at postponing saying goodbye to Waras friends, the logistics of having so many guests had simply not occurred to me.

Daud always helped me in the kitchen in the evenings and Hassan and Abdul Ali were willing kitchen assistants, preparing the salads and slicing up the vast mounds of melons that were required.

Knowing how important it was for a host to be seen to push the boat out by killing something for guests, I felt I should make an effort. Unable to face dealing with a whole goat, I asked Daud to buy some chickens.

Afghan chickens are exceedingly tough. Pressure cooking them for hours still produces something the consistency of leather. The birds are, of course, free range, but poor feeding and all the running around searching for food turns what little fat they have to solid muscle. A feature in the *Guardian Weekly* about tenderising turkeys in Africa by giving them alcohol caught my eye, so we tried our Afghan chickens on Uzbek wine. They loved it, and it worked so amazingly well we enjoyed tender chicken for the first time in years.

I warned Daud not to disclose to our guests what the chickens were washing down their daily bread and grain with – half a bottle a day between them!

Six birds were devoured at a single sitting – including most of the bones, which Afghans crunch up until only tiny splinters remain. Everyone praised the tenderness of the meat, deciding that this was because city chickens were killed at a younger age than country ones.

I felt like a tour guide, taking my group to see the sights of the city, escorting them around the shrine, telling them of its myths and legends.

They were often invited out and wherever they went they were invariably pressed to stay the night.

Fatima, returning from one such overnight visit, said, 'Now I know how you felt in Hazara Jat when people kept insisting you stay the night when you really wanted to go home. It is very difficult to know how to refuse without being rude.'

I was intrigued to learn that she, and the others, felt as I did about this enforced hospitality. I had thought it was because I was a foreigner that hosts were always trying to make me stay for longer, and that it was because I was a foreigner that I did not know how to refuse graciously. Seeing my friends searching desperately for a polite way to refuse an invitation, or cut short a visit was rather enjoyable: they had always left me to flounder alone trying to justify my refusal to stay the night.

Fatima had her new teeth fitted, which made her seem ten years younger. I teased her that people at home would think Hassan had found a new wife in Mazar. She blushed with pleasure. Freed from her usual heavy workload and eating well, she had gained weight, which contributed to making her much healthier looking.

I enjoyed coming home after work to find the women, often with Sharifa, waiting on the veranda for me, ready to tell me about what they had seen and done. Every day brought something new into their lives – the sight of tanks trundling through the streets, or camels (an animal not seen as far north as Waras) pulling carts. The staggering array of foodstuffs and other goods in the bazaar was a source of wonder, as were the women's fashions and hairstyles, which were discussed at great length.

Despite seeing Jemila and Benazir going bare-headed at work, the women kept their own chaddars, often pinned to a small cap under them, firmly in place outside the compound. Kulsom and Yasmin voiced admiration for some of the dress styles but had no desire to emulate them. They were fashions for the city and they were going back to the countryside. 'I'd look silly milking the goats in clothes like Sharifa and Benazir wear,' commented Yasmin with a laugh. 'And they wouldn't last long with the work we have to do.'

The last days went by in a flurry of last-minute shopping, packing and farewells. My adopted Waras 'family' had given me so much more than I could ever repay, but knowing that everyone had enjoyed their city holiday made me feel very glad I had invited them.

David was heart-broken at losing Farid and sobbed loudly. Everyone else was in tears as we hugged and kissed goodbye. Before we had always been able to murmur, 'next year, Insh 'Allah' but this time we all knew there would be no next year. I walked back into our silent, empty house, knowing I would miss them terribly.

Fortunately there was enough going on at work to keep me from brooding. The Mazar health volunteers, who had started out so enthusiastically after their training, soon discovered that the women in the community were less than eager to change their ideas on health care, or seek their advice.

The women felt isolated from each other and from the support of Jemila and the clinic staff now that they no longer attended class, and were becoming discouraged. We invited them to come and talk over the problems. Over tea and biscuits they chattered animatedly to each other until Jemila started to ask them what they had achieved in their health work. An uneasy silence fell as the women, avoiding Jemila's question, gazed steadfastly into their tea glasses, as though inspiration might be discovered there.

Finally, Salma broke the increasingly uncomfortable silence. 'I can't say I've done any work,' she admitted. 'All I've done is suggest that a neighbour who is pregnant came to your antenatal clinic last week.'

Jemila confirmed she had examined the woman. Hanifa said she had taught a mother how to prepare ORS for her son, who had diarrhoea, and another volunteer said she had shown her sister-in-law how to mash potatoes with milk for her baby.

'So you have been working!' exclaimed Jemila with a smile. The women, though they did not feel they had done much, began to look a little more cheerful. They agreed to come together once a fortnight and those meetings were a tremendous success. None of the volunteers ever missed one.

They soon had plenty to report – referrals of malnourished children, expectant mothers, suspected tuberculosis patients. They were delighted when neighbours sought them out, asking advice. It was fascinating to hear how the content of their conversations changed. In the beginning, when they gathered in the large classroom, the women had enquired after each other's families, discussed their own children's ailments and exchanged local gossip. After a few meetings they immediately began, instead, to swap stories about their work – overcoming the difficulties of persuading a child to drink ORS, how someone convinced a young mother she had sufficient breast milk and did not need to buy powdered milk.

As Jemila pointed out one day, 'They were working all along, but hadn't realised it. They expected health care to be more dramatic than it is.'

The highlight of each meeting was the 'drama', a role-play, brilliantly performed by Sharif and Hussain (who played the straight man to Sharif's clowning), used to illustrate a particular health topic. The first sketch, on the benefits of breast over bottle-feeding, featured Sharif playing the part of a mother whose baby often had diarrhoea. From the moment the group first saw big, bearded Sharif, his head swathed in a chaddar, crooning softly to 'her' baby in between demanding powdered milk from the doctor, they started laughing.

When Hussain tried to assure the mother that she had plenty of milk herself, Sharif, leaning forward, said, 'Oh, no doctor, there is no milk there – see for yourself. Look, you can squeeze it – empty.' It was so true to life that the audience dissolved completely. Tears rolling down their cheeks, some were literally rolling on the ground crying with laughter.

Delighted with their success, Sharif and Hussain strove to achieve even greater acclaim for their one-act dramas. Mothers-in-law, portrayed as pouring scorn on new ideas, expecting total obedience from their daughters-in-law, were introduced to howls of delighted recognition from the women. Very few of these women, mostly Kabul refugees, now lived with their in-laws – and they did not want to return to the old ways. Despite the problems of being refugees in their own country – living in cramped rented accommodation, struggling for money, often mourning the loss of family members and friends – these women were enjoying the novelty of living in nuclear family units. No mothers-in-law were going to boss them around any more.

When Latifa, chaddar and hair flying in all directions, rushed in late for a meeting one day, she panted, 'Sorry, I had some work to do.' Suddenly, she flashed a great, beaming smile on us. 'I have just delivered a baby!' she cried in excitement.

A neighbour had gone into labour in the early hours of the morning and her husband had come running for Latifa. 'I was shaking with fright to start with,' she told us. 'Luckily, it was her fourth baby and it just slipped out easily. It was a wonderful feeling.' The others were envious of how much more exciting Latifa's experience was compared to teaching someone how to mix ORS.

When one of the volunteers was offered payment for her midwifery services, she asked the next group meeting what their policy was to be. After a brief discussion the women decided, unanimously, to retain their volunteer title. Salma spoke for them all when she explained, 'The women who come to us for help can't afford to pay fees, otherwise they would go to a private doctor. If we don't help them, no one else will.'

The women began to talk openly about the difficulty of teaching their daughters – and sons – about sex. Benazir spoke for them she said, 'We would feel "shame" talking about such things with our children. I wish we could.

'We warn our daughters to stay away from boys but we don't tell them the feelings they have as they grow up are normal. We try to frighten them into being good, telling them never to bring shame on the family, or that it is against Islam. Mothers don't talk to their sons about such things – God knows what their fathers tell them.

'We know how a young girl feels when a boy shows that he likes her. If nature made us feel like that only after we are married, life would be less dangerous.' The others laughed at this, showing their agreement. Benazir, realizing how closely everyone was listening to her, flushed slightly in embarrassment. But she continued, 'It would be better if we could discuss feelings about sex openly with our daughters and explain to our sons that they have to take responsibility if they act on their feelings before being married.

'I do think boys and girls should wait until they are married, as Islam teaches and Allah wants, but I know they don't always. I don't believe that makes them bad and I would hate to think my son would ruin a young girl's life by making her pregnant.'

The women applauded as she finished. It would be a long time before the women felt able to talk about sex with their children, but at least they were beginning to think about it in a positive way. Despite Benazir's wonderful speech in class, though, she still retained a deeply prudish streak, as did Jemila.

Benazir was changing her daughter Malika's nappy in the staff room one day, allowing her baby the joy of kicking her bare legs in the air. When Hussain, himself the father of two daughters, came into the room, both women threw their chaddars over a startled Malika, who roared her protest at this uncalled for behaviour.

Seeing the look of consternation on the women's faces, Hussain hastily retreated. 'Why did you do that?' I asked, freeing the child from her cloth prison. Jemila and Benazir both had the grace to look sheepish as they explained that it wouldn't be proper for a man to see Malika's private parts. And so, before she was even able to walk, Malika had started learning the lessons that would teach her to be ashamed of her body. Such entrenched attitudes would take time to change, but change they undoubtedly would.

21

Where are the Dollars?

WHILE SO TOTALLY absorbed in our busy lives, the larger drama of Afghanistan's war often seemed very remote. Then, in September, we were forced to take notice, when Taliban, surprising everyone, took control of the city of Herat.

The governor of the city, Ismail Khan, fled across the border to Iran. If that country's regime had once seemed repressive, it now looked like a bastion of freedom compared with the restrictions Taliban began imposing in Herat.

Satellite dishes and television sets were destroyed in mock 'public hangings'. Music, other than religious, was banned and the streets were festooned with unravelled cassette tape seized by the soldiers. Insisting that *Sharia'ah* (sacred Islamic law) be followed, Taliban, without allowing the accused any form of judicial defence process, amputated the limbs of thieves. There were public executions, which people were forced to attend. Men accused of murder were shot in the back by relatives of the victim. Others were hanged, from a tall construction crane, dying slowly and horribly.

Girls' schools and health training projects for women were closed. Women were ordered to leave their jobs and remain at home. If they ventured out they had to veil themselves completely and be accompanied by a male relative. Taliban denied that their regime oppressed women, stripping them of basic rights. Women, they said, were like precious flowers, which should be protected and nurtured so that they would bloom. This flourishing of women, however, could only happen if they were kept safely at home.

Every day, new horror stories reached us. The women in Mazar felt the first flicker of fear. 'What if . . .?' was asked a dozen times a day. The Kabul government ordered Taliban

to leave Herat, warning that if they did not, they would bomb
the city. Taliban's reply was to issue the same warning to the
government – leave Kabul, or we shall attack.

While male colleagues discussed the possible political
repercussions, the women wondered how they would feed their
families if Taliban reached Mazar. Latifa's husband rarely had
a job, Sharifa's had disappeared, Benazir's family could not
survive without her income. Even Maryam, who did not go
out to work, was often left alone in the city when Naeem went
to Hazara Jat. Then, she, with no male relative to hand, was
responsible for the shopping and everything else that meant
going outside her home. Naeem's daughter, Shanaz, would see
her dream of becoming a doctor disappear. Every girl and
woman would be affected if Taliban succeeded in their aim of
taking total control of the country.

A few weeks later, Naeem and Farid went south to meet a
shipment of medical supplies coming across the border from
Pakistan. After making a final pre-winter tour of the clinics,
they found that to return to Mazar they had to come via
Herat, as fighting – not against Taliban but between factions of
Parties opposed to the extremists – had closed all other routes.
I was astonished to hear Farid extol the virtues of Taliban's
rule over the city and surrounding areas. 'We had no problems
on the road,' he declared happily. 'Taliban doesn't take money
by force from travellers and they have stopped all the robbing
and looting on the road.'

Farid had viewed things from his perspective as a driver,
appreciating the trouble-free journey, but giving no thought
to how Taliban's repressive regime affected people in other
ways, especially women. I thought about his friendship with
Sharifa, wondering if it bothered him at all that Taliban would
likely have her stoned to death for adultery? Even if it they had
never actually consummated their affair, it was unlikely such
zealots would worry unduly if it was only hearsay and the four
witnesses did not exist to testify.

I wished I could ask him about that, but instead merely
asked, 'Is that all that is important? What about how they treat

women? If they took control of Mazar next week, who would feed your friend (I laid heavy emphasis on the word 'friend') Sharifa and her children if she was not allowed to work?' Farid, confused and feeling himself under attack, subsided into silence.

Naeem, while also appreciating the ease of travelling in Taliban controlled areas, was horrified by the fundamentalist regime. 'If there was any chance of them reaching Mazar-i-Sharif I would take my family away,' he said emphatically. 'There is no way they could live under such conditions.'

The Kabul government was powerless to force Taliban out of Herat and their talk of retaliation soon evaporated. The other parties were not prepared to ally themselves with President Rabbani even though they too opposed Taliban. Without a full-scale war to report on, the international media lost interest.

Winter was approaching, a time when there tended to be a lull in Afghanistan's civil strife, and it seemed that, despite their propaganda and rhetoric, Taliban were unable to take Kabul as swiftly as they hoped.

What was happening in Herat, Kandahar and other Taliban areas, slowly slid out of focus as the people of Mazar once more began to concentrate on their own lives and immediate problems.

By now, everyone had begun the necessary preparations for the cold weather. Sharifa asked for a salary advance to enable her to buy in wood for the winter months. She took a few days leave and, with help from her neighbours (and Farid), worked hard chopping and stacking it. Then she 'mudded' her roof, by adding extra layers of mud to make it watertight – a messy, cold, wet job. She was proud of herself by the time she finished. 'Women can manage without a husband,' she said, with evident satisfaction when the task was done, 'although I am lucky to have good friends to help me.'

Nothing had been heard from Jawad for months, but Sharifa no longer worried herself sick about him. She had, however, received a letter from Marzia in Iran. She had had a baby girl, at which news we all rejoiced – delighted that Ghulam Ali could

not boast about having fathered a son. Marzia wrote that she
had been unhappy in the house she shared with Ghulam Ali's
second wife but had now moved to a different town to live in
the home of his first wife, where things were better. We agreed,
reading between the lines, that Ghulam Ali was not with her.

Though she would always worry about her little sister,
Sharifa was reassured that things were not as bad as she had
feared. Her own life was peaceful and contented. She enjoyed
her work and was able to support her family – even buying
them new clothes occasionally – and had far fewer unexplained
aches and pains than before. She was as happy as I had ever
known her.

That all changed the day her husband strolled into the
house one evening and greeted her casually before handing out
sweets to the children. 'It was as if he had only gone out five
minutes before for cigarettes!' exclaimed Sharifa in wonder. I
touched the sleeve of the smart new outfit she was wearing.

'At least he brought you a present,' I said with a smile. She
shook her head.

'Oh, no! He didn't. One of the *kharijee* volunteers gave me
this before she left. I put it on this morning to show him that
while he was away I managed quite well without him. He
doesn't know I didn't buy it.'

Poor Sharifa was so confused she did not know how she felt
about Jawad's unexpected return. 'It's as if he was just waiting
until all the work for winter was done,' she remarked. 'He
didn't have to do a thing. If only he would find a job and things
could be like they used to be, in Kabul, it would be all right.
We used to be happy together in those days.' She sighed and
shook her head, adding wearily, 'But I think those happy times
are gone and I hate the thought of the arguments and fights
starting again. He has come home without any money and is
already telling me to bring cigarettes back for him.

'Not that it matters what I want – he is the man and he will
make the decisions. He can decide to go away and come back
whenever he feels like it and I can't do anything about it.'

'At least, if he does leave again, you know that you can

manage on your own. It won't be like last time,' I pointed out. It was the only consolation I could think of.

Farid chose this time to announce his engagement, which must have done little to cheer Sharifa, who, because of the secrecy of their affair, was denied the opportunity to vent her feelings by talking to her friends about him.

The next morning I heard sounds of retching from the bathroom in the office and I realised Sharifa was not the only one facing fresh troubles. Latifa emerged, her complexion a horrid grey colour.

'Pregnant?' I whispered. She nodded, miserably. 'Two months.'

'Oh, Latifa,' I replied, 'I am sorry. What will you do?'

She shrugged resignedly. 'What can I do?' she asked. 'I can't face another pregnancy. I am still breast feeding Ahmad and I'm already exhausted.'

This time Latifa was not going to be thwarted by her husband and, requesting a few days leave, took herself to the doctor who had terminated Sharifa's pregnancy. As with Sharifa, the initial visit did not bring about a complete abortion. After two days of cramping pain and nausea, but no bleeding, Latifa returned to the doctor, demanding that she do the job properly. For days afterwards, she looked dreadful and I was afraid she was going to end up seriously ill. The thought of food made her too nauseous to eat and she became terribly thin and weak. Even Reza seemed disinclined to continue his hate campaign, and there was an uneasy truce between them.

It was some weeks before Latifa began to eat properly again, gradually regain some colour in her cheeks, and look healthier. One evening, when she came to collect her children from our compound, I commented on the fact that she was putting on weight. 'Yes,' she agreed, 'but I am not happy about it. I am afraid I have an infection after seeing that doctor. Maybe her hands were not clean or something. I have a lot of swelling in my stomach, although there is no pain.'

Not wanting to go to a gynaecologist at the hospital in case the doctor realised that she had recently terminated a pregnancy, she asked Jemila to examine her. I saw her emerge from the consulting room, her face registering shocked dismay. It was not an infection the doctor had left inside, it was the baby, and Jemila calculated she was almost five months' pregnant.

For a few days, a distracted Latifa went about her work like a zombie. One morning, she did not come in. Sharifa told me she gone to see a doctor who lived in the camp. She was there for two days and nights, during which time she went to hell and back.

The woman who carried out the abortion injected a cocktail of drugs to induce labour, which Latifa had endured, in agony, for twenty-four hours before expelling the foetus. 'It was a girl,' she whispered, when I visited her at home. 'I saw her before the doctor took her away.'

Latifa remained at home for a day, mourning the death of her daughter, then returned to work. I begged her to take more time off until she was stronger, but she refused. 'If I stay at home I think too much. It is better to keep busy, although I'll never forget seeing that little dead baby in the doctor's hands for as long as I live.'

Latifa slowly recovered physically from her ordeal, but the mental anguish remained with her long after that. 'I didn't know I would feel like this,' she said. 'I know I couldn't have coped with another pregnancy and another child, but now, I feel sad all the time. It feels like there is a big wound inside me that will never heal. If Sharifa's doctor had done her work properly the first time, before it looked like a real baby, I would not have felt like this,' she wept.

The women gathered round Latifa, offering as much comfort and emotional support as possible. Eventually, the depression became less severe and she was able to laugh again. But she had changed, and up to the time I left Afghanistan I never again saw the old, teasing, fun-loving Latifa I had first met.

I felt a tremendous admiration for Benazir, who spent extra time with Latifa, trying to assure her that her decision to terminate her pregnancy had not been wrong or sinful.

Although she had never had an abortion herself, she seemed to empathise even more than the others and attempted to assuage Latifa's sense of guilt.

Benazir was now working with several mothers whose children were malnourished – some severely so. She went about her teaching tasks calmly and confidently. She, more than any of the health volunteers, was deeply interested in child development, understanding that the more a baby was stimulated, the quicker its progress. I often heard her encourage mothers to talk to their infants, to tell them the names of everything they saw around them, to sing to them and to play with them. And when it came to persuading mothers to accept new ideas about feeding their children, she had the patience of a saint.

Although she and Murad appeared to get along well most of the time, there were occasions when he drove her to distraction – like when he decided to dabble in a business venture with her money.

Murad had met a man who made a lot of money from trading goods between Mazar and Kabul. With a groan of despair, Benazir told me, 'He thinks he can do the same. He has no idea about doing business, but he has gone to Kabul with the money I have saved since starting work. He is convinced he will be rich when he comes back.'

It was several weeks before he returned. Torn between crying and laughing, Benazir explained how her worst fears had been realised. 'He bought some carpets, but they were of such poor quality no one in Mazar (where excellent quality carpets were widely available) will buy them. He invested most of the money in potatoes because, when he reached Kabul he found they were much cheaper than in Mazar.

'The man has no brain. Everyone knows that the new potatoes are expensive but the price always goes down. How could my husband not know this?'

I asked if the potatoes could not still be sold, so that at least some of the money would be recouped. Benazir shook her head. 'Even if he sold the lot, he would barely break even, but', she wailed 'we can't even do that. When I opened a sack to see the quality, the rotten smell nearly made me faint.' Shaking her head in wonder at her husband's stupidity, she added, 'He bought the potatoes as soon as he reached Kabul, weeks ago. Not one was left fit to eat. I knew he shouldn't have gone. Men are useless creatures.'

For days, Sharif, Nauroz and Hussain teased Benazir, making jokes about potatoes, offering her recipes for tasty potato dishes. Although she laughed with them, I knew that inside she was crying over how Murad had thrown away the money that had taken a year to save. I knew he had a very uncomfortable time at home before she finally forgave him.

In the meantime, when we had finally stopped worrying about them, the thieves returned.

The night they came back, I had, unusually gone to bed early. Daud and I often sat talking until late but that night, feeling tired, I had cut short our evening chat. Jon was watching television in the living room opposite the bedroom, with David sleeping by his side.

I fell asleep to the sound of the wind blowing hard outside, then shortly afterwards some noise awoke me. I heard the door open and sat up, sleepy and confused, half expecting it to be Daud asking if he should put the generator on as the electricity had gone off.

The beam of a powerful torch blinded me. Then I saw the Kalashnikov pointed at me. 'Ki asteed?' – Who are you? – I asked, as though armed robbers should make proper introductions.

Two men swiftly crossed the room ordering me to shut up and lie down. For a moment, I understood the fear of rape that Chaman had felt when the soldiers began to advance down the mountain towards us. Almost paralysed with terror I turned over to lie face down as ordered and felt my arms being tied behind my back. The Kalashnikov was pressing against the back of my neck and a pistol was pushed into my ear. I heard the sound of the safety bolt of the gun being released and was aware of the dreadful sound of my own harsh breathing.

I remember praying, 'God, if they are going to kill me, please don't let me be afraid.' It seemed vitally important that I not be afraid at the moment of death.

In hoarse whispers the two men demanded to know where the dollars were. 'We don't have any . . . ask my husband . . .' then, remembering David was in the next room, repeated, 'we don't have any dollars.' I wondered why Jon, Daud or Abbas, the *chowkidar*, didn't come and get me out of this mess, not knowing that that they had already been trussed up in various locations about the house.

The men began to search the room, emptying the trunks we used for storage, throwing their contents around. After each fruitless search (we really didn't have any dollars) they returned to stick that pistol in my ear again, demanding where we kept our dollars.

Somehow, despite my terror, other thoughts began circling in my brain. I told them that we never kept money in the house but money was always kept locked in a safe in our office. Desperate to get them out of our house, I helpfully gave them the address and clear instructions on how to get there.

In the middle of my urging them to go and rob the office I suddenly realised I had made a grammatical error in a couple of sentences and found myself apologising for this, before repeating them correctly.

While they had been ransacking the trunks I had discovered the cloth binding my arms was loose enough to allow some movement. When the men left the room, I realised that by wriggling my arms I could loosen my bonds enough to slip an arm out. I reached for the alarm button under the mattress. At that point, I was even more terrified than when the pistol was in my ear. I did not know where the men were – would they rush back in and shoot me? Were they, even now, tying up Jon and David, and would they shoot them? Or would they run as soon as the alarm sounded?

I risked it, sliding my arm back into its binding immediately I had pressed the button. The sound seemed very loud in the silence, though instead of buzzing continuously it stopped after only seconds. Had the battery been low, I wondered? We had become careless about security. There was the sound of running feet, past my room, up the stairs to the roof – then silence again.

In the living room they had bound Jon, who had fallen asleep while watching television, with electric flex. Mercifully they had left David, still asleep, untouched. Even when they had rolled Jon around to check for money under cushions they had left David alone – nice robbers, we told ourselves. We repeated it thankfully a few days later when, in another incident, the householder trying to protect his property was shot in the legs.

In Daud's room we found him and Abbas bound, gagged and blindfolded. As we rushed forward to untie them, I saw a look of absolute terror on Daud's face. He thought the thieves had returned. 'It's all right,' I reassured him. 'They've gone.' So had our video recorder. The television, wrapped in a blanket, had been abandoned as they fled.

Abbas was abject in his apologies. He had been sitting on a chair on the veranda when a figure appeared on the roof, pointing a Kalashnikov at him. Two others climbed down the mulberry tree and pushed him into Daud's room. 'It is all right, Hussain. No one was hurt. No one is blaming you. Please, could you make us some tea?'

The man was such a gibbering wreck, convinced he was going to lose his job, that I finally went to make the tea. I had been hyperventilating so much that my throat was dry and sore and I needed gallons of hot, sweet tea to soothe it.

As after the previous robbery, the thieves were never caught. The police arrived in great numbers and milled around our compound. Two detectives asked questions and expressed shock and concern that I had been tied up. When I overheard one saying to Daud, 'So, you've done it again,' I said they could only question him in the police station if I was present at the interview. The detective agreed, but when I came back with my coat on, he laughed, 'I can't take you to the police station. Don't worry, we're only going to get a statement from him.' Finally they agreed to question Daud and Abbas in a room in our house. That was the end of the investigation.

We put massive wooden shutters up at the window and on the door from the roof through which the thieves had made off. Even so, I was still scared at night. That made me angry – there is something so undignified about being afraid. And when I went shopping with Daud the next day I felt as if everyone knew what had happened and became so upset with people staring at me that I insisted we went home. 'People always stare at you,' pointed out Daud reasonably, but that day and for some time to come, it felt different.

If it hadn't been for the support of friends like Benazir, Jemila, Shoguffa and Sharifa and the work at the clinic I might have left Afghanistan earlier than planned. They did not ask stupid questions, as did a foreign worker with a UN agency who visited, ostensibly to see that I was all right. 'Did they speak English?' she asked, as though armed robbers took lessons before trying to rob foreigners.

Eventually I was able to laugh about some of the sillier aspects of the ordeal. Daud said, 'It's good you made the thieves run away without the television. Now we don't have to miss any episodes of "Santa Barbara".' I thought the daily minutiae of everyday life in Afghanistan contained more drama than any American soap – even if it was without the glamour and wealth.

The women were amused about how I had given directions to the office – the office staff, who had to tighten their own security were less amused. And they laughed when I told them how I had corrected my grammar. 'Habiba would have been very cross if she had heard your mistakes,' commented Sharifa.

Poor Habiba was still searching fruitlessly for a job. We had reached the end of her grammar book before my second journey to Hazara Jat and on my return I had not continued with lessons. She still came to visit me at home, though she never invited me to her house.

Knowing of her concerns about the twins' health, I thought she might be interested in joining the training course at the clinic. But when I asked her, she rather took me aback by

asking, 'What salary are you offering?' Apparently she thought
I was offering her the job of master trainer. When I explained
she would be trained to work as a volunteer, she lost interest.

Her social calls were becoming embarrassing. Apart from
asking about job vacancies, she spent the time telling me how
much she missed seeing me every day or complimenting me
lavishly on everything from the clothes I was wearing to the
tea she was drinking. We shared no common interests and I felt
our conversations were stilted and awkward. I always passed
on any news I had heard about agencies opening and possible
jobs, but she had always already been to see them. However
much I tried to find different topics to talk about, Habiba
managed to switch back to her usual litany of lament.

If she had been remotely interested in the lives of people we
both knew, it would have been easy to while away a couple
of hours exchanging news. Despite the fact that we saw each
other almost every day, I never ran out of things to talk about
with other friends. We shared an endless fascination about
who was pregnant, who had just had a baby, who had rowed
with their neighbour, husband, or mother-in-law, and who had
become engaged or married.

Although we were living in a city, my friends had the same
attitude towards their neighbours as people in the villages
in Hazara Jat – and in my small, rural part of Scotland.
Basically we were nosy, but there was a comforting feeling
of being connected to each other and that everyone cared
about everyone else. In the clinic that feeling of connection
was almost tangible. The team was the nucleus of a huge and
ever-widening network of people – students, volunteers, their
families and their neighbours – each inextricably linked to
the other.

— 22 —
Grabbing the Goat

As MAZAR-I-SHARIF WAS caught in winter's icy grip, we assembled the heaps of summer-stored blackened metal pipes and drums (and some shiny new ones purchased grudgingly at triple the previous year's price) into diesel burning *bukharis* [stoves]. These were Heath Robinsonish affairs, which took up enormous amounts of space.

They gave off a tremendous heat so that rooms became suffocatingly hot. We had the luxury of one installed in the bathroom, which also heated water in an upper tank. Of course they had to be turned off at night, so mornings were not a pleasant experience, especially as we had forgotten to dress our pipes – which run along outside walls in Afghan houses – in their winter woollies.

I came home from work one afternoon to find Daud in a foul temper, struggling to thaw the pipes with a dysfunctional blowtorch. His hands and face were black, as were the walls, which we had painted white only that summer. 'Daud, I think you should forget it for today,' I called out, 'the temperature is already below freezing so it's pointless continuing now.' His temper was not improved by this.

There was no water in the house, not a drop. It was two days before Reza and Abbas, with two industrial sized working blowtorches, succeeded in thawing the pipes. On the first day, a neighbour came to the gate. 'Why didn't you tell us there were going to be men on your roof?' he demanded crossly. 'Our women have to go outside to the latrine – you should have warned us.'

I apologised profusely, though personally I would hardly have thought there was much chance of passions being sparked

in those temperatures. Reza and Abbas considerately turned
their backs whenever a warning shout from the neighbouring
compound alerted them to the fact that women were about to
scuttle across their back yard.

One of the few social activities that made life bearable
during the winter was the weekly *buzkashi* game. No sport
in the world can compare with the drama and excitement of
buzkashi [literally, 'goat grabbing']. Not for the faint hearted,
Afghanistan's national equestrian sport made polo look like a
kindergarten activity.

The basic rules and scoring system were simple. A *chapandaz*
[skilled *buzkashi* player] grabbed the carcass of a dead calf
(supposedly less likely to disintegrate during play then the
traditional goat) from a marked circle and galloped around
a flag positioned several hundred yards distant. Wherever the
calf was dropped, whether by accident or design, a new scrum
developed. The rider, who succeeded in returning the carcass
to its original starting point before his opponents wrested it
from him, scored a 'goal'. The chief guest each week put up the
prize money.

Although it sounded very simple, it took me weeks to grasp
some of the finer points of the game – not helped by the fact
that I was labouring under the impression that there were
two teams on the field. Once Daud had put me right on this
matter and I realised that the sixty odd riders were playing
as individuals, I understood things better. Before long, I was
completely addicted to the sport.

It was undoubtedly a dangerous game, and there were
accidents – riders were kicked, were sometimes thrown or
slipped from the saddle into the maelstrom of slashing hooves.
Yet thanks to a combination of instinct and excellent training,
these wonderful horses never trampled a fallen rider.

Buzkashi symbolised Afghanistan's macho cultural values in
terms of strength, courage, control and superb horsemanship,
and women had no involvement in the sport. However,
that didn't stop Jemila and Miriam (Mustafa's sister) from
accompanying me to the matches on several occasions. Miriam,

unable to stand the cold, soon gave up, but Jemila was almost as keen as I was. Then her mother arrived in Mazar from Pakistan.

Although happy that her mother had joined her, Jemila was less pleased about the curtailment of her free and independent life-style. 'She's very angry that my brother allowed me to go and stay with friends on my own, and she's furious that I've been going to the *buzkashi*.

'Nauroz told her that I was safe with you but she says I've not to go again.'

Not one to give up easily, Jemila persuaded her mother to attend the following Friday's game – though they sat inside a jeep on the sidelines instead of on the platform with us. 'She actually admitted that she enjoyed it,' reported Jemila, 'but it isn't so much fun watching from inside.'

At least Jemila's mother did nothing to curtail her daughter's other passion in life – shopping. A very fashion-conscious young woman, Jemila loved buying clothes, or having them made to her own design at the tailors.

During my last winter in Afghanistan, the latest fashion was for long Iranian coats, buttoned from neck to ankle-length hem, with triangular headscarves worn low on the forehead. I longed to wear such a coat, but no matter how many I tried on, they looked dreadfully frumpish on me – as they also did on the many foreigners who took to wearing them. Maybe it was something to do with the way we moved. Yet on Jemila and Benazir they looked wonderfully elegant.

One day in town we saw two Iranian women coming out of the shrine. As well as their tightly buttoned up, ankle-length black coats, they wore their headscarves low on their foreheads – like a nun's wimple – and pulled tight and knotted under the chin. Maryam nudged me. 'Don't they look beautiful?' And they did. Their black *kohl*-lined eyes were enormous under the severe scarves. Naeem nodded appreciatively. His murmured 'Mmmh, very sexy', was rewarded with a sharp dig in the ribs from Maryam. Goodness knows what the Ayatollahs in Iran would have made of their approved dress code for women suddenly becoming the height of fashion amongst young women in Mazar-i-Sharif.

Fashion was important to the women, even amongst those who wore the *burqa* when venturing outside. From the style of footwear and *tunban* cuff on show one could judge a great deal about the woman hidden beneath the flowing veil. A number of our students arrived at the clinic wearing the *burqa*, often with the headpiece rolled back so that their faces were uncovered. Once indoors, the *burqa* was removed until it was time to go out in the streets again. Worn like this, it seemed more like our having to put on a coat to go outdoors than a symbol of oppression.

I knew women, like Aquila, who worked for the UN, argued vociferously against women wearing the veil. 'It is not', she pointed out, 'an Islamic injunction. Only ignorant men insist on their women covering up. You can be sure that those who are most insistent on their own women keeping purdah are the ones who most like to look at other women.'

I was sure she was correct, but by now I was beginning to feel that the *burqa* issue had little to do with women's freedom and the right to control their lives. Latifa and Sharifa never wore the veil, yet their lives were still controlled in fundamental ways by the actions of their men folk. Latifa's husband had prevented her terminating one pregnancy, then, by not taking responsibility against conception, caused another pregnancy and the subsequent trauma of a late abortion. Sharifa's husband assumed the right to walk away from his marriage and family responsibilities as and when he felt like it.

The women themselves often stressed that Islam did not cause the problems they encountered in life, but the way in which men interpreted it to suit themselves. Latifa had once described it in terms of men's need to control everything and everyone around them. Taliban, still in total control of Herat, were certainly proving that they were determined to exert total control over every aspect of women's lives.

We often talked about how life must be for the hapless

women of that city, questioning Taliban's reasons for their oppression. 'Why,' I asked, 'when there are so many problems in this country almost destroyed by war, are Taliban's laws directed mainly against women?' There was so much they could have done to improve health services and education.

Latifa, Benazir, Jemila and Sharifa were convinced that it was because the extremists were afraid of educated women. 'If we learn to read and write, we can read for ourselves what the Prophet (Peace Be Upon Him) taught us. They don't want that because they know they have been using Islam as an excuse to keep us down,' said Latifa.

Benazir added, 'They are afraid of women becoming educated because then we would be strong. Maybe women would want to share in government as once was nearly possible. They want to keep us weak because then they have all the power and can control everything.'

'They certainly don't care about the country or the people. If women were in power we would end this stupid war and start to build the country again,' said Latifa.

Listening to them I still could not understand why Taliban were so determined to keep women out of public life. Why could they not accept that women had much to offer in all aspects of life in their country?

'Men, too, must be educated to change,' said Jemila. 'Most of these Taliban are illiterate. They can't read the Quran or the *Hadith* either. They have been indoctrinated and accept what they are told by mullahs who have not studied Islam properly.

'They believe the rubbish about women having a stronger sex drive than men and that we have dangerous powers to make men want us. They try to hide women away, but the more they do that the more they want them. Their own ignorance causes their fear of women and makes them push us down.'

Round and round we would go, asking our questions, tossing answers backwards and forwards, but never able to see how things could improve unless Taliban were stopped. Usually such debates ended with one of the women declaring that, 'For sure, they will be stopped. They will never take

Kabul and one day, when the rest of the parties finally stop fighting, Herat will be free again.'

By now Jemila and Benazir had the antenatal and mother and child clinics well established. The health volunteers were working hard, referring pregnant women for check-ups and encouraging mothers to take their infants along to be weighed regularly.

Benazir had introduced coloured 'road to health charts' on which she plotted a child's weight. Mothers of those children on the red for danger curve were invited to attend teaching sessions, which included lessons on nutrition and cooking tasty meals. So, we were accustomed to seeing malnourished children until Najiba arrived one day with her son, Hussain.

At seven months, he weighed only two kilos. Najiba had heard people talking about the work of the health volunteers in the district and, hoping they could do something for her son, she brought him to the clinic.

While Benazir and Jemila gently unwrapped the pathetic bundle of skin and bones in order to weigh him, Najiba explained that until illness struck at four months old, Hussain and his twin sister had been healthy babies. 'His sister died and we thought we would lose Hussain too. Mash 'Allah, he is still with us but he never stopped crying after his sister died.'

Driven half crazy by grief and her surviving baby's never-ending wailing, Najiba gave him opium to quieten his sobs. As she administered increasing doses, Hussain spent most of his days and nights in a drugged stupor. He no longer wanted to feed. Thinking it was because her milk was drying up, Najiba bought expensive powdered milk, which she could ill afford. 'But', she said, 'he just gets thinner and thinner and he always gets diarrhoea.'

Benazir sat talking with Najiba for a long time that day, explaining that she would do all she could to save the child, but could guarantee nothing. 'Also,' she continued, 'unless you promise to trust us and work with us, we shall never succeed.'

Najiba promised she would do anything she was asked if it would help Hussain. Benazir gave a small smile. 'Don't be so quick with your promises. We'll ask you to do things you think are stupid or wrong or even dangerous. You must promise not to visit any more doctors and not give Hussain any more medicines.' Najiba nodded. 'And you must agree to reduce the opium.' Najiba nodded, though with less enthusiasm. We knew it would be dangerous to stop the drug immediately, but hoped that once Hussain was drinking milk and had become stronger, we could work on ending his addiction.

Next day, Benazir asked Najiba to explain how she usually mixed Hussain's feed. 'I put water in the bottle, then a spoonful of powder and shake it,' she replied. 'If it doesn't look very "milky" I add a bit more powder before putting in six spoons of sugar to give him energy.'

Even if Najiba had been literate, she would have been unable to read the instructions, as they were printed on the tin lid in Russian. This sugared water had been Hussain's diet for almost two months. God knows how the child was still alive. Certainly none of us, including the usually optimistic Benazir, expected him to live.

Benazir became Hussain's personal health volunteer. Najiba brought milk from her cow to the clinic every day and the two women, with Najiba's older daughter, took over the clinic kitchen. Benazir taught Najiba how to feed Hussain with diluted cow's milk after boiling it (with the addition of a very *small* amount of sugar, otherwise he refused to touch it). He began to gain weight almost immediately, and was soon eager to feed.

However, it was not all plain sailing. 'I'll have to use powdered milk again,' she announced one morning. 'Our cow is dry.'

Benazir shook her head, 'No, Najiba, it is too expensive and then you might be tempted to use less than Hussain needs. It would be cheaper to buy fresh milk if you can find someone to sell it to you.' By lunchtime, Najiba had persuaded a neighbour to sell enough milk for the baby's daily needs. On another occasion, she complained that Hussain had diarrhoea and asked for medicine. Mustafa said that it was unnecessary, but next day Benazir spotted the bottle of Ampicillin syrup in Najiba's bag. She had bought it in the bazaar.

Najiba was worried that she would not be able to cope with Hussain's constant crying when the opium was withdrawn. Benazir tried to reassure her that now her baby was eating properly, he would not cry so much. 'But babies do cry, you know,' she said. 'You have had several children so you understand you can't have a baby that never cries.' Najiba shrugged, looking desperate.

'You don't know what it was like. It wasn't like normal crying. It never stopped.'

Benazir, her arm round the worried woman, soothed her. 'You must have a break sometimes. When it gets too much, give Hussain to your daughter while you go and sit in another room where you can't hear him.' Najiba was not convinced. 'You don't know what it was like,' she repeated stubbornly. 'It made me crazy.'

Benazir smiled reassuringly, 'Sometimes, no matter how much we love our children, we want to throw them out the window. That is when you need your daughter's help, or your husband's, or a neighbour's.'

Starting to protest that she would never want to hurt her baby, Najiba paused, asking, 'Do you ever feel that way?'

Benazir nodded, 'Every mother does.'

Najiba heaved a huge sigh. 'Oh, I thought I was a really bad mother because sometimes I just could not stand the noise any more. I tried everything to soothe him, but nothing worked and I was afraid I might do something terrible to him to make him stop. No one ever told me it was normal to feel that way.'

Benazir winked at me. This was a topic we had talked about before. Women all over the world are supposed to be born perfect mothers, always loving and kind and able to cope with whatever their babies do. We are not supposed to feel like flinging them out of windows when they won't stop crying, no matter what we try to do for them.

Najiba, greatly relieved to discover she was not a monster, agreed that the time had come to stop the opium. We asked a doctor, a paediatrician working for a health agency, to monitor the withdrawal period. Even with the help of small doses of diazepam, Hussain screamed for thirty-six hours after his last dose of opium wore off. He vomited. He had diarrhoea. We could see him lose weight again before our eyes. We were terrified and not one of us slept for two nights.

Finally, the vomiting and diarrhoea stopped. As if by magic, Hussain stopped crying long enough to start devouring his milk with renewed appetite.

His mother immediately signed herself up for the next training course, eager to learn what the volunteers already knew. Not only that, she brought a young neighbour to the clinic. At twenty, Habiba had three children under three years of age, two of which were already being given opium several times a day. Najiba said, 'I told Habiba that it was understandable she had problems coping with three children so young. I said that if she agreed to stop the opium, we would find a way to share the burden on her when the children were crying.'

Although Benazir was the one who worked most closely with Najiba and Hussain, the volunteers, students and clinic staff had also been very involved. Every day people asked anxiously about Hussain and Najiba.

The day Hussain weighed in at six kilos, his gummy grin (as if *he* had done something really clever) gave everyone a tremendous feeling of achievement. If we had needed any extra motivation, we received it that day. Hussain's gurgling laughter, along with Najiba's joy and Benazir's pride made the last three years seem worthwhile.

Suddenly, everything I did, was for the last time. I watched my last *buzkashi* match. I attended my last meeting of the volunteers. Then the farewell *mehmanis*, which I hated, began.

When Jemila announced that the volunteers wanted to give a lunch, I said I couldn't bear one more farewell party. On my last day at work in the clinic, I had lunch with the staff as usual and Sharif tried his best to keep us laughing. Jemila disappeared for a few moments, then beckoned me to follow her. In the guestroom sat the volunteers, looking very anxious. Jemila had warned them I might be angry with them for coming to say goodbye. But they had insisted, saying they wanted to give some *nishani* [remembrance gifts].

We talked together for the last time. They made me laugh when they announced their decision to take over the fortnightly dramas themselves. 'Well,' said Salma, 'we think we could do it just as well as Sharif and Hussain. Maybe one day we shall invite women from the district to come and see us perform.'

They made me cry when they spoke of their determination to carry on with their work, their plans for the future.

'Taliban won't stop us,' declared Benazir, 'They have been at the gates of Kabul for months, but still they could not take the city. They cannot stop us working for the women and children of Afghanistan.'

I was so proud to know these women, so full of bravery and hope and determination. And, as we wept, I was glad they had risked my wrath to come and say goodbye one last time.

— 23 —
Women's Voices Should Not Be Heard

EVEN AFTER TALIBAN captured Mazar-i-Sharif, and much of the rest of Afghanistan, I was able, through various means, to keep in touch with most of my women friends. There were some, like Marzia in Iran, with whom direct contact was no longer possible, and, with the exception of Latifa, I at least always received news indirectly about everyone.

Latifa, having had enough of Reza's campaign against her, had found a new job shortly after I left Afghanistan. I was pleased for her, especially when I heard from her new boss about how happy she was. It seemed that at last the old, sparkling Latifa had returned. The last direct communication I had of her was when she wrote to tell me that 'my duty is at home now'. Mustafa, still working in Mazar, wrote to say he did not know where she is. It may be that he is afraid to make enquiries about a woman.

Daud fled the city and returned safely to Waras. He does not know what, if anything, his future holds. His dreams of going to university are now no more than that. Our telephone rang very early one Sunday morning a few months ago. It was Daud. My first wild, optimistic hopes that he had reached Britain were dashed when he said, 'Mum? I'm calling from Kabul. How are you?'

He had gone to the capital to find out if the schools and colleges had re-opened and if there was any possibility of continuing his education. There wasn't. 'The only thing these people are teaching in school is what *they* call Islam. There is no education. They do not think they need doctors or teachers or engineers in this new Afghanistan.' I was terrified someone in the public call office would have him arrested, and begged him not to talk openly against the Taliban regime. He returned to Waras, where he helps on the land, does some voluntary teaching and dreams of somehow getting out and doing something worthwhile with his life.

In the meantime, as we are able to correspond with reasonable frequency, he keeps me up to date with what is happening in the lives of my women friends. Although Taliban is in control of Hazara Jat, it is too vast and inhospitable a region to allow them to control it fully. For most people, then, life continues almost as before. Only now there is no longer a feeling of moving forward, a hope that education might allow people a chance to do better. And for the women, there is still the same daily round of hard work in the house and in the fields.

Gul Sevre's fiancé returned from Iran, despite her fervent prayers that he would stay there, and they are married now. Hassan wrote to say they are happy together – but he would say that, wouldn't he?

The twins' mother, Nickbacht, has had another son, who, according to Suraya, is doing well, Mash 'Allah. Suraya, after years of losing her male babies, finally gave birth to a boy who survived and who seems, according to Daud, to be normal and healthy. Maybe her joy in her son will help make up for not being allowed to train as an official health worker. She at least knows enough about how to bring the child up to be strong and healthy – at least as far as is possible in an area devastated by drought. Daud's last letter, written in July 2000, said there was hardly even water to drink in the area.

Aquila succeeded in making her trip to Pakistan – in pre-Taliban days – to see her daughter Basma. Now, having finished her training in Karachi, Basma is working in Waras, where her midwifery skills are much in demand.

In Mazar-i-Sharif, however, the picture is very different. Although the situation for women is slightly better than for their sisters in Kabul, there is no possibility of the health volunteers continuing their work – the days of being able to move freely around the streets are gone. Even visiting a neighbour a few doors away is no longer possible.

Benazir is still working, though not with Mustafa. She used to write often, asking Daud to write the letters for her in English, but it is a long time since I received any messages from her. In her last, brief note, she wrote:

> Men and women can no longer work together. I am working in a clinic that is only for females and Mustafa and Sharif are in another clinic, only for men. There is no outreach project, no dramas, no meetings – all is finished. The people I work with now did not know you and Jemila has gone away so there is no one I can talk to about you. I miss you.

Jemila had taken her mother to Iran for cancer treatment. It was too late though and she wrote to tell me the doctors could do nothing.

> So [she wrote] *we are going back to Pakistan. When my mother was a refugee in Pakistan before she always said she did not want to die in a foreign country. But how can I take my mother to die in Afghanistan now? This country that Taliban rule is not our homeland anymore. Nothing is forever, one day, Insh 'Allah, Afghanistan will be our home again.*

Her mother died, in Quetta, a few weeks later. Jemila has returned to Iran to join her brothers.

So we kept in touch, but it was not easy and it became more difficult with the passing of time – as if the links between us were becoming weaker. I knew I could not return to Mazar-i-Sharif, but I felt a longing to renew contact with at least some of my friends from Afghanistan. With the millennium fast approaching, we decided to escape the hype by going back to Pakistan.

It was December 1999 and Peshawar, capital of Pakistan's north-west frontier province was covered in a thick blanket of smog. The policemen directing the traffic wore gas masks and – with the sun barely able to break through – it was cold, much colder than I'd expected – but I didn't care.

Almost drunk with the excitement of being with old friends again, I was sitting in an Afghan kebab restaurant, surrounded by Naeem and Maryam and all their family. Their oldest son,

Hassan, was a child no longer, but a serious young man, too old now for childish games, although Hussain and Habib sat giggling with David at one end of the table. Ismail (who might or might not have kissed Latifa) was there too, laughing and chatting.

They'd met us at the airport – Naeem beaming broadly, Maryam, and Fatima, now a beautiful young woman. We had planned to book into Dean's Hotel, where we had stayed several times in the past. A leftover from the days of the Raj, slightly gone to seed, it consisted of a collection of bungalows, each with its own veranda, spread around its spacious grounds. There had been flower gardens and lawns on which to take tea. At the height of the Soviet occupation of Afghanistan, Dean's had been a favourite base for many foreign journalists, eager to make contact with *mujahideen* leaders who could take them 'inside'. About the place hung an air of intrigue. The rooms, though a bit dark and gloomy, still retained a hint of gracious living and I had delighted in the luxury of the huge sunken bath.

Anxious that there may not be a vacancy because we had been unable to get through on the phone to book, we asked Naeem to make Dean's our first stop. Surprisingly, the large wrought-iron gates were closed, though it was only mid-afternoon. Naeem tooted the horn several times and eventually a *chowkidar*, swathed in a blanket and sleepily rubbing his eyes ambled over to peer at us through the gate. The hotel, he informed us, was closed, and had been for two years.

Green's, around the corner had one room left. On the ground floor, overlooking what was once a pleasant courtyard, now being torn up by a gang of workmen, it was dark and dingy. It was also expensive. 'What the hell,' declared Jon recklessly, 'if we're going to fork out that much for a horrible room we may as well spend a bit more and enjoy some luxury.' A patient Naeem turned the Suzuki and headed for the Pearl Continental.

We later gathered together in the grand foyer of the hotel. Once the business of pouring tea, offering milk and sugar was over, an awkwardness descended. Long pauses were followed by half a dozen questions asked simultaneously, as we smiled, each waiting for another to start. Although we had kept in touch regularly, through letters, e-mail and the occasional phone call, there was just too much to talk about. We hardly knew how or where to begin. Finally Naeem asked where we wanted to eat. 'Anywhere with kebabs,' I replied quickly, 'I've been dreaming about proper Afghan kebabs for weeks.'

In the restaurant the waiter came to take our order. When he confessed that the establishment had run out of nan he was taken aback when, instead of being upset with him, Naeem and I burst out laughing. It broke the ice once and for all. Handing Ismail the car key with a request to go to his home and bring back nan, Naeem looked at me, his eyes twinkling with humour at the memory of our first meal together, the day I had arrived with David in Afghanistan. We immediately plunged into a lengthy 'do you remember?' session, recalling the many good times we had shared in Mazar-i-Sharif. There would be time enough later to hear the stories of how tragedy had touched the lives of our friends since Taliban's final victory in Mazar-i-Sharif.

As we left the restaurant I shivered in the cold air. 'I'll have to go shopping tomorrow for warm clothes,' I commented, eliciting such a groan of dismay from David that Maryam laughingly invited him to come and play with the boys instead. Returning to collect him in the afternoon, I could hear, even before I entered the compound, loud whoops, yells and shouts of laughter.

'They've been all right together, then?' I asked Maryam, who had hurried to let me in. Shaking her head in wonder, she replied, 'They've never stopped for a second. I tried to make them sit still long enough to eat something but it was impossible. Come in and have some tea. If we shut the door we may just about be able to hear ourselves talk.' As she poured the tea, Maryam's hand began to tremble. Putting down the teapot she turned to me, her eyes wet with tears. I reached out and we clung together and cried.

She finally broke away, saying, 'I'm sorry, I didn't mean to . . . It's just all the memories . . .'

'It's all right,' I murmured, searching in my bag for tissues. 'I think I needed a good cry.'

Maryam nodded. 'I'll make some fresh tea. This lot's cold now.'

When Taliban forces had tried, and almost succeeded, to take Mazar for the second time, Naeem had taken his family away from the city, as he had always said he would. Reza, I knew, had done the same and his family was still in Jaghoray. Returning to the village from the city had made little difference for Reza's wife – perhaps she even felt happier being close to her relatives again. For Naeem's children, it was impossible. Remaining in Afghanistan would mean the end of Shahnaz's hopes of studying to be a doctor or an engineer.

Naeem had returned to Mazar-i-Sharif but luckily was in Pakistan when Taliban captured the city. The soldiers occupied his house, so there was no going back. As soon as he was able, Naeem moved his family, including his elderly parents, to Peshawar. 'We are lucky,' remarked Maryam, returning with the tea. 'My husband is still alive, when he could have been massacred like so many others. Living in Pakistan is expensive and we worry about the future. Shahnaz and the boys are still able to go to school, though what we'll do about university I don't know.

'Still, we are so much better off than others are. I thank Allah every day that Naeem took us away when he did and that I didn't have to see the dreadful things Sharifa saw.'

Through Naeem I had kept in regular contact with Sharifa after I left Afghanistan. Sometimes she asked him to write a letter in English, though often he would simply include any message from her in his own letters to me. After the fall of Mazar there had been a long, ominous silence. Then, Naeem telephoned me. 'I knew you'd want to know that Sharifa and her sister Chaman have arrived in Peshawar. They are fine and have all the children with them. They will stay some days with us until they decide what to do.'

'What about her husband? Is he with her?'

'He left Mazar when the Taliban came, she doesn't know where he is. Chaman's husband is dead but she doesn't know yet. It is not a good time to tell her.'

'Are they really all right?' I asked, detecting a note of concern in Naeem's voice.

'They've had a difficult time. I think they are still in shock, but I'll write with the full story. I only called to let you know they are safe. Don't worry!'

Naeem never did write with the complete story. Oh, he wrote, often, but only to repeat that the two women and their children were all right. Chaman's husband, he wrote, had not been killed by Taliban but had died of cholera in Bamiyan, where he had gone to join Hisb-i-Wadhat. Of Jawad, there was still no news. Sharifa's letter to me said nothing other than that they were alright. She hoped Jon was well and urged me to kiss David for her.

Later, Naeem had written to say that the sisters had gone to Iran. A few weeks after that, Jawad arrived in Peshawar. The news that his wife and children had escaped to Pakistan reached him in Hazara Jat, on Afghanistan's still remarkably efficient grapevine.

'When Sharifa and Chaman came here and we heard their story, for the first time ever, I saw my husband cry,' said Maryam in an anguished tone. 'He could not write to you about the horrible things that Sharifa witnessed those animals do. I'll tell you some of what she went through,' she declared. She blinked back fresh tears, wiping them away angrily with the back of her hand.

'She was in the bazaar, near the *rowzah* [the shrine] the morning that Taliban captured Mazar. They didn't have to do much to take it as most of the soldiers had already run away without even warning the people. Sharifa suddenly heard shouts and firing and screaming. Taliban were driving round the streets firing at everyone and everything – men, women, children, donkeys, camels, cars. If it was moving, they fired at it. As Sharifa started to run a man fell to the ground in front of her. His blood splashed over her. She said she could feel it warm on her feet. She heard a child screaming for her mother. The screams suddenly stopped, but she didn't dare look round.

'She took shelter in a shop, hiding behind the counter with many other people. She has no idea how long she stayed there, listening to the awful sounds outside. Even when the firing became less, there were still the sounds of the dying groaning and crying for help. Finally, along with some of the others, she came out of the shop. I don't think she knows how she got home. Whenever she heard jeeps coming or firing she hid – in shops, in doorways, even in the gutter. She reached home late in the afternoon. Her sister Chaman, terrified, was there with her children. By then, everyone knew what Taliban was doing.'

I had read many reports, based on interviews with survivors, about the frenzied orgy of killing carried out by Taliban when they first entered Mazar-i-Sharif. The people had known that if the extremists ever succeeded in taking the city they would exact a terrible revenge for their defeat in 1997, but no one could have imagined the utter barbarity with which they behaved. Determined to terrorise the population into submission, the new governor of Mazar, Abdul Manan Niazi, ordered that the hundreds of dead bodies be left where they were. Dogs were seen eating the rotting corpses. Only when they became a health hazard did he allow the bodies to be cleared away. The indiscriminate killings on that first day, 8 August 1998, were followed by the methodical targeting of the Shia Hazaras, blamed for successfully routing Taliban the previous year.

House to house searches were carried out. Thousands of men were carted off to jail, where, later, they were segregated according to race and religion. Pushtoon were automatically released, as were Sunni Uzbek and Tajik, but Hazaras and any other Shia were kept prisoner. When the jail became too overcrowded, prisoners were pushed into metal containers – sometimes between 120 and 150 men – to be trucked to jails in other towns. Several witnesses reported that by the time these containers were opened, after hours in temperatures over forty degrees celsius, most of the prisoners had died of asphyxiation.

'Was Jawad arrested?' I asked Maryam.

'Sharifa had no idea. He had left the house before her in the morning and he didn't return. She didn't know if he had escaped, been arrested or killed. Taliban were searching all the houses looking for guns, and for Hazaras. Someone came to her house to warn her that Taliban were coming to her street next. They had already searched Chaman's street, so the two of them slipped out and hurried to Chaman's house, which had been totally ransacked.

'There were no men left in the street, only women and children. Because they knew it was a Hazara area, Taliban had burst into the houses and dragged the men out. Some were arrested and sent to jail, others were killed immediately. They shot them in the head and in their . . . you know . . . their private parts. Chaman's next-door neighbour was hysterical after seeing her husband killed in front of her. They had slit his throat. Another woman had begged the soldiers to kill her too after they killed her husband and two sons and they had laughed at her saying they wouldn't waste a bullet on her. Then they . . . they . . .'

Maryam stopped. Tears poured, unchecked down her cheeks. Her face, usually so gentle and calm contorted with rage and hatred. She continued, 'They pulled her small boy out of her arms saying, "This one will never fight against us", and they cut off both his hands. Sharifa said the woman went mad with grief. She wouldn't let anyone touch the boy, just held him in her arms while he bled to death. Finally, a relative came and took them away.

'Sharifa was desperate to leave the city but it was impossible to arrange this because they were afraid to go out of the house, and they did not know who they could trust to help them.'

The day that Taliban had occupied the city, it was estimated that upwards of 10,000 people fled – or tried to flee. Taliban bombed the column of refugees from the air, while, from

behind, troops with rocket launchers fired on them. A UN
report by Special Rapporteur Choong-Hyun Paik, said, 'The
road was so packed with cars and people that vehicles drove
over the bodies of persons killed during the bombing raids.
After that, no movement outside the city was possible during
two weeks.' Thank God, Sharifa and Chaman had not tried to
escape in those first days.

'I don't know how they arranged it, or who helped them to
get out,' said Maryam. 'She did not want to tell us because the
people involved were returning to Afghanistan, though not to
Mazar.' She shuddered, 'I can't understand how human beings
can do such things. It is unbelievable.'

Small wonder Naeem had not wanted to write to me about
Sharifa's ordeal. I thought of how sick I had felt while reading
the horrific reports, not realising then that Sharifa had actually
witnessed all of this.

'They are all right now,' said Maryam.

'Can anyone ever be "all right" after that?' I asked.

She shrugged helplessly. 'They are alive. Some women have
been through even worse things. We heard many stories of
Hazara women being raped.

'Marzia is happy to have her sisters with her.' Maryam
smiled suddenly. 'That girl never changes. She was very angry
when Ghulam Ali decided to come and live with her and his
first wife for a while. Then, when he was in the bazaar one day
he was asked for his papers. It seems they were not in order so
the police deported him. Marzia thinks he is in Herat and said
in her letter that she hopes he stays there because life is nicer
without him.

'I wish I could see her again,' I cried, 'and Shahnaz. She must
be a big girl now.'

'Yes, she is starting school next year. I tell you who you can
see, though – your friend Habiba. She came to Peshawar after
the Taliban came to Mazar the first time.'

I thought about it, but decided against looking up Habiba.
We had so little time in Peshawar and already every evening
and most of our days were booked. Besides, after hearing about

Sharifa, I knew I would have little patience with Habiba's tales of woe. 'Maybe next time,' I said.

Next day, Maryam telephoned me at the hotel. 'Can you come to my house. There is someone I think you would like to meet.'

'Not Habiba?'

'No,' she laughed, 'I promise, not Habiba.' She would not tell me any more than that.

The woman who came to open the gate when I rang was Salma, one of the health volunteers from Mazar. We hugged in delight.

'I told you it wasn't Habiba,' laughed Maryam, ushering us into the guestroom where the tea things were already laid out. For once the grapevine had not worked well because Salma and her family had been in Peshawar for almost as long as Maryam, yet she had only learned of their presence in the city a few days before.

We talked for hours, especially about the health course and the volunteers. 'They were wonderful times. We worked hard,' said Salma, 'and we enjoyed it because we could see it was successful. Now, of course, the project is finished, but there are children alive today because of our work and I remind myself of that whenever I am depressed.'

Fatima joined us and I asked what she would do when she matriculated. 'I would like to be an engineer, but my father still thinks I should become a doctor. Both will be needed in Afghanistan.'

'Do you think you will go back?'

Fatima smiled sadly, 'I haven't finished school yet, and then there will be several years in university.' She shot a look at her mother. 'Who knows what will be happening in Afghanistan by that time? I am sure . . . I must believe that Taliban will be pushed out. Then there will be a need for engineers – and doctors – to help repair the damage done to our country.'

Salma smiled at the girl. 'Yes, we must go on hoping, although sometimes it is impossible to believe that things will get better. My cousin and his family came from Kabul. His wife told me that apart from all the restrictions about not going out without being covered in a *burqa* – wearing black socks, because white ones get the Taliban too excited – and having a chaperon, they banned women from speaking in public places. They say that women's voices should not be heard.'